The Coast to Coast Walk

KU-430-579

Martin Wainwright

Aurum

Acknowledgements

Many thanks to John Temple, Maya Czajkowski and Robert Walden, readers of the first edition of this book, for their helpful comments and suggestions. Grateful thanks also to Emma Davidson, who painstakingly worked out the descents and the highest and lowest points for each section of the walk; and to Brenda and Robert Updegraff for meticulous editing and imaginative design. And to Graham Coster of Aurum, who came all the way up Kidsty Pike.

This fully revised and updated edition first published 2012
by Aurum Press Limited
7 Greenland Street, London NW1 0ND
www.aurumpress.co.uk
First published in 2007

Text copyright © Martin Wainwright 2007, 2010, 2012

Photographs copyright © Martin Wainwright 2007, 2010 and 2012, except for the following which are copyright © 2012 the photographer or agency: pages 21, 23, 60, 80, 82, 88, 92, 99, 114, 116 and 142 Alamy; 17 Kendal Museum; 25 Flickr; 46 pauljenkins@PAJPhotography/Flickr; 84 Marc Gelormino, TravelMarx; 119 Anne Shaw Hewitt, Swaledale Folk Museum; 152 Science Museum/Science & Society Picture Library; and 167 Getty Images.

Ordnance Survey® This product includes mapping data licensed from Ordnance Survey® with the permission of the Controller of Her Majesty's Stationery Office. © Crown copyright 2010. All rights reserved. Licence number 43453U.

Ordnance Survey and Travelmaster are registered trademarks and the Ordnance Survey symbol and Explorer trademarks of Ordnance Survey, the national mapping agency of Great Britain.

All rights reserved. No part of this book may be reproduced or utilised in any form or by any means, electronic or mechanical, including photocopying, recording or by any information storage and retrieval system, without permission in writing from Aurum Press Limited.

A catalogue record for this book is available from the British Library.

ISBN 978 1 84513 854 7

Book design by Robert Updegraff
Printed in China

Cover photograph: *Crummock Water from Chapel Crags, between Red Pike and High Stile*
Half-title photograph: *Sheep lead the way down to Keld in upper Swaledale*
Title page photograph: *Pillar, High Cragg and High Stile rise above Haystacks' summit*

Aurum Press want to ensure that these trail guides are always as up to date as possible – but stiles collapse, pubs close and bus services change all the time. If, on walking this path, you discover any important changes that future walkers need to be aware of, do let us know. Either go to our website, **www.aurumpress.co.uk/trailguides**, and add your comments, or, if you take the trouble to drop us a line to:

Trail Guides, Aurum Press, 7 Greenland Street, London NW1 0ND,

we'll send you a free guide of your choice as thanks.

The Coast to Coast Walk

Martin Wainwright is Northern Editor of the *Guardian* and a regular broadcaster on radio and TV. He lives in Leeds and walks regularly in the wild country of the north of England. Married with two grown-up sons, he was the first chair of the National Lottery Charities Board in Yorkshire and the Humber and was awarded the MBE for this work in 2000. He has also edited two collections of *Guardian* Country Diaries for Aurum: *A Lifetime of Mountains* (2005) and *A Gleaming Landscape* (2006), and written *The* [illegible] *The Biography* (2 [illegible] *nture.*

ISLINGTON LIBRARIES

3 0120 02532654 7

Also available:

West Highland Way
The London Loop
The Capital Ring
Camino de Santiago
Skyline London
Criminal London

Contents

How to use this guide

This guide is in three parts:

- The introduction, historical background to the area and advice for walkers.
- The path itself, described in 12 chapters, with maps opposite each route description. This part of the guide also includes information on places of interest. Key sites are numbered in the text and on the maps to make it easy to follow the route description.
- The last part includes useful information, such as local transport, accommodation, organisations involved with the path, and further reading.

The maps for this guide have been specially prepared by the Ordnance Survey® using 1:25 000 scale maps, using their
1:25 000 Explorer™ maps as a base. While using paths you should follow the Country Code, taking due care to avoid damage to property and the natural environment. The line of the Coast to Coast Walk is highlighted in yellow with alternative routes shown as a dotted yellow highlight. Any parts of the path that may be difficult to follow on the ground are clearly indicated in the route description, and important points to watch out for are marked with letters in each chapter, both in the text and on the maps. Should there have been a need to alter the route since publication of this guide for any reason, walkers are advised to follow the waymarks or signs which have been put on the site to indicate this.

Dove Cottage at Grasmere, the former pub where Wordsworth lived from 1799 to 1808.

KEY MAP 1
KEY MAPS
Coast to Coast Path
Chapter start point
0 km
5
0 miles
5
Based on Ordnance Survey Road Map
WORKINGTON
WHITEHAVEN
COCKERMOUTH
CLEATOR MOOR
EGREMONT
St Bees
St Bees Head
Sandwith
Rottington
Flimby
Seaton
Great Broughton
Papcastle
Harrington
Distington
Moresby
Cleator
Egremont Castle
Ennerdale Bridge
Ennerdale Fell
Ennerdale Water
Loweswater
Loweswater Fell
Buttermere
Buttermere Fell
Whinlatter Pass
Lorton
Braithwaite
Portinscale
Newlands Hause
Grange
Seatoller
Honister Pass
Haystacks
Black Sail Pass
Scarth Gap Pass
Pillar
Great Gable
Kirk Fell
Wasdale Head
Wast Water
The Screes
Nether Wasdale
COPELAND FOREST
SCAFELL PIKE
SCA FELL
CUMBRIA
LAKE DISTRICT NATIONAL
Gosforth
Calder Bridge
Beckermet
Braystones
Seascale
Sellafield Sta
Holmrook
Drigg
Gubbergill
Ravenglass
ROMAN BATH HOUSE
Muncaster Castle
Eskdale Green
Eskdale
Boot
Beckfoot
ROMAN FORT
Hardknott Pass
Harter Fell
Ulpha
Broughton
Corney
Waberthwaite
Broad Oak
Kokoarrah
A595
A66
A596
A5086
A591
A594
A597
Carlisle
Penrith
Keswick
Workington
Whitehaven
Maryport
Cockermouth
St Bees Head
Egremont
Ravenglass
LAKE DISTRICT
Ambleside
Windermere
Kendal
Broughton in Furness
Millom
Barrow-in-Furness
Walney Island
Morecambe
Morecambe Bay
Heysham
Lancaster
Carnforth
Ulverston
Hornby
Ingleton
Settle
Skipton
Kirkby Lonsdale
Sedbergh
Kirkby Stephen
Appleby-in-Westmorland
Brough
Barnard Castle
Darlington
Bainbridge
Leyburn
Richmond
Catterick
Scotch Corner
Northallerton
Thirsk
Helmsley
Pickering
Malton
Easingwold
Ripon
Boroughbridge
Masham
Nidderdale
Harrogate
Knaresborough
Stamford Bridge
Howardian Hills
YORKSHIRE DALES
THE PENNINES
North Pennines
Alston
Hexham
Brampton
Wigton
Thursby
Aspatria
Bothel
Solway Coast
SOLWAY FIRTH
Dalbeattie
Gateshead
Sunderland
Seaham
Consett
Chester-le-Street
Durham
Peterlee
Crook
Hartlepool
Bishop Auckland
Newton Aycliffe
Stockton-on-Tees
Middlesbrough
Redcar
Guisborough
Whitby
NORTH YORK MOORS
Wearhead
Forest of Bowland
KEY MAP 1
KEY MAP 2
KEY MAP 3

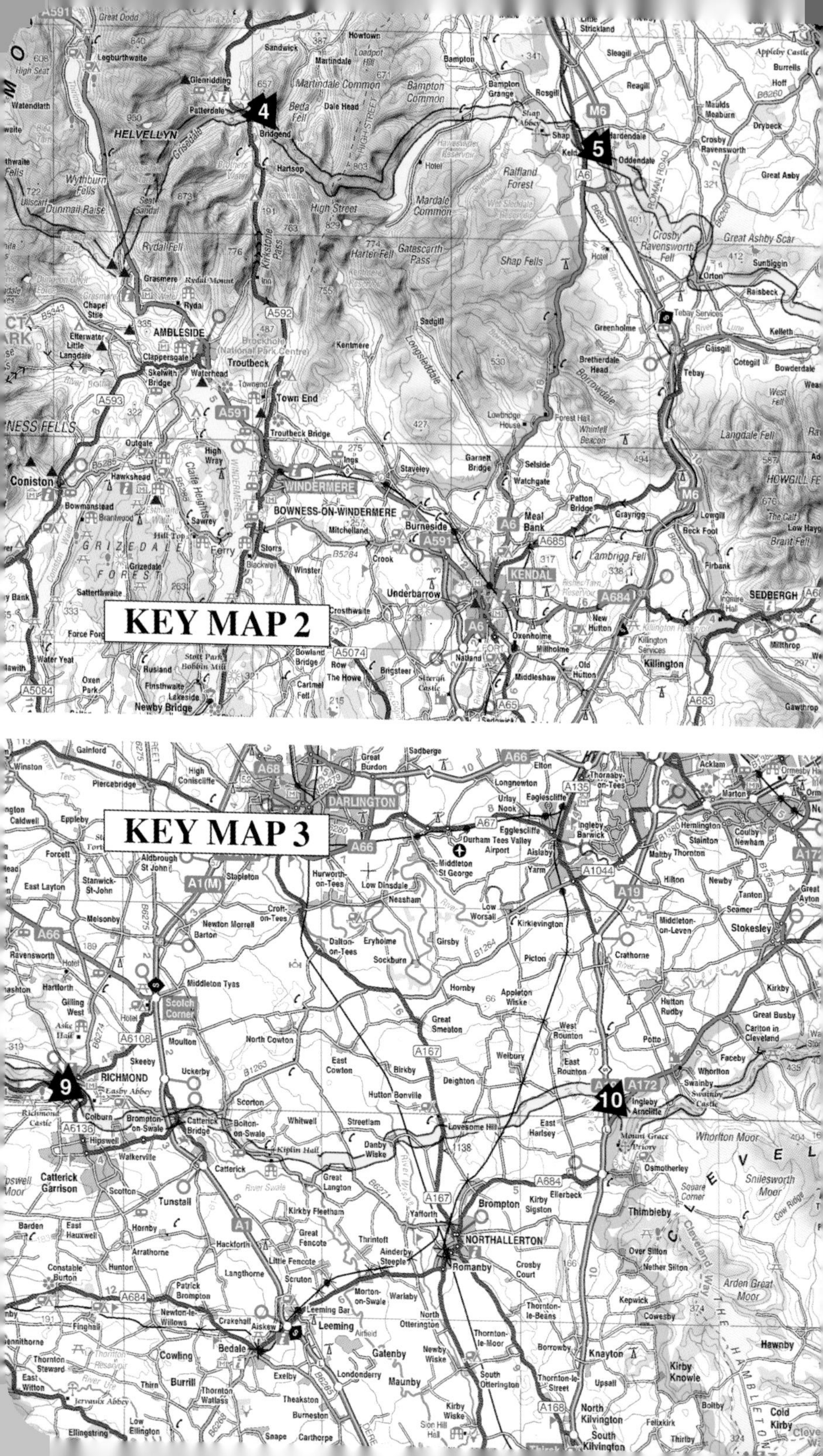

KEY MAP 2
HELVELLYN
AMBLESIDE
Grasmere
Troutbeck
Town End
Troutbeck Bridge
WINDERMERE
BOWNESS-ON-WINDERMERE
Coniston
Hawkshead
KENDAL
SEDBERGH
Patterdale
Glenridding
Bampton
Shap
Orton
Tebay
Kentmere
Staveley
Burneside
Killington
Newby Bridge
KEY MAP 3
DARLINGTON
RICHMOND
NORTHALLERTON
Catterick Garrison
Bedale
Leeming
Yarm
Stokesley
Osmotherley
Scotch Corner
Middleton Tyas
Brompton
Romanby
Thimbleby
Durham Tees Valley Airport

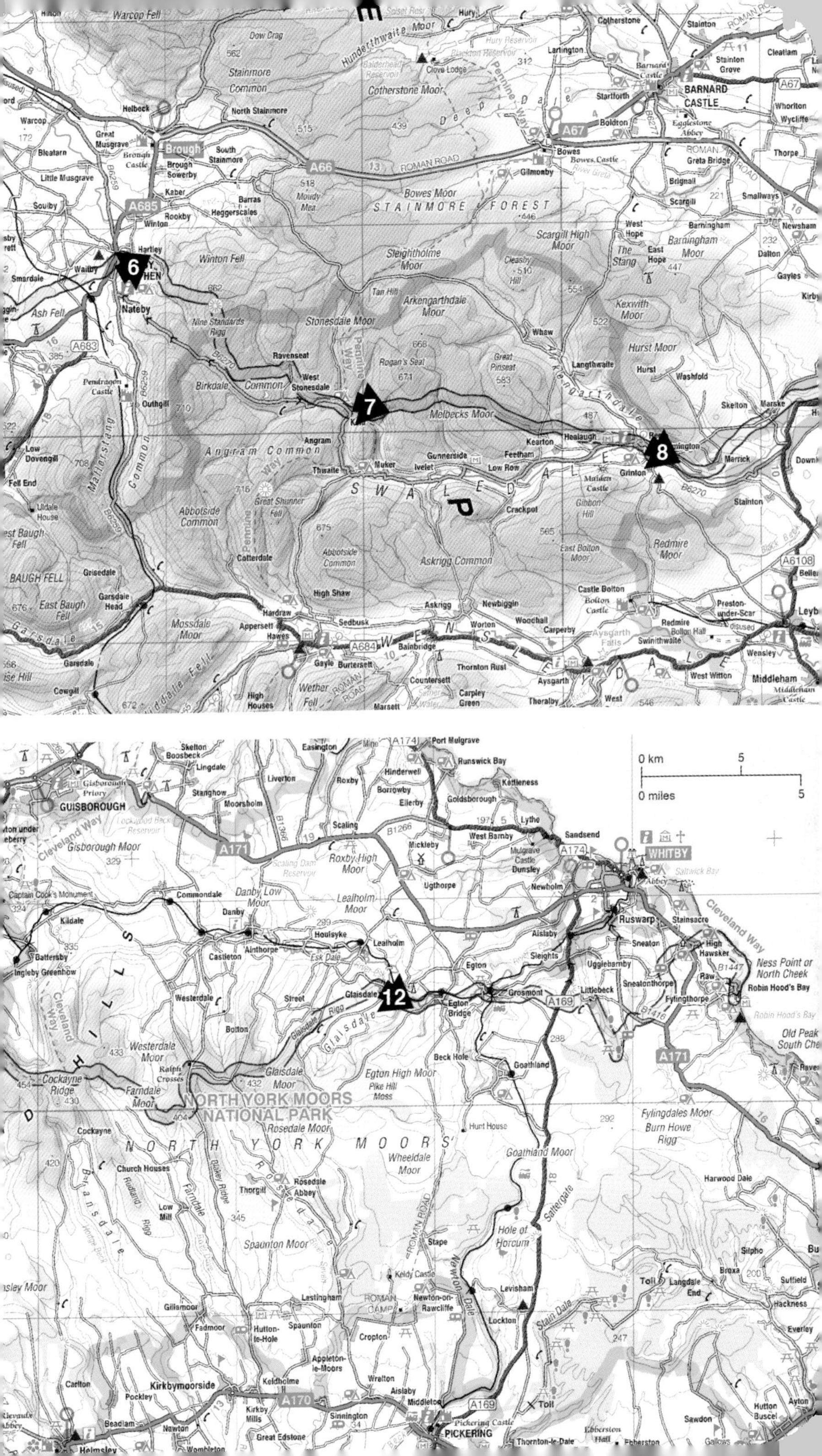

Warcop Fell
Dow Crag
Hunderthwaite Moor
Hury
Cotherstone
Stainton
Cleatlam
Stainmore Common
Clove Lodge
Cotherstone Moor
Lartington
Barnard Castle
Stainton Grove
BARNARD CASTLE
Helbeck
North Stainmore
Deep Dale
Pennine Way
Startforth
Whorlton
Wycliffe
Warcop
Great Musgrave
Brough
Brough Castle
South Stainmore
Brough Sowerby
A66
ROMAN ROAD
A67
Boldron
Egglestone Abbey
Bowes
Bowes Castle
Gilmonby
Greta Bridge
Thorpe
Bleatarn
Little Musgrave
Kaber
Barras
Heggerscales
Moudy Mea
Bowes Moor
STAINMORE FOREST
Brignall
Scargill
Smallways
Soulby
A685
Rookby
Winton
Hartley
Winton Fell
Sleightholme Moor
Scargill High Moor
West Hope
The Stang
East Hope
Barningham
Barningham Moor
Newsham
Dalton
Gayles
Waitby
Smardale
Nateby
Nine Standards Rigg
Tan Hill
Arkengarthdale Moor
Cleasby Hill
Kexwith Moor
Ash Fell
A683
Stonesdale Moor
Whaw
Hurst Moor
Pendragon Castle
Outhgill
Ravenseat
West Stonesdale
Birkdale
Common
Rogan's Seat
Great Pinseat
Langthwaite
Hurst
Washfold
Skelton
Marske
Melbecks Moor
Arkengarthdale
Mallerstang
Low Dovengill
Angram
Angram Common
Thwaite
Muker
Ivelet
Gunnerside
Feetham
Low Row
Kearton
Healaugh
Grinton
Maiden Castle
Marrick
Fell End
Uldale House
Great Shunner Fell
SWALEDALE
Crackpot
Gibbon Hill
Stainton
Abbotside Common
Askrigg Common
East Bolton Moor
Redmire Moor
A6108
Baugh Fell
BAUGH FELL
Grisedale
Cotterdale
East Baugh Fell
Garsdale Head
High Shaw
Castle Bolton
Bolton Castle
Preston-under-Scar
Mossdale Moor
Hardraw
Askrigg
Newbiggin
Woodhall
Carperby
Redmire
Bolton Hall
Leyburn
Garsdale
Appersett
Hawes
Sedbusk
Worton
Aysgarth Falls
Swinithwaite
Wensley
Gayle
Burtersett
A684
Bainbridge
WENSLEYDALE
Thornton Rust
Aysgarth
West Witton
Middleham
Middleham Castle
Cowgill
High Houses
Wether Fell
Countersett
Semer Water
Carpley Green
Thoralby
West
Marsett
Skelton
Boosbeck
Lingdale
Easington
A174
Port Mulgrave
Runswick Bay
Liverton
Hinderwell
Roxby
Borrowby
Kettleness
Gisborough Priory
GUISBOROUGH
Stanghow
Moorsholm
Ellerby
Goldsborough
Lythe
Cleveland Way
Lockwood Beck Reservoir
B1366
Scaling
B1266
West Barnby
Sandsend
WHITBY
Gisborough Moor
A171
Scaling Dam Reservoir
Roxby High Moor
Mickleby
Mulgrave Castle
Dunsley
Saltwick Bay
Abbey
Ugthorpe
Newholm
Captain Cook's Monument
Commondale
Danby Low Moor
Lealholm Moor
Kildale
Danby
Houlsyke
Lealholm
Aislaby
Ruswarp
Stainsacre
Castleton
Ainthorpe
Esk Dale
Egton
Sleights
Sneaton
High Hawsker
Battersby
Ingleby Greenhow
Westerdale
Street
Glaisdale
Egton Bridge
Grosmont
A169
Littlebeck
Ugglebarnby
Sneatonthorpe
Fylingthorpe
Ness Point or North Cheek
Robin Hood's Bay
Raw
B1447
B1416
Botton
Beck Hole
Goathland
Westerdale Moor
Ralph Crosses
Glaisdale Moor
Egton High Moor
Pike Hill Moss
Old Peak or South Cheek
Cockayne Ridge
Farndale Moor
NORTH YORK MOORS NATIONAL PARK
Rosedale Moor
Hunt House
Fylingdales Moor
Burn Howe Rigg
Cockayne
NORTH YORK MOORS
Goathland Moor
Wheeldale Moor
Church Houses
Thorgill
Rosedale Abbey
Blakey Ridge
Rudland Rigg
Low Mill
Farndale
Bransdale
Harwood Dale
Saltergate
Hole of Horcum
Spaunton Moor
ROMAN ROAD
Stape
Silpho
Keldy Castle
Broxa
Suffield
Lastingham
ROMAN CAMP
Newton-on-Rawcliffe
Newton Dale
Levisham
Langdale End
Hackness
Gillamoor
Fadmoor
Hutton-le-Hole
Spaunton
Lockton
Stain Dale
Everley
Cropton
Appleton-le-Moors
Carlton
Kirkbymoorside
Pockley
Keldholme
Wrelton
Aislaby
A170
Middleton
A169
Toll
Hutton Buscel
Ayton
Beadlam
Nawton
Kirkby Mills
Sinnington
Pickering Castle
PICKERING
Sawdon
Helmsley
Great Edstone
Thornton-le-Dale
Ebberston Hall
Ebberston
0 km
5
0 miles
5

Distance checklist

This list should help you in working out distances between your planned overnight stays and in checking your progress along the walk.

	Approx. distance from previous location: miles	km
St Bees		
Cleator	8.5	13.6
Ennerdale Bridge	5.3	8.5
Ennerdale YHA	4.6	7.4
Black Sail YHA	4.0	6.4
Honister YHA	2.5	4.0

Rosthwaite	3.2	5.1	Richmond	10.3	16.5
Grasmere	7.6	12.2	Danby Wiske	13.9	22.2
Patterdale	7.0	11.2	Ingleby Cross	8.7	14.0
Bampton	11.5	18.5	Clay Bank Top	11.0	18.4
Shap	4.1	6.6	Lion Inn, Blakey	9.0	14.4
Orton	7.3	11.7	Glaisdale	9.0	14.4
Kirkby Stephen	12.5	20.1	Grosmont	3.7	5.9
Keld	11.0	17.8	Hawsker	11.1	17.8
Reeth	10.5	17.0	Robin Hood's Bay	4.2	6.7

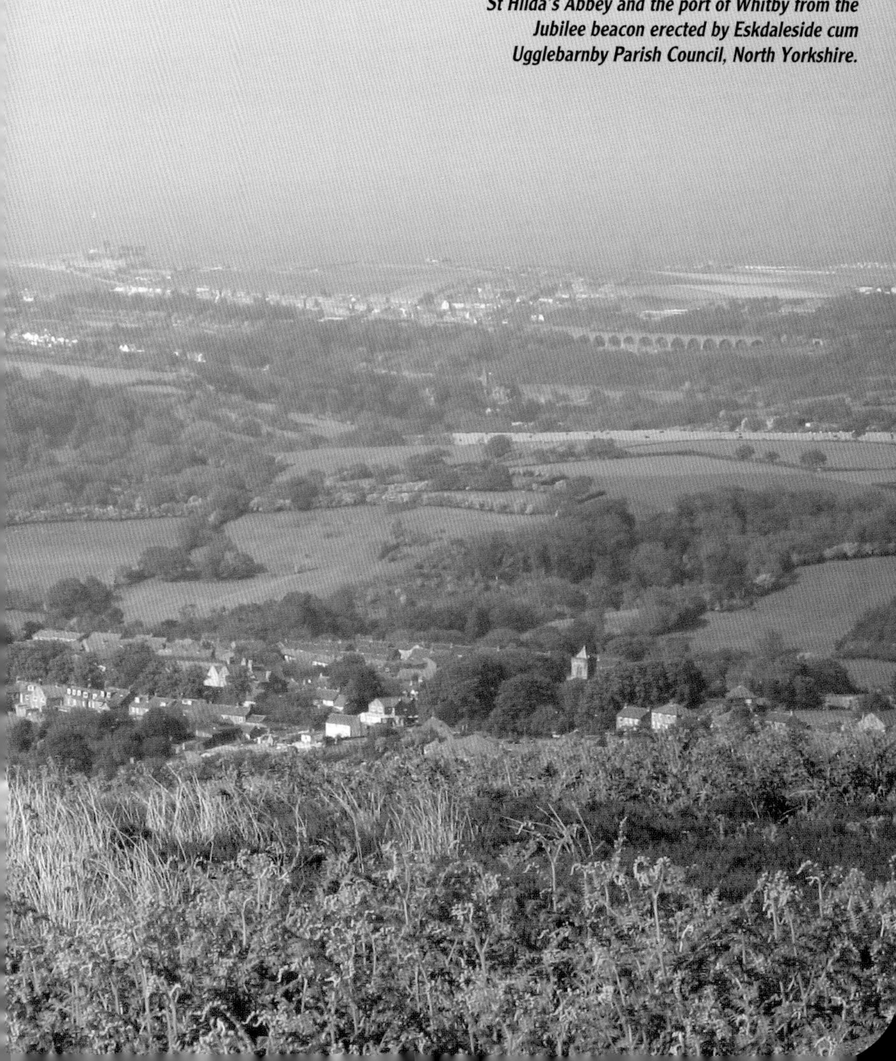

St Hilda's Abbey and the port of Whitby from the Jubilee beacon erected by Eskdaleside cum Ugglebarnby Parish Council, North Yorkshire.

Grasmere – Wordsworth's beloved 'little nook of mountain ground' – from the foot of Tongue Gill where the long haul up the flanks of Helvellyn begins.

PART ONE
Introduction

Route-finding is simple on the paved trod which carries the Coast to Coast, the Cleveland Way and the Lyke Wake Walk together over Cringle Moor.

Introduction – a marvellous notion

The Coast to Coast Walk is unique among Britain's long-distance footpaths in being entirely the invention of one man, albeit that prince among ramblers, Alfred Wainwright. I would like to be able to claim him as a member of my family but he isn't, although I have shared his love of the northern hills in a more modest way since my parents took me up Almscliff Crag near Leeds at the age of four. Almscliff is a small rock outcrop, but so fascinatingly pitted with crevices and overhangs that it was used for training by Edmund Hillary and members of the 1953 Everest expedition only two years before my own ascent (of the easy route, round the back). There is something particularly satisfying about such places, small but unexpectedly rich in history, landscape or wildlife. The Coast to Coast Walk leads to many of them.

It also marches over the finest walking ground in the north of England; in the case of the Lake District, some would say the loveliest in the world. Wainwright regarded this small but infinitely varied part of Britain as Paradise on Earth, and his ambition to tramp from sea to shining sea was never going to take him too far away from it. No sooner have you rounded St Bees Head than your face is set towards the ramparts of Lakeland for the next three, maybe four, glorious days. If you do the route from east to west, an increasingly popular variant, the promise of the lakes and fells will keep you going if night falls too quickly, the temperature plummets or spirits flag.

Wainwright's route also takes in scores of miles through two other national parks, the Yorkshire Dales and the North York Moors, and visits some wonderfully secluded corners off more mundane stretches of the beaten track. It is the creation of a man surprised by joy after years of being trapped by convention in a loveless marriage. He puzzled out the route at a time when his skill and pleasure in such forensic footpath work – mapping, drawing, writing – coincided with remarriage at the age of 63. He and his second wife Betty, originally summoned to his Borough Treasurer's office in Kendal to pay an overlooked bill for a theatre company's hire of a hall, brought one another delight until he died in 1991.

Betty is typically teased in Wainwright's own guide, *A Coast to Coast Walk*, as his 'competent, good-looking chauffeur', but the writer's biographer, Hunter Davies, argues convincingly that her spirit infuses the whole project, which Wainwright researched and wrote in 1971–72 and saw published in 1973. The text has regular sprightly references to the girls of Robin Hood's Bay or the

looking back to Pillar and Ennerdale from Loft Beck

Alfred Wainwright's handwritten guides are extraordinarily meticulous. After completing his first 100 pages in 1953, he was dissatisfied with the style, binned them and started all over again.

need to tidy up before tramping into Richmond in case the walker encounters a modern counterpart of the town's famous Lass. In his 'Personal Notes in Conclusion', a tradition common to all his books, Wainwright contrasts the 'masculine' grandeur of the simple, sturdy Pennine Way with the 'feminine' spirit in which his Coast to Coast Walk reveals its long succession of charms. 'If there is something in you which likes the ladies,' he says, 'the odds are that you will prefer the C-to-C. You may not meet any, but you will be reminded of them.' He could be a chauvinistic old grump, but the point stands.

This walk is also unusual in being a much-enjoyed long-distance path which has no official status, like, for example, a National Trail. This is how Wainwright very much wanted it to be. He disliked the notion of being told where to go and although, ironically, his books have come to serve that very purpose, and in unprecedented detail, he really wanted to encourage others to find similar connections between Britain's millions of miles of right-of-way or open-access land. That assumed a level of confidence and pathfinding enthusiasm which many do not share, but the Coast to Coast remains an excellent instrument for his general idea, particularly since the establishment of a legal 'right to roam' over wild areas (a right which carries the responsibility of sensitive and sensible behaviour). Most walkers will be content with the main route or its most obvious variants, but all along the 192 miles (307 km) there are bypasses, loops and zig-zags which can be followed along the green dots and dashes that mark, respectively, footpaths and bridleways on Ordnance Survey maps. Wainwright also recommended tackling the route in bite-sized chunks, as he did on research journeys with his good-looking chauffeur. But to stay the full course is a richly satisfying experience which you will neither regret nor forget.

Who was Wainwright?

Fame gradually fades, but Alfred Wainwright (1907–91) remains the doyen of modern writers about the Lakes. The seven volumes of his handwritten *Pictorial Guides to the Lakeland Fells* are a masterpiece, illustrated with meticulous line-drawings over which he spent hours. It was this skill which rescued him from a poverty-stricken home in Blackburn, where his mother took in washing and his father, a stonemason whose quarrying business had collapsed, became an alcoholic.

Alfred, the youngest of three children crammed into a two-up, two-down terrace house, won school prizes for his exceptionally neat writing, which also got him a clerical job in the Borough Engineer's department. He was instructed that every page of his ledgers should be fit for framing, and they were. He gradually made his stolid, determined way in local government, eventually becoming the Borough Treasurer of Kendal. But something far more important to him had happened in the meanwhile.

As he describes in his moving memoir *Fellwanderer*, at the age of 23 he joined a cousin on a visit to the Lake District, which he had heard of as a suitable place for a week's break. It was the start of a lifelong love affair – a *real*, passionate love affair which breathes through every line of his wry, witty and sometimes lyrically descriptive text.

Wainwright kept bundles of mountain journals and private sketches until his dissatisfaction with official maps, which missed things out and made minor errors of the sort that infuriate the clerkish mind, sowed the idea of creating his own guides. On the evening of 9 November 1952 (characteristically, he never forgot the date) he started the first page of his

Alfred Wainwright at work on one of his books.

series. The work proceeded at a stately pace for the next 11 years, books appearing at regular intervals. The first was published by a local printer, who accepted the maximum sum Wainwright could raise, £35, and gave the fledgling author no deadline by which to pay the balance of £915. It took Wainwright two years to get the money through sales, but soon word started spreading. The *Westmorland Gazette* in Kendal took over the printing, the little books became sought-after classics, and Wainwright in due course – and greatly to his reluctance – became an industry: coffee-table picture books, a TV portrait and a memorable appearance on Radio 4's *Desert Island Discs* all followed.

Slate blocks ready for riving (splitting into slates) at Honister in the Lake District.

His record choices for his desert island included 'Oh, What a Beautiful Mornin'' from *Oklahoma!* and 'The Happy Wanderer', sung by a boys' choir, but in truth Wainwright's life was far from happy outside his books. He admitted in later life that his obsession with them wrecked his first marriage and gave him the name for grumpy ill-will which was part of his public image to the end. Those who knew him well never found him like that, and his best-known memorial among walkers suggests a more generous side to his character. For years, everyone who completed the marathon Pennine Way at Kirk Yetholm received half a pint of beer at his expense. He honoured the landlord's bills until his death, by which time the *jeu d'esprit* had cost him over £15,000. Note well his final words to Coast to Coasters in his guide: 'You can rest on your laurels in the Bay Hotel with a pint but (let there be no misunderstanding about this) you do so at your own expense. It's no use saying "Charge it to Wainwright" as you did at the Border Hotel at Kirk Yetholm. No sonny, that game won't work here. Pay for your own. I'm skint.'

The six sections

Wainwright's Coast to Coast Walk crosses six distinct sub-regions of northern England, three on each side of the Pennines. It begins by traversing the Cumbrian coastal rim, gentle countryside and unspectacular once the high sea cliffs of St Bees Head have been left behind. More interesting than the woods and fields are the many traces of industry past and present, from Sellafield nuclear reprocessing plant

Hundreds of stone monuments – crosses, boundary markers and here, on Blakey Ridge, an ancient signpost – mark the landscape of the North York Moors.

smoking and steaming to the south, to rows of former miners' cottages at Cleator. The section ends on the 'quiet frontier' of the Lake District national park. The Ennerdale Bridge area takes time to reach from the park's tourist honeypots like Windermere and Keswick, and much of its clientele comes from Carlisle, Barrow and the rest of its western doorstep.

The second sub-region is the Lake District itself. The walk drives straight across the heart of the park, skilfully using passes which were packhorse and quarrymen's routes for centuries. The surroundings are utterly spectacular for three whole days, but there is also a fascinating sub-text of human activity and history. Much of it again involves heavy industry – slate, graphite mining

A station of the cross at St Hedda's Church in the 'old Catholic' stronghold of Egton Bridge.

and chemical works – which seem unlikely in this Paradise but have played (and in slate's case continue to play) an essential economic role.

The final section west of the Pennines is the limestone plateau between the ramparts of the Lakes and the Pennines. Here you will see traditional sheep farming at its best, beautifully maintained drystone walls and a lovely landscape, which is only less visited than it deserves because of its breathtaking neighbours, the Lakes and the northern Yorkshire Dales. It has something particularly special too: the elusive traces of our prehistoric ancestors, whose settlements, burial mounds and other monuments, still unexplained, abound on the high ground.

So to the Dales and their wonderful mixture of deep, green valleys intersecting airy moors, farming country too but with the complicated and fascinating regime of the grouse moors and extraordinary relics of an entirely different past. Although you can take the pretty riverside alternative down Swaledale, Wainwright rightly forged his main route through the fascinating remains of lead mines and stone quarries on the fellsides, picturesque now but the Sheffields or Rotherhams of their day.

Richmond's mighty castle and Georgian streets introduce the fifth section, the rich farming country which lies like a flat green pancake between the Pennines and the North York Moors. Many walkers imagine that this 30-mile (48-km) stretch will be a dreary slog and Wainwright, frustrated by blocked paths and stiles entwined in barbed wire, was forced to plod 8 miles (13 km) of it along tarmac back roads. This is no longer necessary, and navigating between the farms and their always-friendly occupants gives this section an interest not present in other parts of the walk. Unexpectedly, I found it a highlight.

And so to the final stretch, the North York Moors. I think this has to acknowledge the overall supremacy of the Lakes, but it makes a marvellous finish, especially if your walk is in August when the heather turns the entire world purple and honey scented. The paths are exceptionally good here – almost too good for those who like exploring – and there is also, yet again, a rich historical legacy. Old stones, carved crosses, an abandoned mineral railway which provides the 5 fastest and easiest miles of the whole path. And to finish, cliffs as high and sea-besieged as those of St Bees and a fine choice of pubs, cafés or just interesting places to sit and swell with pride in the narrow lanes of Robin Hood's Bay.

Flora and fauna

Any walk which threads through almost 200 miles (322 km) of the English countryside will offer the chance of encountering a rich variety of wildlife. They will see you. Whether you see them depends on how watchful you are – and how quiet. There is no need to creep along like a Trappist monk, but a little stealth in places such as Ennerdale, Borrowdale and on the Yorkshire moor tops may pay dividends. If you can psych yourself up for an early start, you are much more likely to see shy mammals, such as the red squirrel in the Lakes and deer along many parts of the trail. Walk until twilight and you will certainly see hedgehogs and bats, probably the pipistrelle although there are 13 other native species.

There are good chances of seeing red squirrels at Rosthwaite and along Haweswater.

The white scuts of rabbits bob out of your path along much of the route and hares, bigger and more lolloping, frequent the cliff tops at both ends. Look out for foxes close to farming areas. They are often surprisingly nonchalant about walkers and may take their time strolling off. Badgers have setts close to parts of the walk, with Patterdale probably offering the best chance of a sighting, but they are much shyer than foxes. If something small and light brown scoots across the path ahead of you, it will be a stoat or weasel; very rarely you may encounter the horrible but riveting sight of a stoat dancing in front of its favourite prey, a terrified, hypnotised rabbit. Smaller and darker brown mammals travelling at high speed will be mice, voles or shrews. The water vole makes an occasional appearance on the Swale and Esk and if you are very lucky, Swaledale may also give you a sighting of otters. The jackpot among mammals is the pine marten, whose droppings have been found recently in Ennerdale. It is most likely to be high up in the trees, and not just the pines.

Among the reptiles, lizards turn up in surprisingly damp places, including stretches of the old mineral railway on the North York Moors. In hot sunshine, you may spot Britain's only poisonous snake, the adder, which should be given a wide berth. It is far more frightened of you than the other way round and most bites happen when someone inadvertently treads on a basking snake. This is a very rare accident and adder venom is designed to kill only small prey such as mice or shrews, but medical help should be sought as quickly as possible.

Birds provide the most exciting opportunity of all the walk's potential encounters with wildlife: a solitary golden eagle still flies above Riggindale and the steep descent from Kidsty Pike to Haweswater. There was a nesting pair, but the bird's mate died and the outlook for the lonely eagle, much the most southerly in Britain, is not good. It is also shy, unlike the noisy seabird colonies which start the walk. The Royal Society for the Protection of Birds has some brilliantly sited observation points on St Bees Head, where guillemots and black guillemots, fulmars, razorbills, kittiwakes and a small number of puffins with their brightly coloured, barcoded beaks live in squabbling families on white, mess-stained ledges. Another certain encounter en route is the gaudy pheasant and you are bound to see raptors, big buzzards circling over the crags in the Lakes and Pennines, and merlins and peregrine falcons streaking like fighter jets across the heather. Kestrels, recognisable from their unique ability to hover, are common. The other great concentration of birds is on the grouse moors of the Pennines and North York Moors, whose largely invisible but careful management encourages lapwings, with their tumbling flight and 'peewit' cry, curlews with beaks like slender surgical scissors, and less obvious species, including the golden plover, snipe, dunlin, ring ouzel and redshank. The red grouse frequently panics its way out of your path with a tremendous amount of noise ending in the famous 'Go back, go back' cackle. Black grouse, alas now rare, are more decorously behaved, but the noise level on the moors can be

Wood anemones grow in profusion in spring in the woods beside the Swale at Richmond.

surprising, especially during the nesting season when lapwings and curlews will follow you for ages, with their initially haunting shrieks of alarm gradually driving you mad.

On the bleakest stretches of the walk, you may be surprisingly comforted by insects. A beautiful iridescent green beetle inhabits Urra Moor, where the gravelly path and scorched heather can seem a bit grim out of the flowering season. Small day-flying moths also liven up the moors in summer and you may encounter the bright green Emperor moth caterpillar, its silkworm-like cocoon or the adult with large, eyed wings zig-zagging about the heather. Another common caterpillar is the furry blue-banded larva of the Drinker moth, which creeps up blades of grass to enjoy the dew.

A curlew in flight. They will become familiar along the path.

As for flora, you may have read from time to time in metropolitan newspapers about the supposed death of the English hedgerow. It is in glorious life along the Coast to Coast, sharing top billing with woodland flowers and a catalogue of more unusual species on the limestone plateau between Shap and the Pennines, and on the crags and moorland of the higher stretches. Snowdrops give way to daffodils, followed by bluebells and wild anemones. In May and June the verges are a froth of hawthorn blossom and cow parsley. Red campion adds a brighter splash, as do the vivid clumps of gorse on the sea cliffs and the 'halfway' slopes between the fells and moors and the sheep intakes. Specifically interesting to botanists are the damp meadows on the Cumbrian coastal rim, the dank oakwoods of Borrowdale which form a small temperate rainforest and the starry saxifrage on the climb up to Lining Crag in Borrowdale. Look too for unusual ferns in the clint and grike limestone pavements between Shap and Orton.

Time spent on a little preliminary research into the animals and plants of Cumbria and North Yorkshire would be well spent. The relationship between the geology and plants, from the red sandstone of Cumbria to the flinty, fossily cliffs south of Whitby, is particularly instructive. Finally, if your knapsack is not already bursting, consider slipping in a small pair of binoculars.

When to go

The walking season really starts in late April, when B&Bs, youth hostels and other path-related businesses finish spring-cleaning and open their doors. Earlier travellers will enjoy some sensational moments, especially on clear days in winter, but much of the staying and feeding infrastructure is shut. Things wind down by the end of September, although late autumn can combine 'Indian summer' spells with beautiful colours – the russet of dying bracken and the pale hay yellow of exhausted grass.

If you are lucky with the weather, spring is a lovely time to do the Coast to Coast, with the path unlikely to be busy until late May and overnight rooms easier to find at short notice. Everything, from flowers to lambs, seems young and fresh. The weather, however, has a long history of dumping on this cheerful scene. Make sure you have head-to-toe waterproofs.

It also rains unpredictably throughout the British summer; I am writing this on a late June day when the temperature in Leeds would be more appropriate to March or November. But the chances of prolonged good weather are better than at any other time and this is much the most popular season for the walk. As a result, you must book beds, baggage-carrying, etc., well in advance; and being busy, the path may put some people off, especially where it coincides with other long-distance trails in the Lakes and the North York Moors. On the other hand, you get a very nice, varied and interesting type of person on the walk (otherwise why would you be doing it?). You will make friends from all over the world.

Autumn has the advantages of spring, with the freshness replaced by the brief but wonderful show of colours as the foliage dies. Not Vermont; it's much subtler. September in particular often sees a period of calm, pleasant weather and all those noisy children have gone back to school. Winter is for the experienced walker. The rewards of a snow-covered passage are great, but must be earned. I spent a slidy hour getting to Greenup Edge from Borrowdale up a path which had become a frozen waterfall. Views through gaps in the swirling mist were unforgettable, but before enjoying these conditions, get well acquainted with mountain craft and the use of a compass.

National weather conditions and forecasts for up to six months ahead can be found on the Meteorological Office website www.metoffice.com. There are a number of premium-rate national weather lines and more local information is provided by the three national parks (see Useful Information, pages 182–88).

Safety first

Which brings me to equipment, and by far the most important thing to take with you is Common Sense. Never be rash on mountains or in remote places. Discretion should always be the better part of valour. But you are your own best judge of your capabilities and Wainwright would have been saddened by well-meaning advisers who tell you never to walk on your own or always to wear stout boots. Footwear is a matter of personal comfort (but make sure you keep your feet dry, if necessary with waterproof socks).

Solitary walking is one of life's finest pleasures. The sort of people who should not walk alone, because of the risk of accident, are very unlikely to do so because they will almost certainly find the prospect frightening or unappealing. Those who do sally forth on their own are likely to be more careful, instinctively. They will also see things which others miss because of noise or distraction. Wainwright almost always made solo trips.

In rainy England, it is important to keep dry. Waterproof clothing is very lightweight nowadays and (as above) make sure that it includes socks. I hesitate to lay down the law about clothing otherwise, but several lightish layers – T-shirt, shirt, sweater – give greater warmth and flexibility than one big chunky sweater or heavy anorak. A cap or hat is useful, especially on sunny days. Sunburn and heat headaches are possible, even in the north of England.

The best present you can give yourself in advance is learning to use a compass and overcoming any fear of mist. It is liberating to feel that you can navigate safely in poor visibility, a skill which will see you through the whole of the Coast to Coast. Problem places are few: at low level, the humble farmland round Stanley Pond and between Naddle Bridge and Shap needs concentration, as do the Graystone Hills on what is likely to be your final day. In higher and wilder country, the top of Loft Beck, the 'Wythburn trap' between Borrowdale and Grasmere, and the bogs after Nine Standards Rigg also require care. I am very grateful to readers for highlighting places where they had problems and suggesting revisions, especially John Temple, Maya Czajkowski and her fiancé Paul, and Robert Walden. Paul proposed to Maya on the beach at St Bees, and I'm delighted to say that a fortnight with this book ended with them more certain than ever of one another.

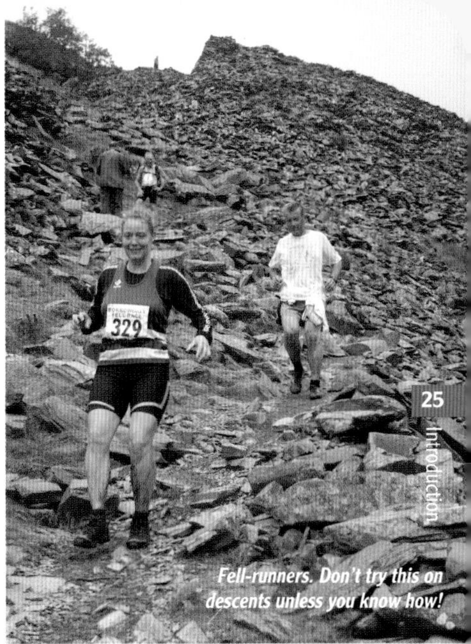

Fell-runners. Don't try this on descents unless you know how!

Robert sent comments on his entire walk in the summer of 2011 which were so genial, thorough and helpful that I have hidden a very small engraved medallion to him on the route which I hope one day ends up in the British Museum. Two of his observations particularly struck me: the amount of cheerful co-operation between walkers previously unknown to one another; and the number of times that he saw Coast to Coasters make small but potentially time-consuming errors because they were deep in chat. No need to be Trappist, but in stretches with twists and turns, it really pays to concentrate. It also pays really to study the maps in advance, checking out the contours and working out distances and rough times. Having said all that, it is prudent to avoid the high-level route alternatives above Ennerdale and over Helvellyn in foul weather.

Other backpack items should include the map or maps, a water bottle, chocolate, Kendal mint cake or similar blood-sugar boost, fruit, torch with spare batteries, penknife, string, toilet paper, pen and basic first aid kit (plasters, antiseptic cream). Some people feel reassured by taking a lightweight survival or 'bivvy' bag, which will almost certainly remain unused. GPS equipment is useful but not essential and perhaps best kept as a back-up. You are in England not Antarctica, and remember that Wainwright even spurned the use of a compass. Beyond this, your packing depends on whether you are self-sufficient or using friends or one of the many portering services which ferry your heavy gear from stop to stop (see Useful Information, pages 182–92).

Three other top items: a mobile phone (although reception can be poor or non-existent high up); a lightweight stick – extremely useful when crossing streams and going downhill; and money. Most stopping places take cards, but there are long stretches without cashpoints, e.g. between St Bees and Grasmere.

Which way?

The overwhelming majority of Coast to Coasters walk west to east for three reasons: (a) Wainwright did it that way; (b) as he wrote, it is better to have the prevailing weather at your back and not in your face; (c) you don't get the afternoon and evening sun in your eyes. Those who walk the other way are usually either (a) people who have done the trail before by the usual west–east route, or (b) those who feel the Lake District is so much the finest stretch that it should be saved until last.

Weighing these up, I unhesitatingly recommend west–east, unless you are a second-timer. The Lakes remain a highlight and one which stays with you for the rest of the walk. And the Cleveland escarpment, Eskdale villages and Littlebeck's long valley provide a marvellous finale. Wainwright's walk is much too subtle to 'save best till last'. And anyway, if you do walk east to west, there's a whole lot still to do once you have left the Lakes National Park boundary at Dent Fell behind.

A final plea

You will, alas, notice litter along the walk, and when it consists of high-energy drink bottles or cereal-bar wrappings, there can be little doubt who are the culprits. Please respect the Country Code and don't be shy about clearing up other walkers' litter if you come across it. The Coast to Coast has largely been a triumph in the long and often tetchy relationship between the English countryside and its visitors; each of us can add to this excellent reputation.

On that score, it is greatly appreciated if you use local facilities, for example Cleator Family Store in Cleator which has become a sort of mini-clubhouse for walkers, or the Lord Stones Café between Carlton and Cringle Moors, with its famous warm baps stuffed with black pudding. No economy can rely on charity, but if you face a choice between bringing your own supplies or buying en route, please opt for the latter.

In my experience, local people are also very interested in Coast to Coasters, because of the fantastic range of nationalities and types who undertake the walk every year. In turn, you will learn a lot from a brief interruption in your pounding progress to chat with a farmer at his gate or a gamekeeper pursuing his solitary, fascinating business on the lonely moors.

Food for free: bilberries grow in thousands by the path on the Cleveland escarpment, delicious but, with each berry separate, the devil to pick.

The sweep of the Swale above Ivelet Wood, between Keld and Muker, seen from the ruins of the deerkeeper's lodge at Crackpot Hall.

PART TWO

The Coast to Coast Walk

1 St Bees to Ennerdale Bridge

via the sea cliffs and Cleator • 6–7 hours
13.8 miles (22.1 km)

Ascent 2,315 feet (705 metres)
Descent 1,657 feet (505 metres)
Lowest point St Bees: 33 feet (10 metres)
Highest point Dent: 1,148 feet (350 metres)

An exhilarating stride along sea cliffs leads to a stint of orienteering across farmland, through small towns recovering from industrial collapse and over an outlying minor fell to a secret valley and the gates of Lakeland.

The walk sets off in fine style over a bridge across Rottington Beck and up wooden-shuttered earthen steps at the northern end of St Bees' grey shale and sandy beach. Grass and gorse accompany a switchback along the cliff edge round both buttresses of St Bees Head, south and north. The path is unmistakable, tramped to such an extent that in places it forms a vivid furrow in the red sandstone, changing after the lighthouse to a duller brown. Don't stray beyond the cliff fence; you can see the rich variety of seabirds from a brilliantly sited RSPB watching place not far beyond Fleswick Bay, complete with a colour poster to help non-ornithologists. Binoculars are a boon here and at two similar sites along this stretch, which is all an RSPB reserve – another reason for keeping to the path, which provides plenty of excitement without any need for diversions, except, perhaps, a brief look at the lighthouse, 150 yards up a gentle grassy slope. It was the last coal-fired light in the country, changed to oil in 1822 after mariners complained that the smoke from the small grate often obscured its beams.

Soon after the initial steps, the Pattering Holes **1** form unexplained fissures, fenced off to the right of the path opposite the skeletal remains of a coastguard post. Looking back, the towers of Sellafield nuclear plant rise in front of Black Combe, spookily in morning mist or at twilight, while breakfast smells drift over from the immense caravan park by Rottington Beck. On a clear day the Isle of Man is just visible on the sea horizon, often marked by a thin pelmet of cloud. The gradients are a gentle rehearsal for what lies ahead (just wait until Dent Fell in two hours' time . . .) and the only place needing care, especially in or after wet weather, is the hairpin path round the picturesque fissure of Fleswick Bay **A**. The path gets slippery, but you can scramble carefully down to the beach to get closer to the birds, examine the fine, wave-eroded pebbles and enjoy the mosses and plants hanging from the 300-foot (90-metre) cliffs. If you forgot to dip your boots in the sea and pick up a shell or pebble to take to Robin Hood's Bay, this is your last chance.

The RSPB birdwatching bays follow **2** and the path continues clearly ahead. The only navigational issue on this stretch may be a feeling beyond the lighthouse **3** that you have gone too far and should have turned right, inland. Don't worry. There are regular CtoC waymarks in a vivid turquoise-green, which is, fortunately, unique to this stretch of the walk, and you can also reassure yourself by checking the position of the prominent transmitter mast **B** to your right. The point where the walk

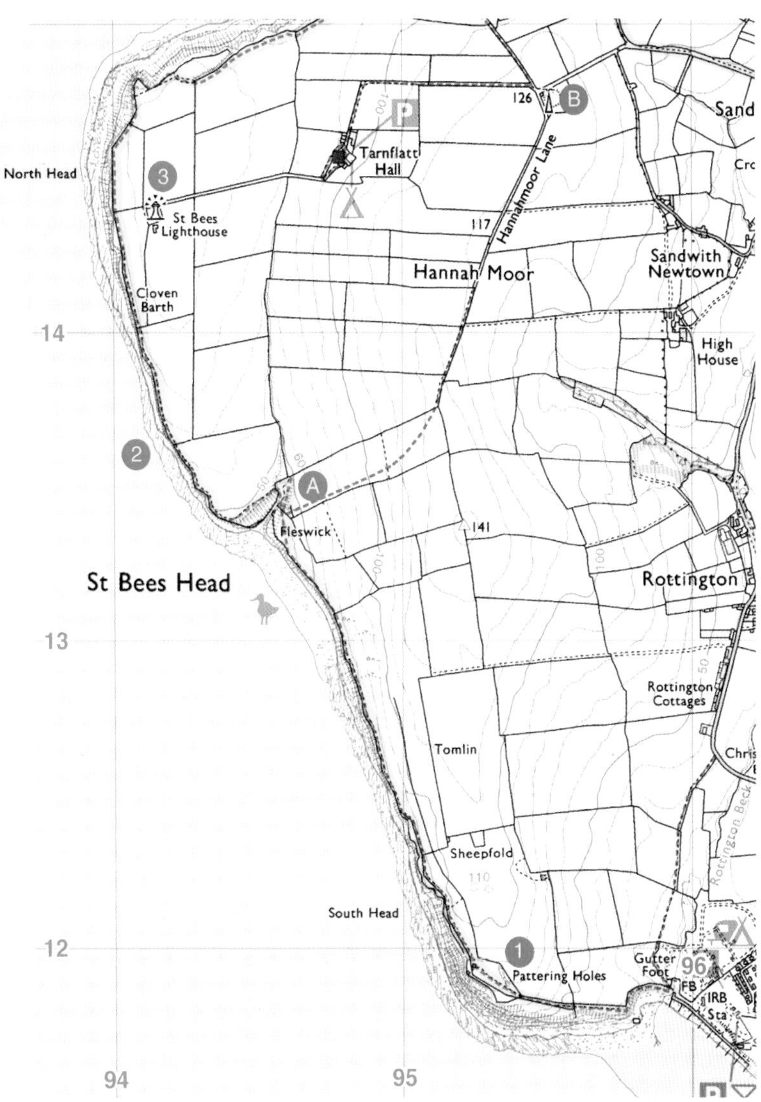

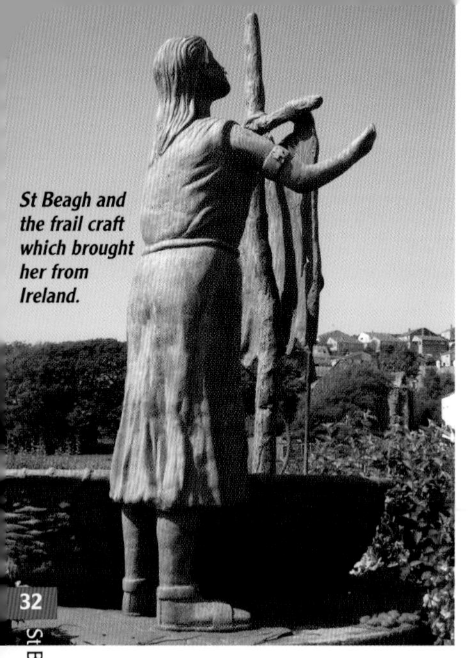

St Beagh and the frail craft which brought her from Ireland.

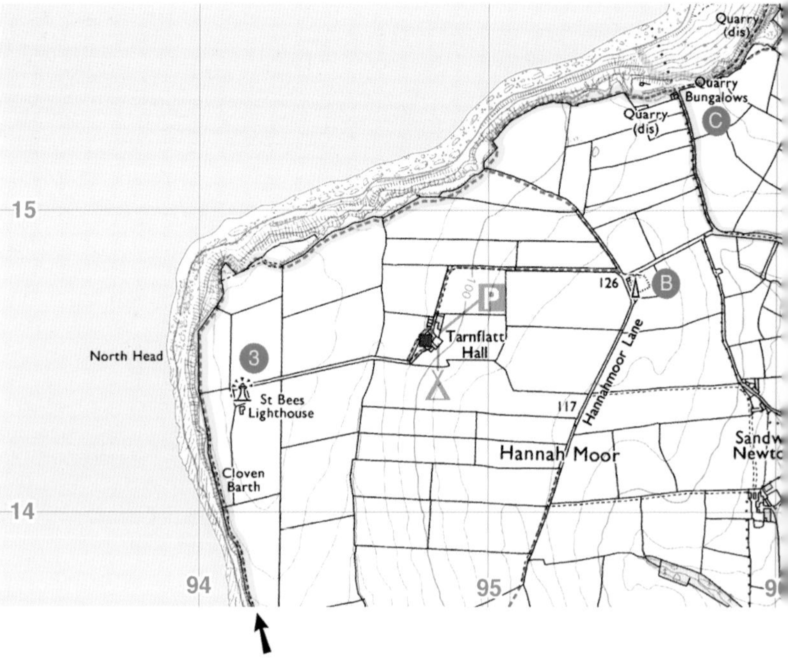

turns east, and sets its face at last towards Robin Hood's Bay, is unmistakable. The path leads to the fenced brink of working Birkham quarry, stone from which faces 19th-century commercial buildings in many northern cities. Whitehaven is dramatically revealed beyond, and here is a dramatic fact about it: Jonathan Swift, the author of *Gulliver's Travels*, caused a national kidnap scare here when he was only one year old. His nurse had to visit a sick relative in the town in a rush and, being exceptionally fond of baby Jonathan, took him with her from Dublin without telling his mother, who understandably panicked. All was well in the end. Skirt the quarry on the seaward side and round to a lane prominently marked 'Sandwith' **C**, which soon turns left into the metalled lighthouse service road. Striding downhill to Sandwith (pronounced Sanith), walkers get a clear view of the next 3 miles (5 km), culminating in Dent Fell, the small but steep Lakeland outlyer directly athwart the route. Tonsured like a monk, with bare, sheep-cropped grass above encircling fir plantations, it is your objective for the next couple of hours, getting nearer and larger until the arrow-straight wall which accompanies the path to its summit is clear. This provides reassurance on the cunning but zig-zag route pioneered by Wainwright across farmland between Sandwith and the next village, Moor Top. Route-finding needs concentration, even though the distance is short and the general direction clear.

Turn left at Sandwith past The Dog and Partridge (closed but plans to reopen are afoot), then right up Lanehead to Byerstead Road – often busy, so take care crossing to the green lane opposite which leads to Demesne Farm. Keep left in front of the farm, then right on a track marked CtoC. Cross the B5345 on to a metalled track to Bell House Farm. Pass the farm – walkers have warned of a dog here – to reach a cattle grid and take the waymarked right fork to a gate. Be ready to peel off to the left from the main track as it starts to bend at **D**, on a less distinct path down the field side to two gates. Go through the right one, by a Coast to Coast signpost, and down left beside the fence to the obvious underpass beneath the railway (a good place for sheltering in rain).

Now bear half-left across the meadow towards a dozen trees which help hide Stanley Pond, clear on the map but low-lying and fringed with long grass and reeds. Honking waterfowl may help mark its presence. Follow the hedgerow on your right to its north-eastern corner, through a gate and across a narrow bridge to walk between Stanley Pond and a smaller pool. Stay close to the hedge and then fence on your left all the way to the large copse ahead, where a stile and gate take you left into a mire of mud and sheep droppings. The hedges here are full of wildlife,

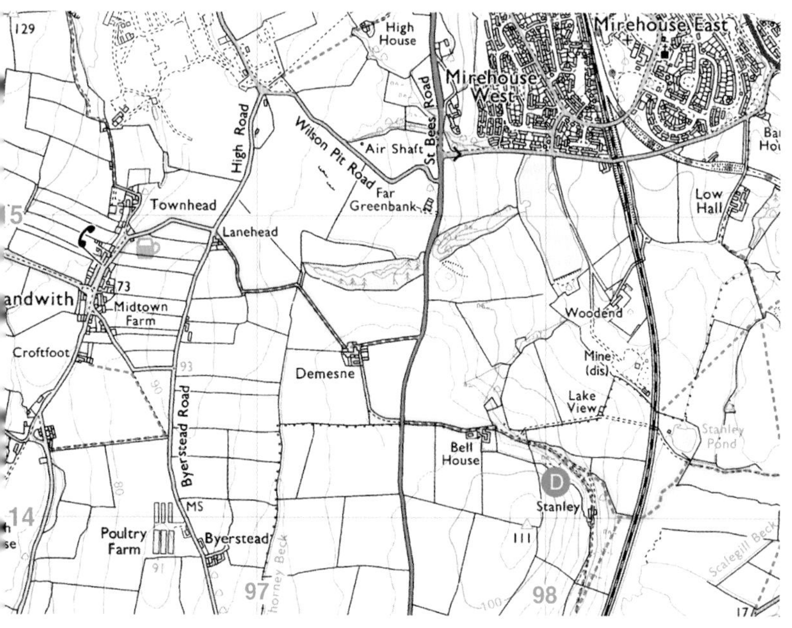

including tiny goldcrests, like wrens in party clothes, and the meadows in the broad valley are a paradise for botanists in spring and summer. They are often also a squelchy bog and anyone who fails to wear waterproof boots or oversocks may learn a lesson. Follow the edge of the copse left, ignoring a track which leads into the trees, A small post with a white arrow marks your way ahead, then after some 50 yards angle half-left uphill across the field to a gate and then down to cross Scalegill Beck by a large wall on the right **E**. Pass beneath another railway, this time a disused line which is now the excellent Whitehaven–Ennerdale cycleway.

The main route follows a farm track straight ahead, across the often busy A595 to – blimey, already! – a statue of a Coast to Coaster, erected in 2007 but already missing part of its nose. It looks as though it was sculpted from the mud through which you have just squelched. Then into Moor Row (friendly shop, bakery and café which much appreciate walkers' custom) along tarmac Scalegill Road. Take a bow, too; the village was one of the top ten places in the UK to raise children according to a 2011 internet survey, with the chance to meet walkers from all over the world an important part of that. Turn right where this angles into the village's main street, and climb gently out of Moor Row on the Egremont road until an obvious footpath sign on the left at **F**, shortly after passing a modern farmhouse on your left, points up a couple of steps to a kissing-gate in the hedge. Go through, turn right and follow the field boundary with the hedge on your right, down to Cleator, whose roofs lie below, snug beneath Dent Fell.

A quieter and more rural alternative is to scramble up on to the cycle track back at the underpass, turning left and using it to bypass Moor Row either partly, in which case you leave it (right) at its junction with Dalziell Street, or wholly by using the Egremont Extension disused railway to the point where it crosses the field path down to Cleator.

This passes through a succession of Robin Hood kissing-gates, a compact design which unfortunately doesn't take account of the fact that a full pack almost doubles a walker's size. It may be all right for the slim folk of Cleator, but I had to climb the rungs until my pack reached over the top bar. In extremis, you will just have to take the thing off. More in the spirit of the Coast to Coast, the 'bypass' of Cleator cricket ground is called Wainwright Passage, which leads to the main street after passing the fine red sandstone church of St Leonard on the right **4**. Largely modern, the church has some interesting 12th-century remains and a stained-glass window depicting Lord Egremont making his infamously mean offer of snow-covered land to St Bega (see page 40).

Cleator has the classic modest terraces of a working village flung up quickly in the huge expansion of this area, which saw the local population grow from some 800 to over 17,500 during an iron ore and coal-mining boom between 1840 and 1880. Its economic rug was pulled from under it with the decline of both industries from the 1930s onwards and it still has a forlorn air, although new employment is slowly taking up the slack. The Coast to Coast has been a tonic and you will get a specially friendly welcome from Cleator Family Store where they keep a walker's logbook. In early March, mine was only the third entry of the year, with 903 signatures the previous season, a little under a tenth of the estimated annual tally of walkers.

If you started late, or spent time pottering round St Bees, the Cleator area (including Egremont, 1½ miles (2.5 km) south and with more B&Bs) is a possible first halt, but most walkers will press on to enjoy the taster of Lakeland which lies between here and Ennerdale Bridge. Turn left up the main street, then right into Kiln Brow and right again over Blackhow Bridge, across the burbling River Ehen whose waters have not long left Ennerdale Water. Now comes the first real upward haul, but Dent Fell kindly refrains from adding route-finding

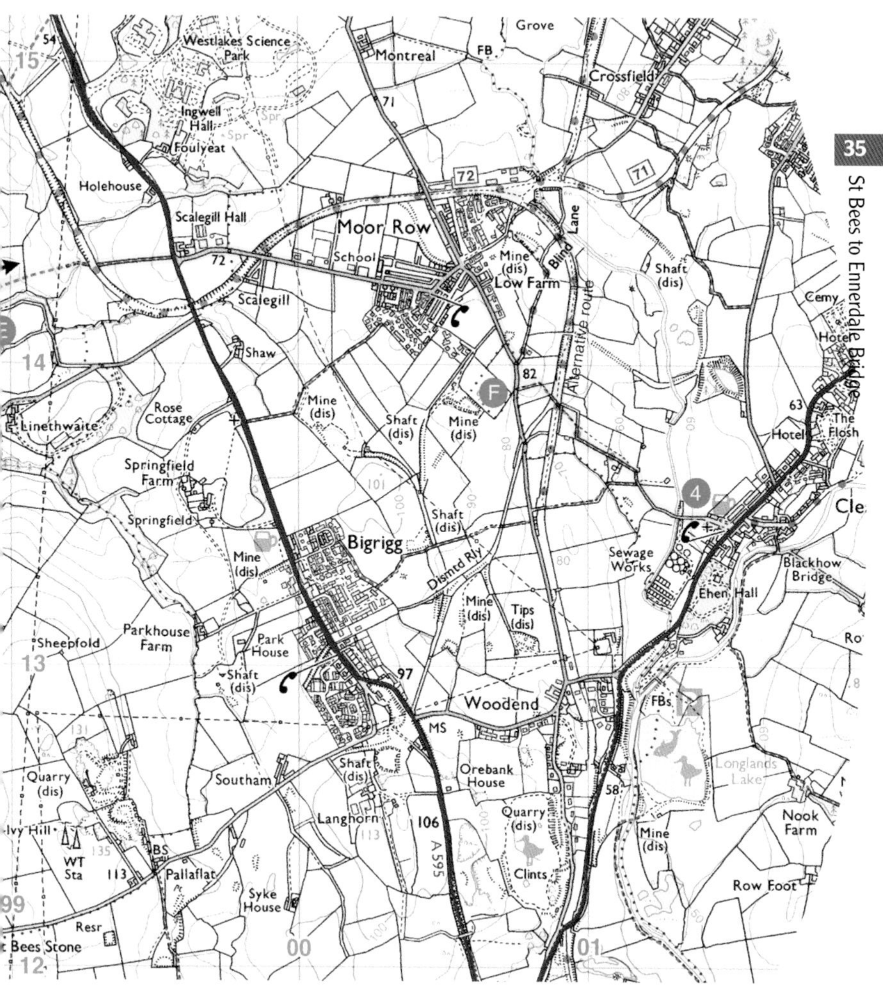

Looking back to the sea and St Bees from the gentle outlying fells of Lakeland above the hidden 'secret valley' of Nannycatch Gate.

problems to the toll it takes on tired legs. The track leads obviously up to Blackhow Farm, where a signed right turn between buildings leads to a path that rises into the forest. Where this curves right, a path signed Dent Fell **G** cuts off left and then, signed again, strikes straight uphill. If you stick with the original path at **G** you will reach the summit too; it's one of those choices of which Wainwright approved. On a wet day the dark firs on either side, despised for their uniformity and unnaturally close-packed military ranks, provide excellent shelter for a break. It is dry as a house only a yard or two in and countless small branches make pegs for soaked kit. Needless to say, leave no trace of any brief stay in this hushed, church-like refuge and never light any sort of flame.

Once beyond the tree line, march on up to the fine Egyptian pyramid of a cairn on the west summit and then traverse south-eastwards over stepping stones across boggy patches to its poor relation on the fell's true top **H**. The path curves gently left down the open slope beyond, through stumps of recently felled firs to the tree line, where a deer fence leads off to the left. Cross this by very high A-steps and traverse left along the path to a very steep descent by slither and bump down into the pretty haven of

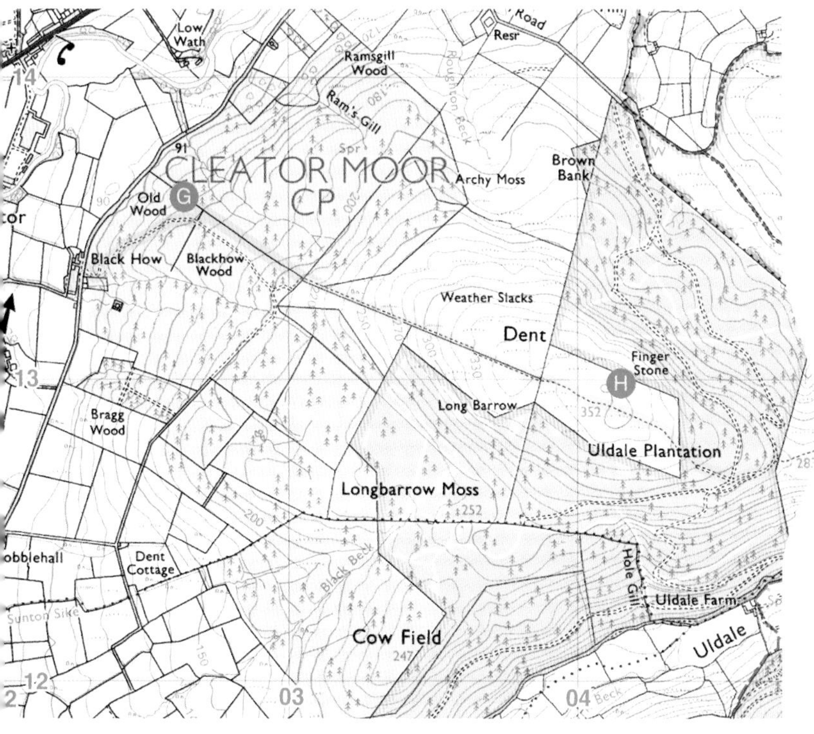

Kinniside or Blakeley Raise stone circle, reconstructed in 1925 by Dr Quine of nearby Frizington.

Ulldale. Only those equipped to 'bottom' down by sliding on strongly made jackets or trousers will enjoy this. Console yourself with the view ahead or by thinking how dreadful this brief stretch is for Coast to Coasters coming the other way.

The route now turns to the left, running along the valley bottom to Nannycatch Gate, a spot as delectable as its name, where three steep-sided valleys meet, their becks dancing along beneath the rocks of Raven Crag. Strong walkers planning to end the day at High Gillerthwaite or Black Sail youth hostels can target this little paradise for picnic lunch, with a good chance of seeing kestrels or buzzards. Don't ease off too much, though, because this is not, as you might have thought, the head of a valley running gently north-eastwards down to Ennerdale Bridge. Ulldale drains the other way, to the west, and you must climb out of it before the route finally drops down past Kinniside stone circle (a 20th-century doctor's well-sited reconstruction) **5** to the village or surrounding farms offering B&B where non-hostellers are likely to end their first day.

The traditional path follows the left (western) bank of Nannycatch Beck from the Gate up to Kinniside, keeping to the right of the wall, but in recent years there have been diversions (well signed and due to forestry or other estate work) up steep farm tracks to Sillathwaite and the metalled fell road which then curves round to Kinniside. These are a little longer but provide good views. The final drop to Ennerdale Bridge fringing Hickbarley Forest takes a pleasant path near but separate from the road, saving you from ankle-jarring tarmac or (as a down-to-earth notice warns on the cattle grid at the end of the open fell) an early death from fast cars.

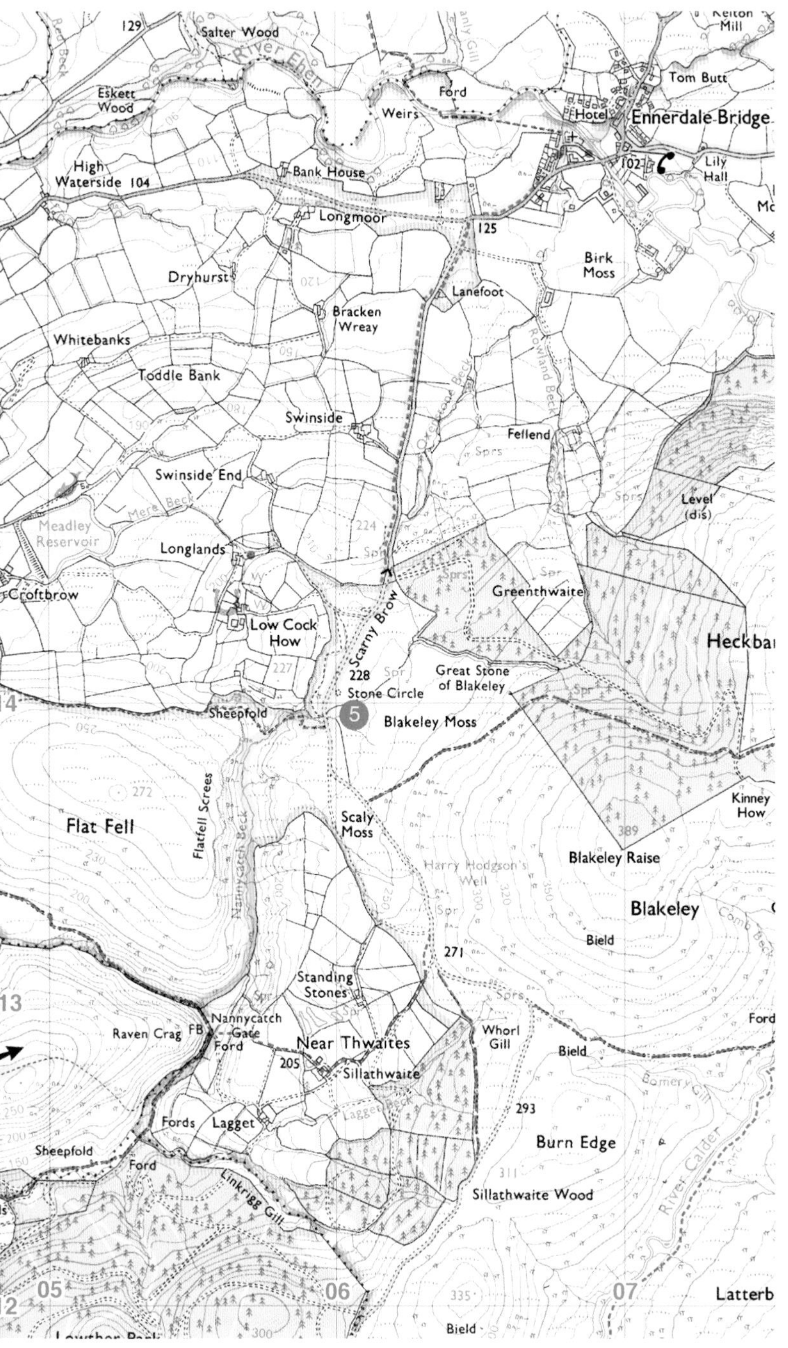

Salter Wood
River Ehen
Eskett Wood
Ford
Weirs
Hotel
Ennerdale Bridge
Tom Butt
Lily Hall
High Waterside 104
Bank House
Longmoor
125
Birk Moss
Dryhurst
Lanefoot
Bracken Wreay
Whitebanks
Toddle Bank
Rowland Beck
Swinside
Fellend
Swinside End
Level (dis)
Meadley Reservoir
Mere Beck
Longlands
Croftbrow
Greenthwaite
Low Cock How
Scarny Brow
Heckbar
228
Stone Circle
Great Stone of Blakeley
Sheepfold
Blakeley Moss
Flat Fell
Flatfell Screes
Scaly Moss
Kinney How
389
Blakeley Raise
Harry Hodgson's Well
Blakeley
Bield
Nannycatch Beck
271
Standing Stones
Nannycatch Gate
Raven Crag
FB
Ford
Near Thwaites
Whorl Gill
205
Sillathwaite
Bield
Lagget Beck
293
Fords
Lagget
Burn Edge
Sheepfold
Ford
Linkrigg Gill
Sillathwaite Wood
River Calder
05
06
07
335
Latterb
Bield

St Bees – saint and place

St Bees, often locally pronounced 'bears', is a mishearing of Bega, the name of an Irish princess who fled home and landed here after her father betrothed her to a Norwegian for political reasons. Round-cheeked and mop-haired, her bronze statue stands beside her very unsuitable boat a few yards towards the sea from the railway station, where many Coast to Coasters arrive. As the stained glass in Cleator church shows, she got the better of Lord Egremont, who thought he was clever in offering her, on midsummer's day, as much land as was covered with snow the following morning. Needless to say, there was the mother of all blizzards overnight. More substantial proof of Bega's existence can be found in the 12th-century *Life and Miracles of St Bega the Virgin* at the British Museum, and in traces of St Bees Abbey, which survived devastation by Danes and Scottish raiders before succumbing to Henry VIII in 1539.

The finest relic is the red sandstone Priory Church which had its roof stolen by Henry but was later restored. It has splendid Norman features, including the Great West Door and a carved lintel known as the Dragon Stone. Opposite stand the handsome buildings of St Bees School, founded in 1583 by Edmund Grindal who started life in the oldest house left in the town, at the junction of Cross Street and Finkle Street, and ended it at Lambeth Palace as Archbishop of Canterbury during the reign of Queen Elizabeth I. We will meet more young lads later in the walk who grew up along the route of the Coast to Coast and rose to the top job in the Church of England.

Originally a local grammar, St Bees has taken the familiar path of becoming a public school, i.e. private. Another idiosyncrasy of English usage may engage you as you stroll down to the sea: why did the nation which adds a 'greengrocer's apostrophe' in so many inappropriate places remove it from somewhere which should surely be St Bee's?

The town is still primarily agricultural, with an interesting stone-built circular pinfold, or sheep pen, surviving from the 17th century on Outbrigg. There is a little commuting to Carlisle, Barrow and Sellafield, and a low-key seafront but with lovely wide sands, divided by groynes in a perfect picture of the English bucket-and-spade nirvana. The shops will appreciate your custom and you in turn may be grateful for the only cash machine between here and Grasmere. Like many small British towns, St Bees has a magnificent website packed with information about everything from the town's fascinating near-miss as a Socialist utopia in 1895 (the parish council was gradually going to buy up the entire place) to the locally based craftsman who designed organs for St John's and King's Colleges in Cambridge. See www.stbees.org.uk.

The Great West Door of St Mary and St Bega's Church dates from 1160.

Thousands of seabirds soar, squabble and stain the pink and red stone cliffs of the RSPB reserve at St Bees' North Head.

Between the sea and the hills

The 5.57am train north from Barrow-in-Furness is always packed as far as Sellafield. But from the nuclear plant to the next halt, St Bees, where you have to ask the conductor if you want the train to stop, I shared all three carriages with just one elderly woman and a schoolboy. This tells the modern story of the largely forgotten edge of Cumbria which you traverse on your first day of the Coast to Coast. It has known sudden great prosperity, equally sudden slumps and years of drowsing most of the time.

Like a plain child with a beautiful sister, it has to live with the proximity of the Lake District. Visitors want to go there, not here. It is no good protesting that the region's greatest son, William Wordsworth, was a Cockermouth boy. Some people dutifully examine his birthplace, but not a fraction of the crocodiles which tour Rydal Mount or Dove Cottage. In today's crowded and market-hyped world, however, the peace and quiet of Ennerdale Bridge or Nannycatch Gate is a tonic for anyone jaded by the Beatrix Potter, cream-tea merry-go-round of Ambleside or Bowness.

Peripheral Cumbria has always earned a living from the earth, first through farming and then by mining coal. Victorian pits brought so much wealth that their owners actually adorned their buildings above ground as if they were small palaces. The fashionable London architect Sydney Smirke came to Whitehaven in 1850 to design the Candlestick chimney, a pit ventilation shaft which is still a local landmark. Industry also brought a tradition of hard work and inventiveness: Britain's first detergents were manufactured in 1941 at Preston Isle, south of Whitehaven, when an Austrian refugee called Frank Schon, later Lord Schon, and partner Fred Marzillier set up the Marchon chemical works which are clearly seen from the Coast to Coast. Creating more than 2,000 jobs, the new industry was a well-timed successor to worked-out coal seams, along with Kangol (silK, ANGora,woOL) which made berets and then seat belts here from 1938 to 2009 when production moved overseas.

Nothing could wholly compensate for the collapse, however, which was as rapid as the original 'Black Klondyke' between 1840 and 1880. In the 1930s, thousands moved to find work in the Yorkshire pits and later the new Northamptonshire steel town of Corby. Recently, the Sellafield nuclear complex has been a mainstay of the local economy, though many doubt its future. Such worries have encouraged the development of smaller hi-tech industries which compete for the pool of expert labour.

Birds at Fleswick Bay

England's only nesting colony of black guillemots is at Fleswick Bay between St Bees' north and south heads, with early mornings in April and May the best time to see the birds. From May until late July there are over 100 nesting cormorants on the noisy cliffs, thousands of fork-tailed kittiwakes, soaring fulmars and – on the cliff top – whitethroats, as well as linnets, rock pipits and stonechats.

2 Ennerdale Bridge to Rosthwaite

via Black Sail and Honister • 6–7 hours
14.3 miles (22.9 km)

Ascent 1,740 feet (530 metres)

Descent 1,772 feet 540 (metres)

Lowest point Rosthwaite: 295 feet (90 metres)

Highest point Moses' Trod: 2,067 feet (630 metres)

Past a lonely lake to the remote youth hostel of Black Sail, one of the most beautiful places to stay in Britain, then over a high pass with ravishing mountain views to Honister slate mine and down into the lovely valley of Borrowdale.

The walk leaves Ennerdale Bridge on the Croasdale road, marked by an elegant early 20th-century roadsign opposite the village school on the left. After about 700 yards (640 metres), turn right and follow the metalled road to the lake as it zig-zags to a bridge over the River Ehen and then the politely inconspicuous water-treatment plant, which cost £12 million

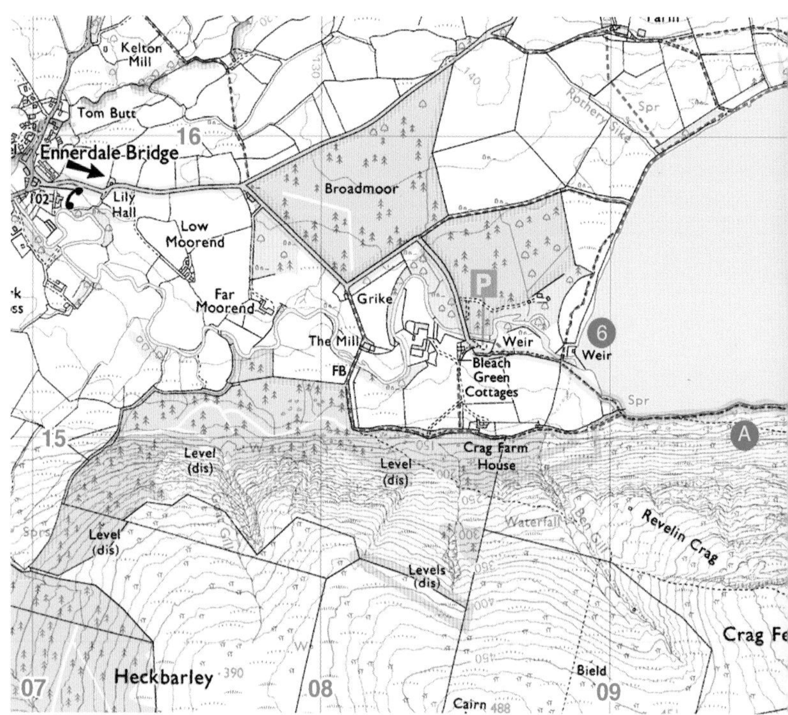

and supplies more than 60,000 households but is hardly to be seen, even from close by **6**. Here the path divides: turn left for the northern shore path, which skirts the lake without incident or obstacle to Gillerthwaite at the far end, and is pleasant but definitely second best. Between April and October it is also likely to be busier with day-trippers. Most Coast to Coasters will prefer the southern shore.

The path to this runs straight ahead to a little scrambling round the foot of Angler's Crag, which has a long-standing accident record of sprains on rock made slippery by rain. Recent work has made the sinuous route clearer and safer and most walkers should have no difficulty. Just don't rush. An attraction of this 'low road' is the chance to sit on Robin Hood's Chair **7**, a stone outcrop into the lake and another of many moments when the man in Lincoln green watches over your progress to his alleged bay. (As with all his memorials, there is no evidence that he was ever here, but who cares?) If you have worries about the rocks, a clear diversionary path **A** slants up to the top of Angler's Crag and down the other side, a bit of a slog so early in the day but rewarded by good views of the Buttermere fells opposite and some of the giants further up Ennerdale. Beyond the junction of the two paths a kissing-gate leads to a pretty spinney of stunted woodland growing from a wilderness of rough

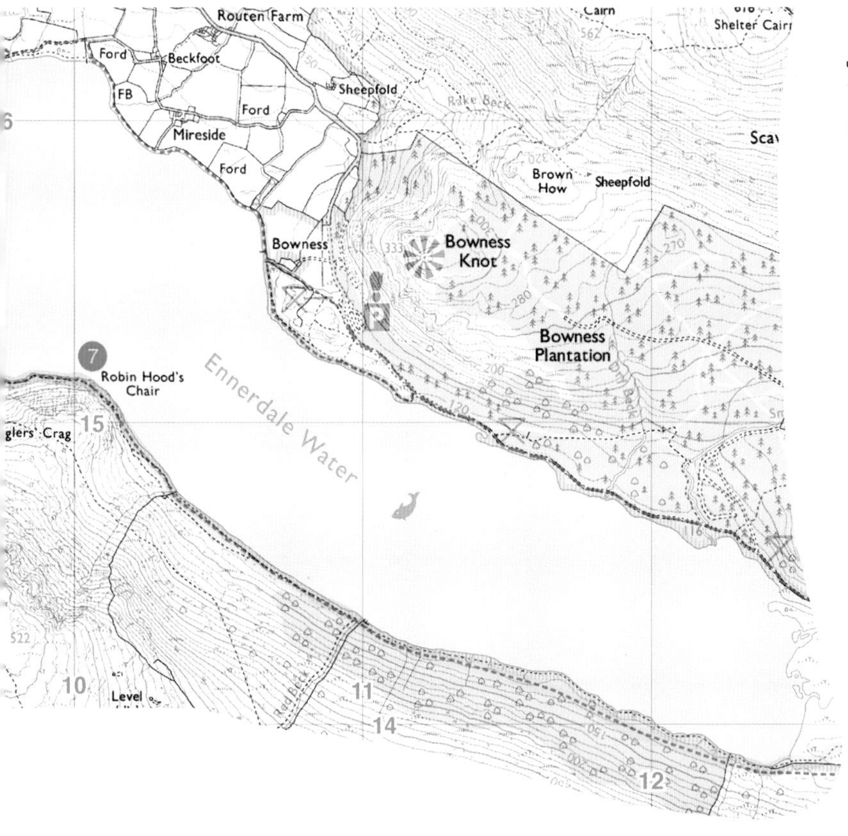

boulders cloaked in moss and lichen. Becks and little waterfalls splash through, crossed by large stepping stones when in spate. Birdsong in season is marvellous here. I had goldcrests fluting away, blackbirds providing the main music and a woodpecker on percussion.

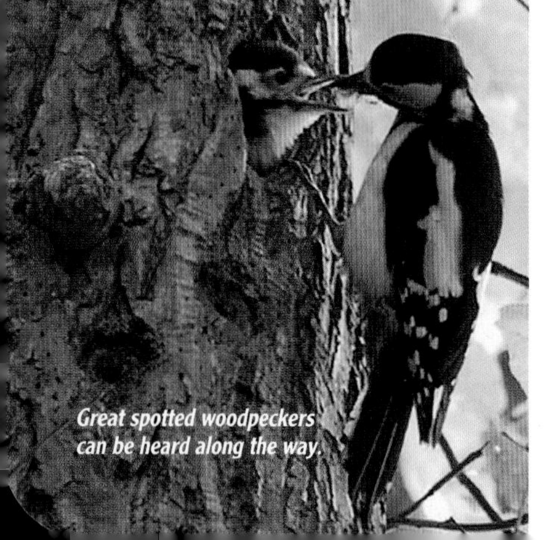

Great spotted woodpeckers can be heard along the way.

At the end of the lake follow the route carefully because you need to hit one of the two bridges across the wide and lively River Liza, unless you prefer to take the path along the right-hand bank of the river for some 4 miles (6.4 km) to a ford shortly before Black Sail. This is a beautiful and less-used route, with a footbridge a little further beyond the ford if the Liza is in spate, and your best chance of seeing the elusive pine marten. The usual path, however, crosses a little grassland **B** before either turning left on the track which comes out of the forestry plantation on your right or – better – turning right into the plantation then sharp left and left again after only about 50 yards, through a gate marked Forestry Commission with an instruction to leash

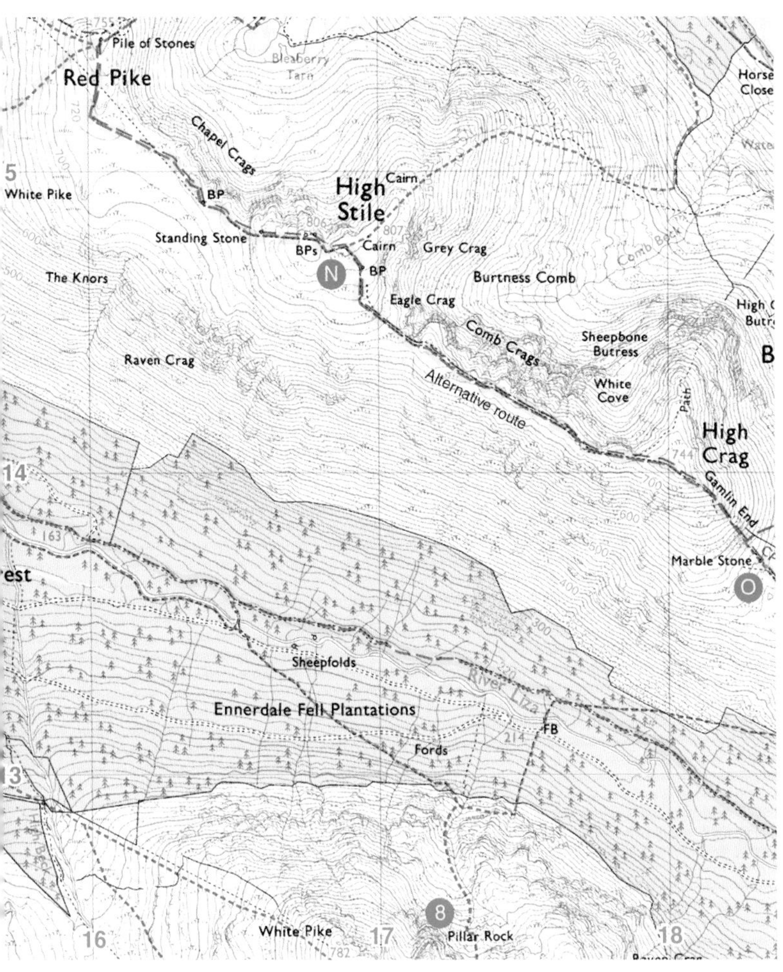

dogs. From here a grassy path curves across the meadow straight to a narrow footbridge over the river. Aim across the next field, crossing a small rivulet by a broken bridge, for a stile which takes you into Low Gillerthwaite Farm – an outdoor activities centre which can put up walkers overnight when not full of schoolchildren – and up to the main Ennerdale track.

This takes forestry jeeps up to Black Sail and is wide and easy walking. Much scorn has been poured on the evergreen planting here, notably by Alfred Wainwright, but things are better now than in his day. Much of the high-level tree-planting has been harvested, leaving a tidemark of stumps and felling debris (excellent for beetles and other inconspicuous wildlife) on the flanks of the grand mountains which line the trod. Here are Haycock, Scoat Fell, Steeple, Pillar and the tower of Pillar Rock **8** with its curiously flat ledge right above your

Black Sail! All Hail!

head. Meanwhile, tantalising glimpses of high-altitude becks and more huge fells at the head of the valley come and go as the track snakes along and the height of the surrounding trees rises and falls.

And then you are suddenly out of the trees and at Black Sail **9**, perhaps the loveliest place to stay in the entire Lake District – but book well ahead because the tiny youth hostel sleeps only 16 and is closed except for block-bookings between the end of October and Easter. A former shepherd's bothy, it sits with a green, sheep-nibbled grass terrace on its lap and homely touches such as a birdnut feeder during the winter. A very welcome seat honours the memory of a Leeds youth worker who sat here awestruck by the panorama as a young man and returned to make nearly half a million feet of ascents with needy children from his city. Fittingly, Black Sail is a place where humanity's domination of nature is reversed – the hut is insignificant in its vast, wild setting, watched over by Great Gable with Kirk Fell, Green Gable and Brandreth occupying the side thrones. The adage about faith moving mountains is also turned on its head. Memories of this lovely place will move and sustain you in any difficult times you may endure. 'Black Sail, All Hail,' as my grandfather used to chant at the end of a long poem about Lake District glories.

Leaving Black Sail is a wrench and the next step of the walk makes it worse. Follow an initially indistinct path straight ahead **C**, instead of the more obvious track which leads to a footbridge across the Liza but then heads off to Wasdale. Your route aims towards the conspicuous silver thread of Tongue Beck high above on the flank of Green Gable. The path crosses hummocky terrain, becoming more distinct until an unsuspected ravine **D** opens up in the fellside on your left. This is Loft Beck, which alas you must climb following the right-hand side of the Beck on a clear, recently repaired stone stairway. Bless the Lake District's marvellous path improvers in your hour of pain and promise to make a donation to the mountain rescue collection boxes which await you at Honister slate mine.

I was worried about the route from the top of the beck, as my crossing of this high and largely featureless land was shrouded in thick mist. I need not have been. An extremely well-cairned path leads off to the right from the top of Loft Beck. After pausing to admire the view back for almost the last time, follow the unfailing heaps of stones in a gentle north-easterly curve round the flanks of Brandreth and Grey Knotts, hitting a stile **E** to cross the modern and otherwise impassable sheep fence which cuts across your route. There are wonderful views from here **10** in clear weather – or, even better, through sudden openings in the mist – back to Ennerdale, along the ridge from Haystacks to High Stile and down into the lovely valley of Buttermere. Slate workings lie directly ahead and below, but they are not Honister and if you divert to inspect them you will have a haul back up. Don't worry if the cairns seem to go on for a long time. They do. You will not miss the arrival from the right of the even more distinct path called Moses' Trod, named after a smuggler and moonshine whisky distiller and the old route for slate convoys to Wasdale Head and the coast. The paths combine at a T-junction with an extra flourish of cairns **F** and you follow the trod left (north) down a gradual descent to the skeletal

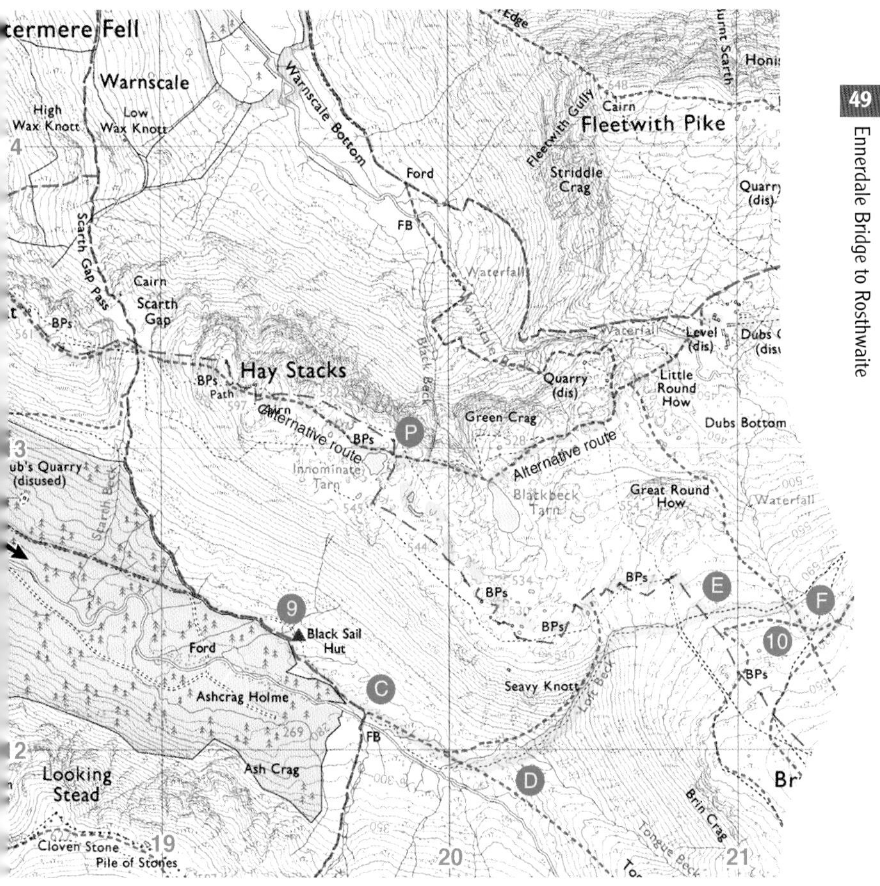

ruins of the old drum house which contained the mechanism for the slate tramway **11**. Turn sharp right here and follow the splendidly angled tramway ramp straight down to Honister mine **12** and the motor road pass between Buttermere and Borrowdale. The very last part is a steep but well-engineered zig-zag over rock.

Great joy awaits you here, with hot drinks, food, the chance to buy a little slate Coast to Coast coaster, two roaring fires in season, plus rocking chairs; and because the floor is slate you don't even have to take off your boots.

Don't relax too much, though, because there is still quite a long descent to Rosthwaite. The road loops widely down but you can leave it within five minutes by taking the old road which forks off to the left **G** and keeps to higher ground until a short and steep descent at Seatoller which welcomes you back into civilisation with a

'Wad' under Siege

Seatoller was the site of Britain's most closely guarded mine in the 17th and 18th centuries, when ferocious penalties met any attempt to steal 'wad', the world's best graphite, which was found here in large quantities. Militarily sensitive, in mouldings for cannon and musket balls, it was also prized by pencil-makers, including the famous Keswick company just up the valley at the head of Derwentwater. Flooding the market would have destroyed businesses, so armed men were stationed in a guardhouse, miners searched repeatedly and theft punished by transportation to Australia. One smuggler, Black Sal, was said to have been hunted to his death by hounds, but another dug a fake copper mine and made a secret, and profitable, door into the wad workings.

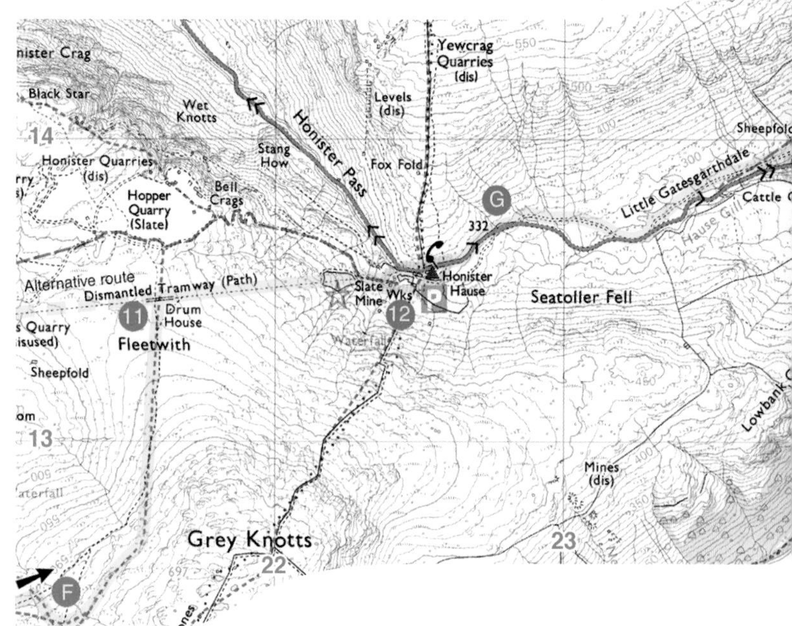

Neighbourhood Watch notice and, on the afternoon I arrived, wheeliebins put out for collection. But there is one brief finale to come which recalls exhilarating scrambles earlier in the day.

Turn left into Seatoller car park and leave at the far end up a short track to a stile (not the small one in the fence on the right) **H**. Keep right at a fork in the obvious path signed Rosthwaite and amble down through lovely woodland to the racing Derwent. Here comes the tingle factor. The path turns for 25 yards into a cautious clamber over smooth, water-worn rocks with a chain bolted into the miniature cliff face above the river to help you past a narrow furrow where you can put only one foot at a time **I**. It's safe and well thought out, but be careful: you may be more tired than you think after your long day and the river is always icy cold.

Cross the Derwent just after Rosthwaite youth hostel (the fourth you have passed today) then follow the clearly marked path to the outlying fringe of Rosthwaite village **J** – houses which mark your return from the wild with names like Home Cottage and The Nook. Sheep will probably examine you across two final paddocks before you take a last look at the Jaws of Borrowdale on your left and turn into the main street.

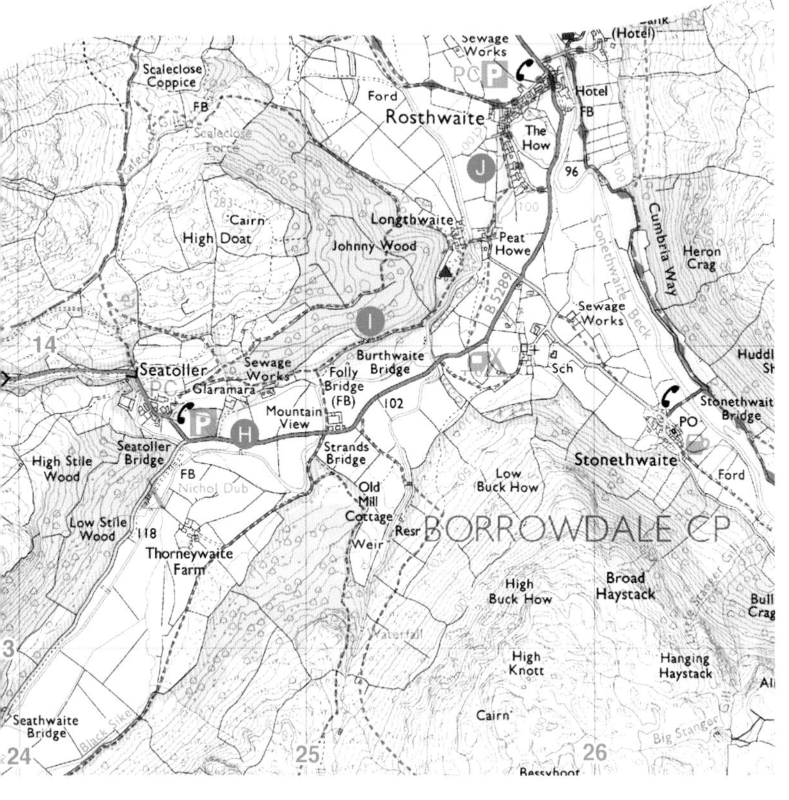

High-level alternative

The 'standard' Coast-to-Coast route through the Lakes is enough of a pleasure for many walkers, and I enjoyed its thoughtful traverse of passes – partly because this is how people used to get from A to B, whether with pedlar's packs or pannier ponies. It was a waste of time and money for them to divert to bag a peak. But many others, these days, only have to look at a mountain to want to get to the top; and the ranges between Ennerdale Bridge and Haweswater are among the loveliest in the world. Alfred Wainwright, who knew them as well as anyone ever has, left instructions for his ashes to be scattered at a particularly ravishing place on this high road: Haystacks' uniquely un-named summit pool, Innominate Tarn. 'If you, dear reader, should get a bit of grit in your boots when you are crossing Haystacks,' he wrote, 'treat it with respect. It might be me.'

The tarn is a highlight of the first of the three high-level alternatives on the Coast to Coast through Lakeland. The other two are described at the end of the next chapter. All are best undertaken in clear weather, even if you enjoy the challenge of mountain mist. There is much fun to be had from scrambling or ticking off a list of summits, but the greatest pleasure comes from the wonderful views. They are both intimate, as in the rocky chaos of Haystacks, and far-reaching, way ahead and back over the satisfyingly mighty tract of land you have already covered, to the sea.

The first alternative – Red Pike to the top of Loft Beck – starts at the former cattle grid **K** (see maps on pages 46–49) on the forest track to Black Sail shortly after Ennerdale youth hostel. Turn left up a path which clambers steeply up the side of Red Pike, following a stream, until a large and prominent cairn on the left bank **L**. Cross the stream here and continue beside it, following cairns uphill and taking care not to angle right until the cairns do **M**. Leaving the stream early leads you on to a dead end amid dangerous scree. Staying with the cairns takes you safely north-east across grass to the summit of Red Pike. Note that the path climbs straight up the slope at right angles to the contour lines until the ridge is reached, when it veers slightly to the left. Hooray – you are on the ridge, and although it's a switchback from now on, you will stay well above the valley below.

From the summit, follow old boundary posts south-east to the highest summit on the ridge, High Stile **N**, with Chapel Crags on your left and grand views in all directions if the weather is kind. The direction continues gently south-east over Comb Crags to High Cragg, just a little lower than Red Pike and followed by rocky steps down past a tarn on the right **O**. After a gentler descent, more steps lead steeply to Scarth Gap and then an invigorating slope upwards, with some scrambling, to Haystacks, its small summit tarn and then Innominate Tarn a little below. The path skirts to the left of the water and then curves right **P**, threads between two small tarnlets and heads south-east towards the Brandreth fence, keeping it on the right. The final stretch before joining the low-level route from Black Sail at the fence stile above Loft Beck is often horribly boggy. Stick with the fence, where the ground is usually firmer, until you reach the stile **E** on the main route – not the first, but identifiable by the cairns stretching away on both sides. You are back on the 'standard' path, turning left to head for Honister.

Taking this diversion adds between 1½ and 2 miles (3.2 km) to the route, or an average of two hours, and Wainwright recommended it for fit walkers in good weather. Its greatest disadvantage – missing Black Sail – can be put right by dropping down right at Scarth Gap for a night at the lonely hostel, remembering to check availability in advance.

An excellent path from **P** to **11** via Dubs Quarry is a good alternative ending to the high-level route (see maps pages 46, 47, 49 and 50).

Alfred Wainwright's ashes were scattered at Innominate Tarn on Haystacks, his favourite peak.

3 Rosthwaite to Patterdale

via Grasmere • 8–9 hours/5 to Grasmere
14.6 miles (23.2 km) to Grasmere

Ascent 1,970 feet (600 metres)
Descent 3,084 feet (94 metres)
Lowest point Grasmere: 295 feet (90 metres)
Highest point Greenup Edge: 2,001 feet (610 metres)

Switchback over two passes surrounded by outstanding mountain walks, climbing first from Borrowdale to Wordsworth's Grasmere, then past the cliffs of Helvellyn to the quiet southern shores of Ullswater.

This section, across the heart of Lakeland, may be taken as one day or two. There is time to make the journey in a day, even in winter, but dividing it at Grasmere allows for more diversions to the wealth of peaks beside the trail, or gives a breather after your energetic start to the trek. Grasmere is packed with places to stay and eat, even if its tourism may come as a shock after several hours in the wild.

Take up the route at the start of the Keswick road from Rosthwaite, turning right by Hazelbank, crossing the Derwent on a sturdy bridge and then turning right again for a prolonged meander upstream. The gravelled track fringes woodland and, if you are quiet and lucky, you may see red squirrels. The waterfalls get better and better, especially after you pass Stonethwaite (another good alternative for overnight stays) and the Langstrath Beck comes tumbling in to join Greenup Gill at a heavenly spot **13**.

The path strikes from here at an angle up the slopes of Greenup Edge, one of those perfect gradients for early in the day, gaining height but not taking too much toll of legs and puff. If humans could walk backwards more easily, the view down into Borrowdale would entrance you all the way up. As it is, the precipices of Eagle Crag **14** form an increasingly grand foreground to your right. If, like me, you encounter mist, the vexations of route-finding have a silver lining in spectacular cloud effects – sudden glimpses of distant mountains such as snow-covered Blencathra; mist boiling up from a corrie or lifting gently from a ridge like a veil. If you get above the cloud, the subtly different layers are delightful to watch and, should the sun be shining, you may see a Brocken Spectre – your shadow vastly inflated on to the mist below and surrounded by a 'glory' or circular rainbow, or even occasionally a double one. Each walker can see only their own spectre, a phenomenon first recorded in the Brocken mountains of Germany.

As the recently repaired and very well-engineered path rises, two pyramid hillocks become larger ahead **A**. They mark the edge of a desolate but lovely hanging valley, an unexpected bowl high

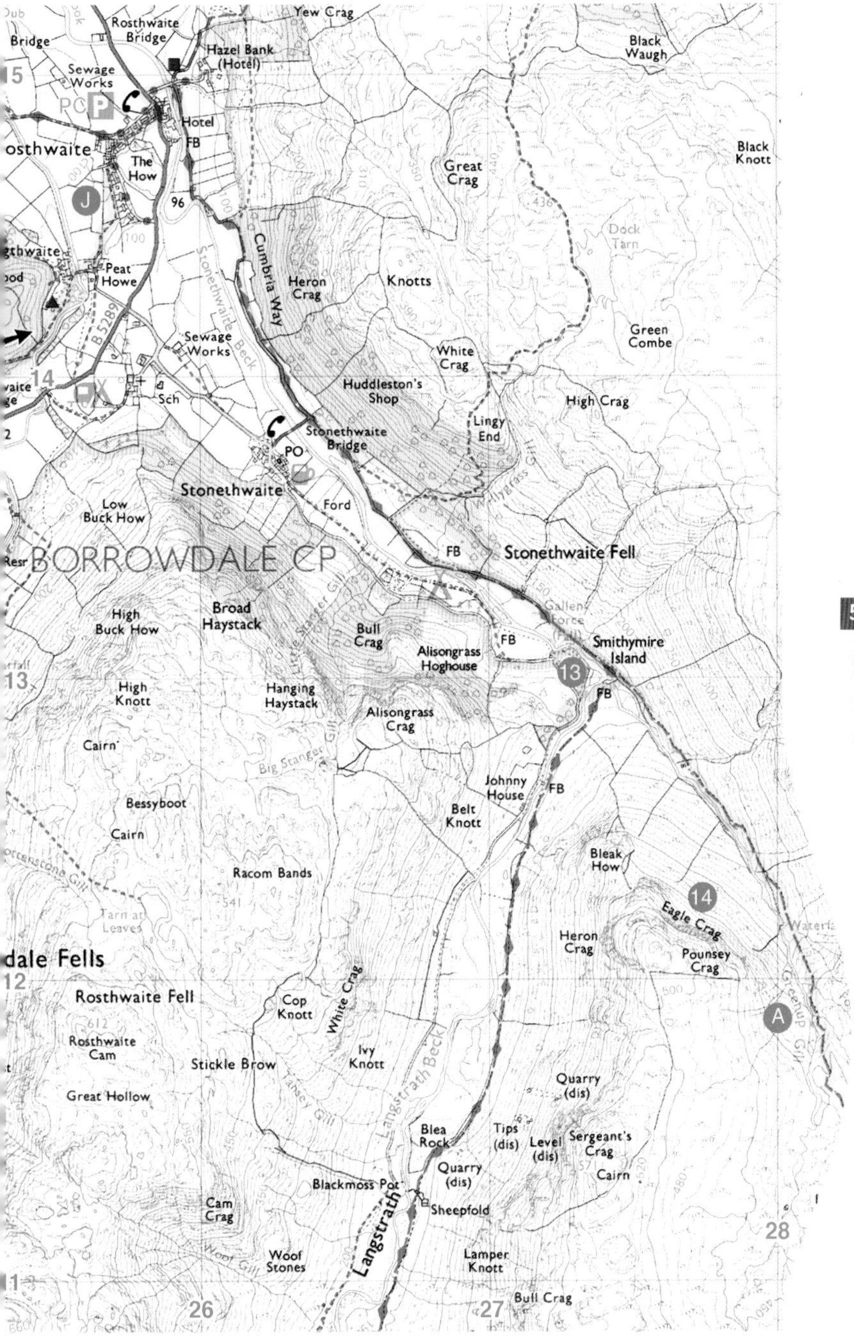

Yew Crag
Rosthwaite Bridge
Bridge
Hazel Bank (Hotel)
Sewage Works
Black Waugh
Hotel
FB
Rosthwaite
The How
Great Crag
Black Knott
96
J
Dock Tarn
Peat Howe
Cumbria Way
Heron Crag
Knotts
B 5289
Stonethwaite Beck
Sewage Works
Green Combe
White Crag
Huddleston's Shop
High Crag
Sch
Lingy End
Stonethwaite Bridge
PO
Wythburn Gill
Stonethwaite
Ford
Low Buck How
BORROWDALE CP
FB
Stonethwaite Fell
High Buck How
Broad Haystack
Galleny Force (Fall)
Bull Crag
FB
Smithymire Island
Alisongrass Hoghouse
13
High Knott
Hanging Haystack
FB
Alisongrass Crag
Cairn
Big Stanger Gill
Johnny House
FB
Belt Knott
Bessyboot
Cairn
Bleak How
Racom Bands
14
Eagle Crag
Tarn at Leaves
Heron Crag
Pounsey Crag
dale Fells
Rosthwaite Fell
Greenup Gill
A
Cop Knott
White Crag
Rosthwaite Cam
Ivy Knott
Stickle Brow
Langstrath Beck
Quarry (dis)
Great Hollow
Blea Rock
Tips (dis)
Level (dis)
Sergeant's Crag
Quarry (dis)
Cairn
Blackmoss Pot
Cam Crag
Sheepfold
Langstrath
Woof Stones
Lamper Knott
Bull Crag
26
27
28

Herdwicks, Swaledales and other hardy mountain breeds of sheep rest in the rich valley pastures near Rosthwaite, divided into intakes by drystone walls.

up the fellside, perfect for a picnic on a sunny day. This is the place for designing your dream castle amid the drumlins, oblivious of how to connect mains services or pay for a cable car, although nature has got here first: Lining Crag **15** stands like a fortress by your next step up. Again, the noble path engineers have saved you from a nasty scree scramble by making stone steps – only hazardous in winter when they can become an impassable staircase of ice. Arriving in just such conditions, I scrambled to the left and then upwards via steep hummocks of frozen grass. In warmer weather, look out for clumps of starry saxifrage.

The hard work is over at the top of the crag, where the path continues on its straight, south-east course at a gentler gradient, clear initially and then marked with cairns – but only small ones; add a stone to each if you can. Navigation is fine in good weather but in mist make carefully from cairn to cairn, trust your map and if necessary check occasionally with a compass. The old iron posts of two fences are important landmarks; the first come soon after the summit of Lining Crag and mark the top of Greenup Edge **B**. Here the path bears slightly left (east) and then contours gently round to the right, again with rather small cairns and across the infant Flour Gill and a succession of smaller becks descending to your left. Do not follow these tempting streams. You would be falling into what Wainwright calls the 'Wythburn trap'. They lead uncomfortably down into the Wythburn valley, which comes out well north of Grasmere. Our path leads, sometimes boggily, to the narrow col at the head of Far Easedale, luckily marked by two metal posts distinctively close together which were once a stile in another fence **C**. The way is straight through these, becoming clearer at once and plunging eagerly downhill.

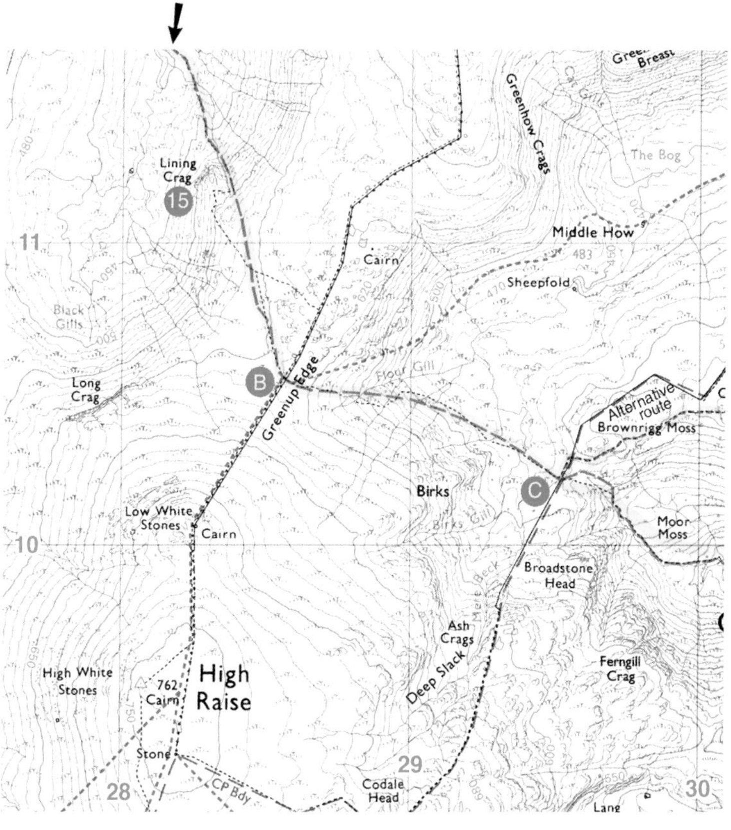

An excellent alternative, preferrable in clear conditions, strikes off left here, initially by the old fenceposts and then along the ridge from Calf Crag to Gibson Knott and bristling little Helm Crag (see pages 61–62).

Descending Far Easedale by the main route, signs of gentler civilisation soon appear: first the sheep (though in summer you will have met them higher up), then trees and birds. The becks are a lovely succession of pools and cascades, invigorating for summer dips (but don't plunge straight in if you are hot from walking; even at the warmest time of year, the water is extremely cold). Reaching flat ground and farmhouses, the valley curls round the end of Helm Crag, with a fine view on your right of Sour Milk Gill **16**

tumbling down from Easedale Tarn, and reaches Goody Bridge. Walkers hastening on for Patterdale turn left here **D**, bypassing Grasmere (though if necessary getting food and drink at The Traveller's Rest on the A591, just below the start of the ascent to Grisedale Hause). Otherwise go straight on for the final five minutes into the village and be ready to remove your boots at the many polite eateries.

Versatile Gingerbread

Grasmere gingerbread, a good alternative to Kendal mint cake for energy boosting, uses Sarah Nelson's secret recipe, developed with encouragement from a French chef employed by Lady Farquhar and passed on after Sarah's death in 1904, aged 88. A keen reformer, she made gingerbread alphabets to teach local children to read.

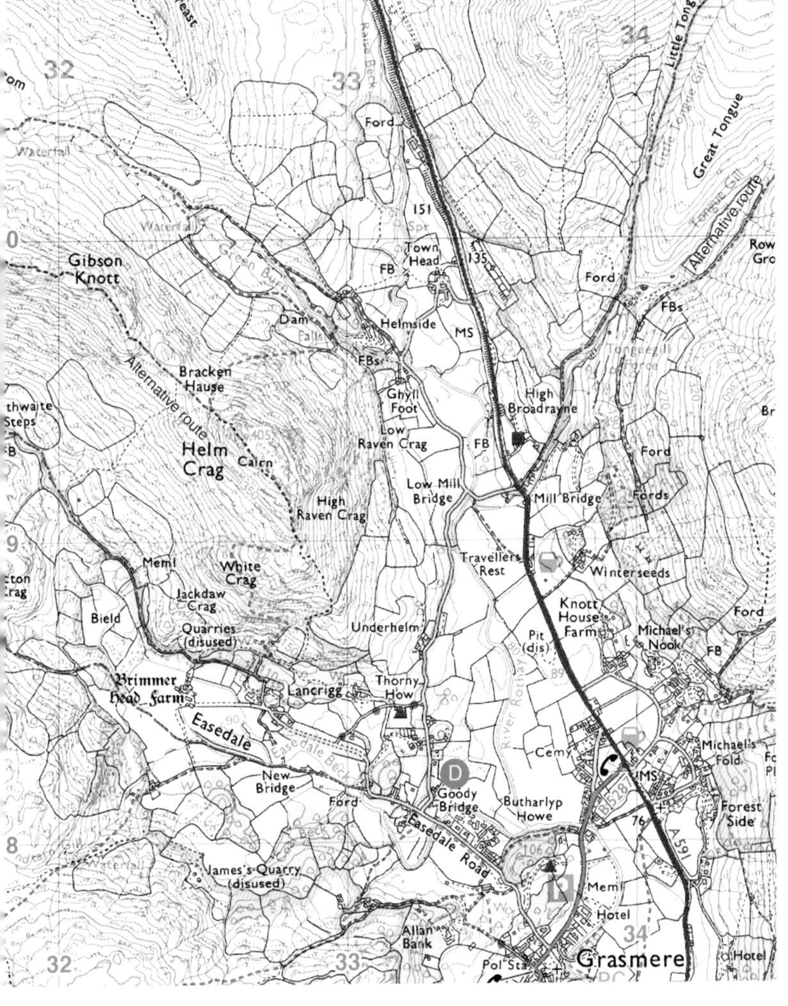

Grasmere is awash with attractions, the best being Dove Cottage, Wordsworth's well-preserved home, which has a new and stylish adjoining museum **17**.

The climb to Patterdale starts directly opposite the junction of the pretty lane from Goody Bridge to the A591 **E**. Either retrace your steps to Goody Bridge or continue through Grasmere up Broadgate to the main road and a short haul alongside the rushing traffic, past The Traveller's Rest. Clear signing, 'Bridleway to Patterdale', marks the right turn by some cottages to the start of the Victorians' pony track to the summit of Helvellyn and the old route across the pass. A stony track mounts briskly upwards with the grassy slopes of Seat Sandal on the left.

William Wordsworth towards the end of his life. The laureate of the Lakes survived into the age of the camera.

At a footbridge over Little Tongue Gill **F** you can choose between the pony route (left) or the Tongue Gill variant (right). The ponies' old path climbs straight up beside Little Tongue Gill to just above the obvious line of crags on the right, where it turns right on to a clear path **G** which contours round Seat Sandal's upper slopes.

From the path above the crags, which switchbacks slightly, you can clearly see the alternative route marching up the far side of Tongue Gill and crossing the dramatic, slender waterfalls at a safely level point. Although I have marked it on the map opposite as the variant, this is the way I prefer to go. The gradient is gentler than the in-your-face pony route and the waterfalls are marvellous for a rest or picnic. Hurry and get there before anyone else does. There's only room for one party. The paths meet just below what appears to be the head of the pass, but isn't **H**. One of the Lake District's notorious false summits reveals a final dip and then a steep ascent through a jumble of rocks (unobtrusively 'stone-staircased' in the worst places) to the actual saddle between Fairfield (on the right) and Seat Sandal and the start of the descent along the right-hand side of Grisedale Tarn..

This is Grisedale Hause (Pass) and it is now downhill all the way, a relief to me because rain started here – abrupt change in the weather is common at passes – which sluiced for the next two hours all the way to The White Lion at Patterdale.

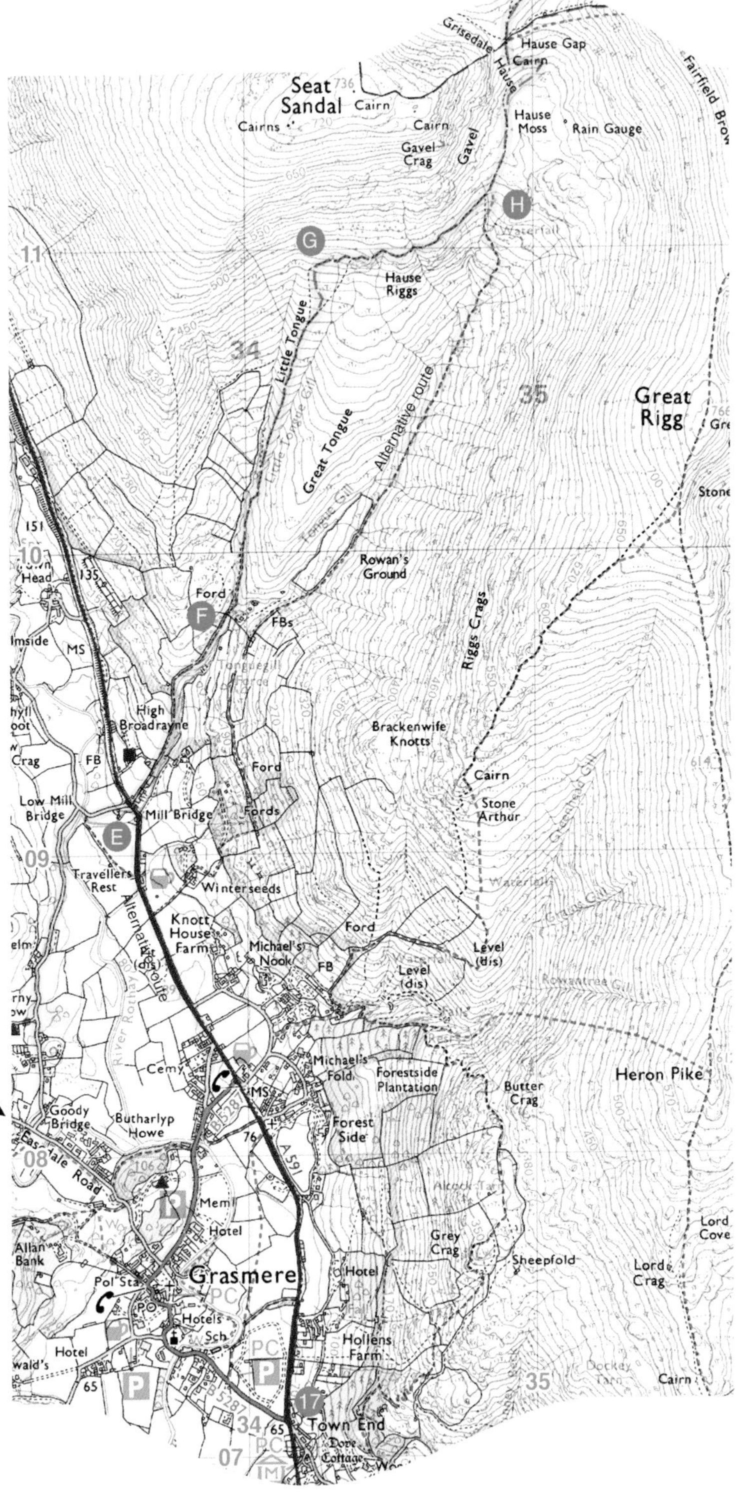

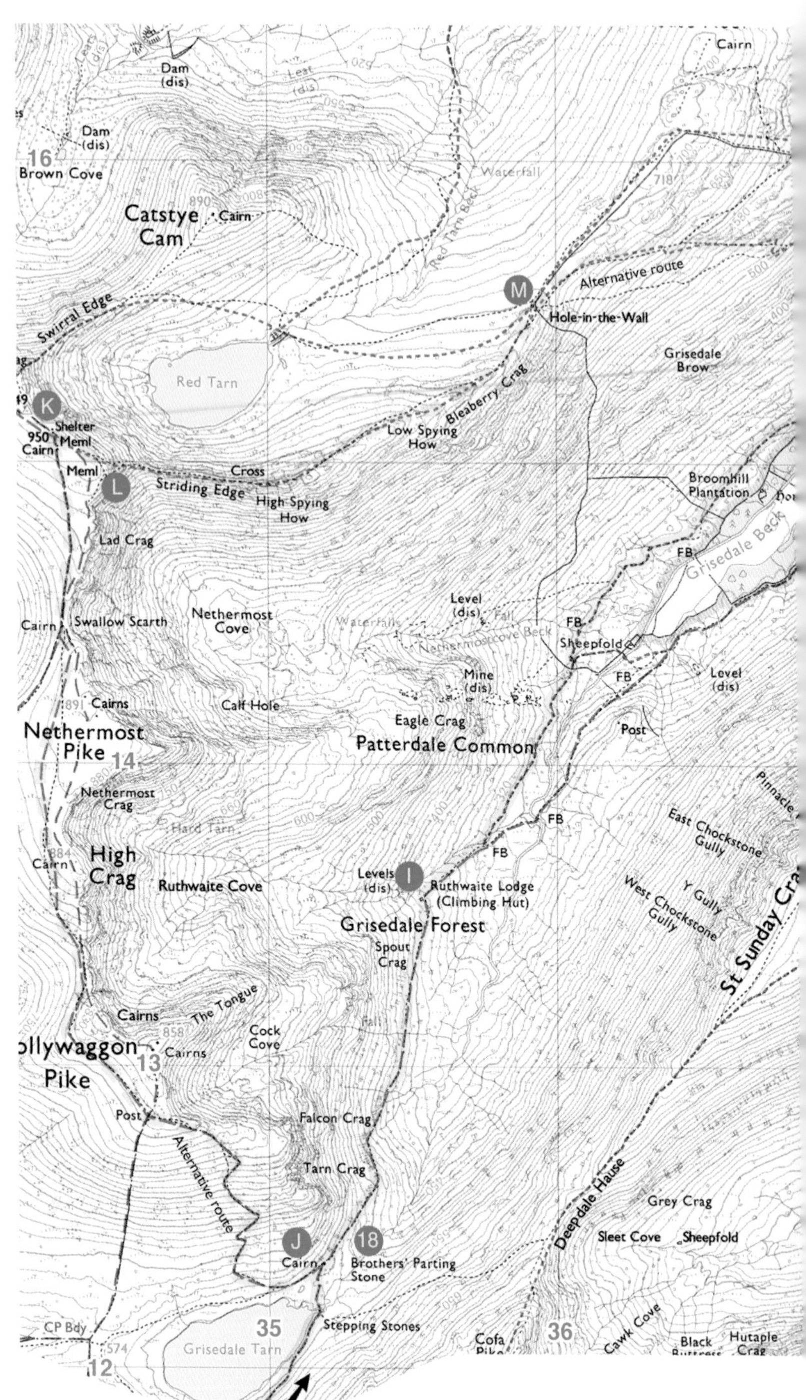
Cairn
Dam (dis)
Dam (dis)
16
Brown Cove
Catstye Cam
Cairn
Waterfall
Red Tarn Beck
M
Alternative route
Hole-in-the-Wall
Swirral Edge
Red Tarn
Grisedale Brow
K
Shelter
950 Meml
Cairn
Bleaberry Crag
Low Spying How
Meml
L
Cross
Striding Edge
High Spying How
Broomhill Plantation
Grisedale Beck
FB
Lad Crag
Level (dis)
Cairn
Swallow Scarth
Nethermost Cove
Waterfalls
Nethermostcove Beck
FB
Sheepfold
FB
Level (dis)
Mine (dis)
Cairns
Calf Hole
Eagle Crag
Post
Nethermost Pike
14
Patterdale Common
Pinnacle
Nethermost Crag
Hard Tarn
FB
East Chockstone Gully
FB
Cairn
High Crag
Ruthwaite Cove
Levels (dis)
I
Ruthwaite Lodge (Climbing Hut)
Y Gully
West Chockstone Gully
St Sunday Crag
Grisedale Forest
Spout Crag
Cairns
The Tongue
Cock Cove
Fall
Nethermost Pike
Dollywaggon Pike
Cairns
13
Post
Falcon Crag
Alternative route
Tarn Crag
Deepdale Hause
Grey Crag
Sleet Cove
Sheepfold
J
18
Cairn
Brothers' Parting Stone
35
Stepping Stones
CP Bdy
Grisedale Tarn
12
Cofa Pike
36
Cawk Cove
Black Buttress
Hutaple Crag

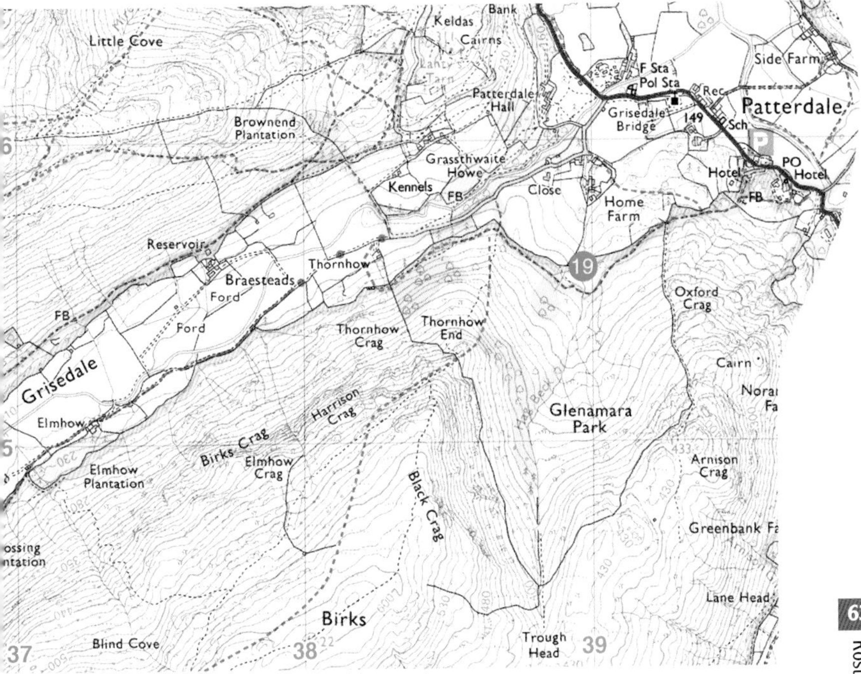

Grisedale Tarn, a lonely outpost at the best of times, was frozen and the snow-streaked flanks of the high mountains around it disappeared into thick mist 200 feet (61 metres) overhead. The desolation was tremendous. But the path skirting the tarn to the right and then descending gently into Grisedale itself is unmistakable. A short way down, a faint track leads 50 yards to the right to Brothers' Parting **18**, a stone which marks where William Wordsworth said goodbye to his brother John for what proved to be the last time. John was a sea captain who drowned in 1805 when his ship, the *Earl of Abergavenny*, went down. Wordsworth's commemorative verses are carved on the rock but have worn to almost nothing.

A little further on Ruthwaite Lodge Outward Bound hut **I** marks a fork in the path. Both ways lead down the valley; in poor weather the right-hand route is more sheltered and soon becomes a wide jeep track; in normal conditions, the left fork is prettier and keeps to a higher contour all the way down the valley's left flank. The paths meet at the bottom, and join the steep tarmac road downhill which may be left after 350 yards (275 metres) through a gate on the right where a path winds through the pleasantly landscaped delights of Glenamara Park **19** to Patterdale village centre.

High-level alternatives

One of Lakeland's dearest mountains, Helm Crag, rises grandly above Grasmere, with an excitingly serrated crest and air of importance which belies its modest 1,299 feet (396 metres). It is also known, from the shape of its rocky peak, as The Lion and the Lamb, and this is a good way of describing these two high-level stretches, albeit in reverse order.

The lamb includes Helm Crag itself and is certainly to be preferred to the 'standard' route down Easedale from Greenup Edge and Wythburn unless you are very tired. At the abandoned stile **C** (see pages 58–59) which marks the head of Far Easedale, turn left on to a narrow path which switchbacks over Calf Crag, Gibson Knott and finally Helm Crag – an exhilarating ridgewalk where the way forward is obvious in clear conditions and hard to lose even in foul weather (although there is less point in spending the extra hour if you are denied views). At Helm Crag, the path wends along the jumble of rocks at the summit, keeping most of them to the left, and then makes a

The Lion and the Lamb crown the summit of Helm Crag's exhilarating, spiky ridge on the high-level alternative path above Grasmere.

U-turn to drop down a grassy slope to further zig-zags on a clear path which has replaced the old and badly eroded one. The main, Far Easedale, path is joined at a signed junction from which a broad track descends past cottages to the road.

The lion (see pages 62–63), the second of these high-level variations, is best avoided by inexperienced fellwalkers in bad conditions because of the care needed on Striding Edge. Take a weather check before deciding whether to leave the main path at the end of Grisedale Tarn **J**, where a steep path leads straight into a steep and energy-sapping zig-zag up the flank of Dollywagon Pike. The worst is first; once on the Pike's broad shoulder, the route becomes an uplifting stride along a gradual but increasingly awesome ascent with sweeping views in good conditions – far away to the left and steeply down to the right into the grim fastnesses of Ruthwaite and Nethermost Coves. This is very fine mountain country and soon you are on the summit of England's third highest peak, Helvellyn, with further breathtaking views to the north and east, stretching away from the shapely daughter summit of Catstycam (or Catchedicam, both suitably lovely names). The sense of achievement may be slightly diluted by the fact that you are highly unlikely to be alone. This is the most popular of all the Lakeland giants and tourists have arrived by pony, handcart and even aeroplane, as a plaque recalls, when two intrepid pilots landed and then flew off with written confirmation of their feat from the Professor of Greek at Manchester University, who happened to have walked up Striding Edge.

Down the Edge is where you go now. Don't be frightened by its reputation, but steer clear in icy conditions or in rain and mist if you or your party are not used to either or both. The initial descent from Helvellyn summit is steep and nasty scree **K**, and the end of the Edge **L** involves one of those foot-in-mouth scrambles which you don't really want anyone to photograph. But once up (and anyone can manage it) the narrow ridge is easy to negotiate, with the path keeping slightly below the crest for those who don't want to creep along the top. It isn't very far down on the left-hand side to Red Tarn, and the final stretch is marvellous, along wide flat slabs to the stony track which leads to the Hole in the Wall gap **M** and a long, gentle slant down the right flank of Birkhouse Moor to the bottom of Grisedale, where a bridge reunites you with the Coast to Coast's main route. Wainwright, a clumsy but cautious walker himself, calls the Edge 'the best quarter-mile between St Bees and Robin Hood's Bay.' But there have been many accidents here in bad weather, evidenced by an ominous number of memorials. If you decide not to take this high road, be consoled by the fact that you are still in one piece. A third high-level route, offered in the Wainwright spirit of finding your own alternative (ideally with the help of his infallible *The Eastern Fells*), is to turn right instead of left at Grisedale and climb St Sunday Crag, descending its ridge to Patterdale with wonderful views of Ullswater in good weather.

4 Patterdale to Shap

via Haweswater • 7 hours
15 miles (24 km)

Ascent 3,265 (995 metres)
Descent 1,837 feet (560 metres)
Lowest point Patterdale: 525 feet (160 metres)
Highest point Kidsty Pike: 2,560 feet (780 metres)

A final, high-level farewell to the Lake District, with the chance of seeing wild deer and a golden eagle before following the flooded valley of Haweswater and route-finding across meadows to medieval Shap Abbey and Shap village.

This is the longest haul so far and the greatest ascent to the highest point of the whole Coast to Coast journey, excluding variants: the summit of Kidsty Pike – 2,560 feet (780 metres). The hardest work is all in the first part of the day, but after a picnic lunch (for there are no pubs or cafés within a morning's walk unless you start very early) most walkers need reserves of stamina for the long switchback along the side of Haweswater and tricky navigation on the final stretch for those going all the way to Shap, rather than stopping at Burnbanks or Bampton, which has become a popular alternative.

The path leaves Patterdale by a turning left off the Ambleside road, a metalled lane to the hamlet of Rooking, past a beautifully laid field hedge on the left. At the cottages turn left, then very soon right on to the fell path, signed to Boredale Hause and Angle Tarn **A**. The well-used track rises at that ideal angle encountered on the start of Greenup Edge and Grisedale Hause, gaining height rapidly but without unpleasant steepness. An early fork into two paths joins up again a little further on; the higher one has the

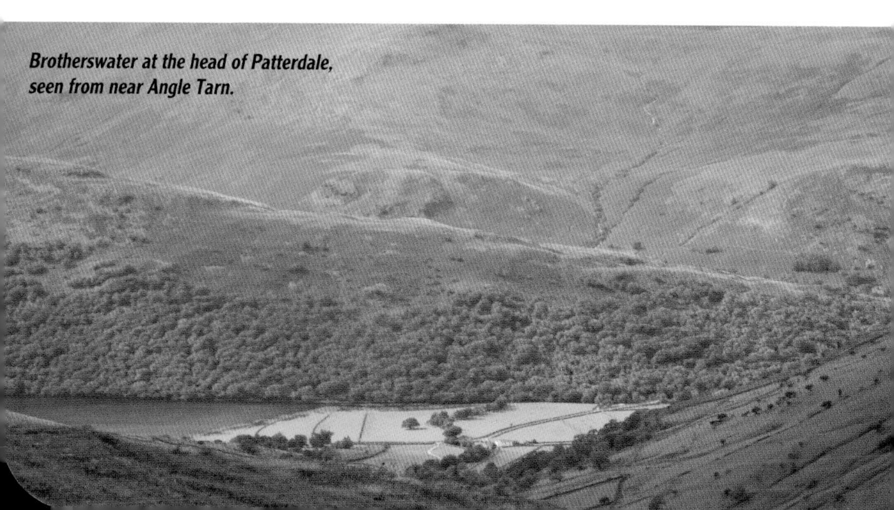

Brotherswater at the head of Patterdale, seen from near Angle Tarn.

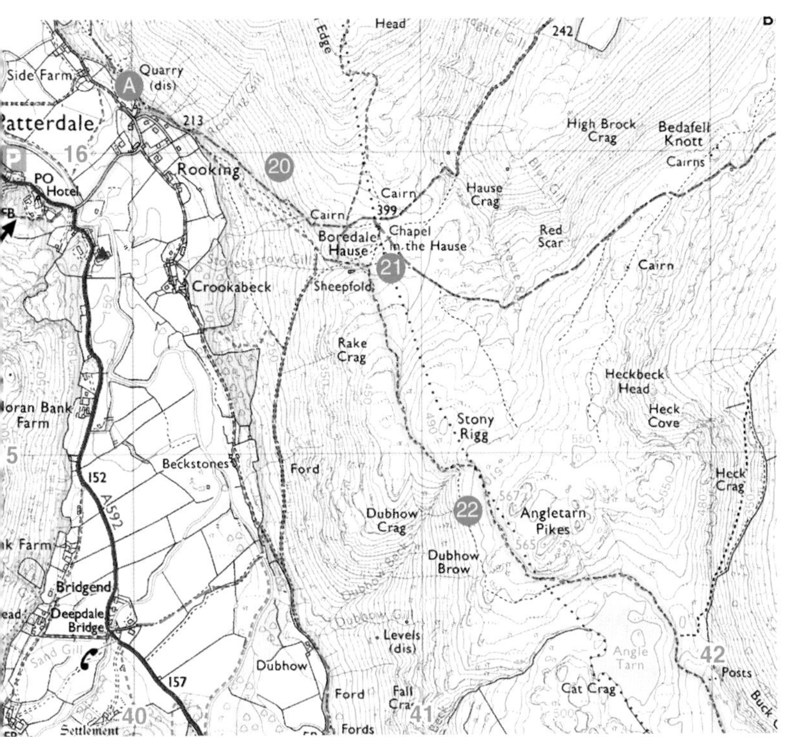

advantage of an elegant Victorian seat **20** with a lovely view of Patterdale, Helvellyn and the southern tip of Ullswater; a shame that it is rather early for a rest. At Boredale Hause, the top of this first ascent, the remains of the old Chapel-in-the-Hause **21** now look like nothing more than a sheepfold but add atmosphere, and the view back is even better than from the seat, now including Brotherswater and the southern approach to the Kirkstone Pass.

The path heads right, briefly south-east and then almost due south, rising up the fell (ignore a path descending south-east, which leads back to the valley) past occasional cairns and latterly through hummocky small hills. Don't just look down at your feet or back at the view, though. On the northern shoulder of Angle Tarn Pikes, my wife, who had joined me at Patterdale, nudged me and pointed out three very small wind-farm turbines on the skyline. Then one of them moved. They were deer from the wild herd which roams these fells, their necks and long straight ears making that Mercedes-Benz shape characteristic of a modern windmill's blades. If you are quiet and watchful, you should see some too. As they dropped out of sight behind the ridge, we followed the path below Angle Tarn Pikes **22**, a modest outcrop of rocks where you look back to a view which uniquely includes both tips of Ullswater, England's longest lake. Then drop down gently to the beautiful tarn with its archipelago of islands and often a flock of honking Canada geese or other waterfowl.

The Straits of Riggindale (foreground) form a narrow pass which took the Roman road between Ambleside and Brougham across the spine of the eastern fells.

Still very distinct, the route swings round the left shore and up a gentle slope to Saura Crag and along the contour above Prison and Sulphury Gills, which are less exciting than they sound. Climb over the shoulder of the Knott, above yet another lake down to the right, Hayeswater **23** (not to be confused with Haweswater, although also a reservoir). If you are having a rest day in Patterdale, you can return from the junction halfway up The Knott via a beautiful path down to Hayeswater and Hartsop, recently extended in its lower reaches by a permissive diversion to an old slate mine and the site of Hartsop's cornmill by Pasture Beck. This is a delightful way back to Patterdale, with lovely picnic spots along Hayeswater Gill.

Continuing round The Knott, with the option of a brief hike up to the summit if you are energetic, the path drops to the dramatic Straits of Riggindale **B**, a place to sit for a while and imagine the Roman legionaries tramping across this narrow ridge on their skilfully engineered road between Ambleside and Brougham, now known as High Street; you can see it marching south, clear and straight, along the spine of the mountain which shares its name. We go the other way, executing a neat hairpin just before the Straits and heading left above the steep crags and precipes over Twopenny Crag. This is the likeliest spot to see the last Lakes golden eagle soaring in search of prey from its eyrie in the Riggindale rocks, sadly a bachelor apartment since the death of the bird's mate in 2004. The path continues up to the perky summit

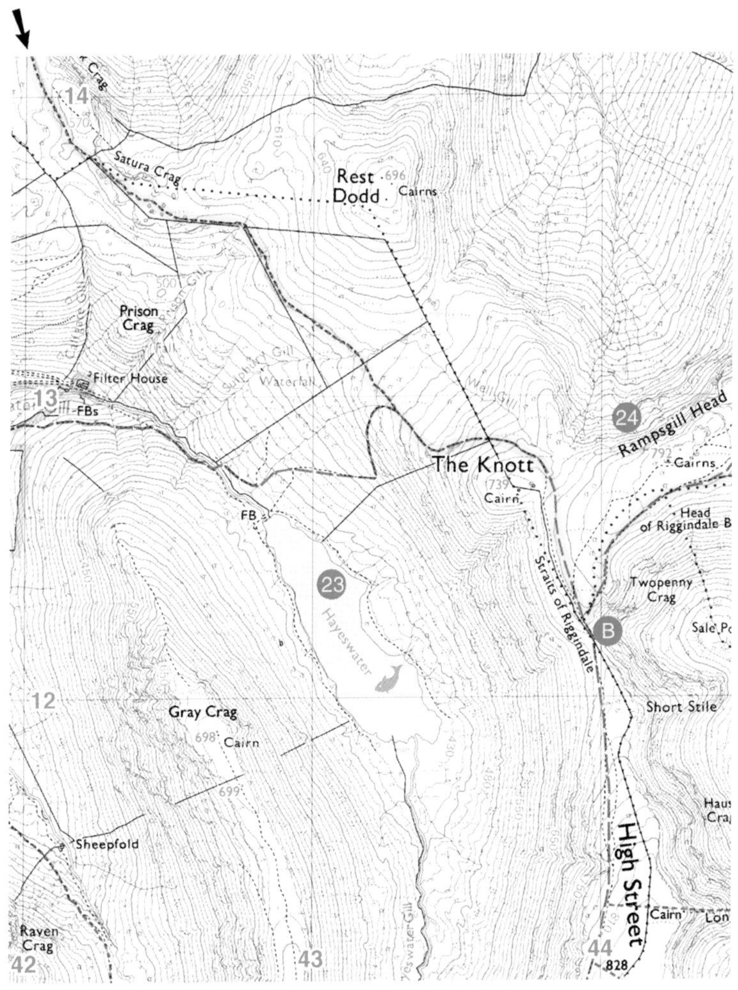

of Kidsty Pike **C**, a sharp little point which you see in backward glances virtually all the way to the Pennines. Stop and raise a glass of whatever you have in your knapsack, even if it's only beck water; at 2,560 feet (780 metres) this is the highest point of the 'standard' walk. Nothing to come will beat it, although it is by no means downhill all the way from here.

Kidsty Pike is much less dramatic close-to than from a distance. Visitors see all too plainly that it is really a shoulder which cheekily takes the glory from its higher but little-known parent, Rampsgill Head **24**. The east ridge leads down past a rocky patch at Kidsty Howes, bearing gently left through grass and then steeply to the beck and a stone bridge to the gradually vanishing ruins

Local Histories

The drama of the flooding of Mardale Green is superbly told in Sarah Hall's novel *Haweswater*, and there is an excellent history of Burnbanks, *Cast Iron Community*, by Bampton and District Local History Society.

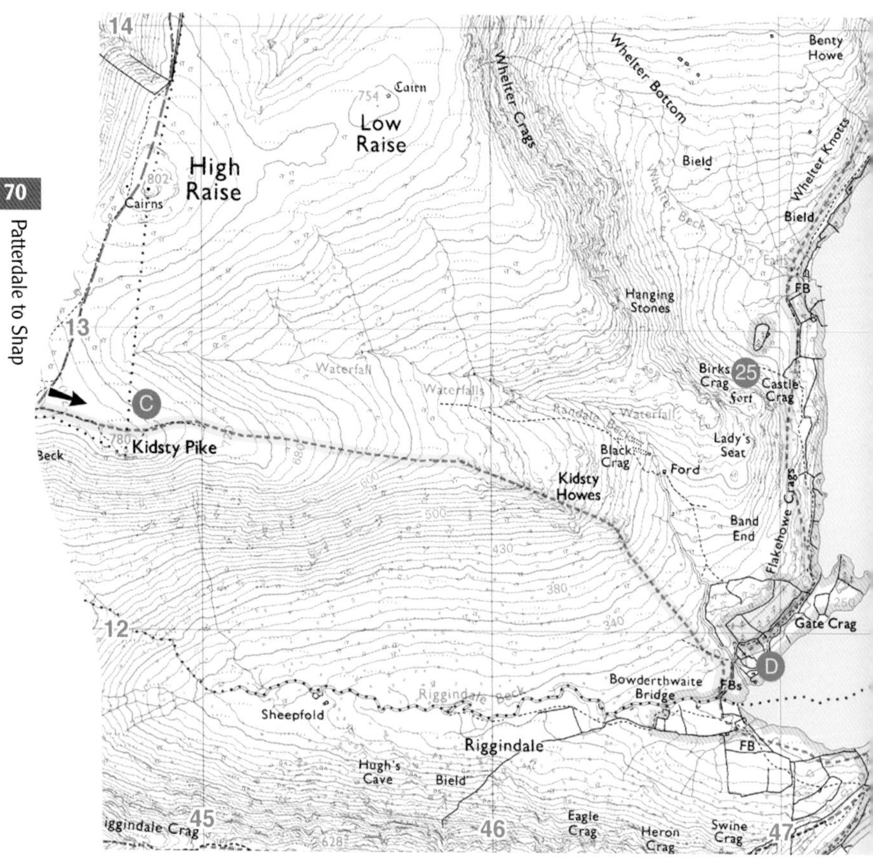

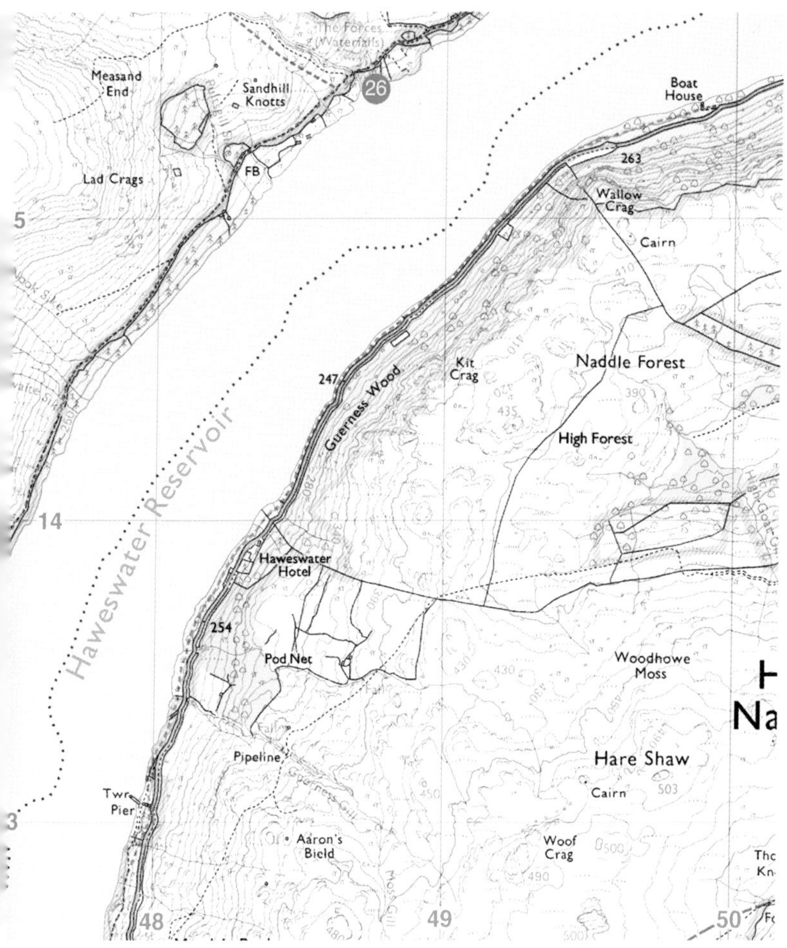

of Riggindale Farm **D**. This was one of many victims of the great stretch of water in front of you; serene and beautiful, Haweswater is artificial, a reservoir built in the early 1930s for Manchester, extending the much smaller natural lake, amid fury at the drowning of Mardale village, where the annual sports on the whaleback top of High Street used to be organised at The Dun Bull inn.

The route switchbacks left along the bank of the lake, taxing after the long haul from Patterdale. It can seem an age before you reach Burnbanks, the site of the fascinating navvies' village, made of iron houses and described on a noticeboard, which was flung up for the building of the nearby dam. On the way, Birks Crag **25** once had a British fort on its summit and at Measand Bridge there are fine waterfalls **26** on the beck which make a pleasant place to rest.

Approaching Burnbanks, the path becomes a track which leads through a gate and stile to a gap in the wall on the right. This is marked by a Coast to Coast sign **E**, the first since way back before Ennerdale Bridge, because the Lake District discourages such waymarks. The path from here leads through tranquil woodland to the road and a stile to reach Naddle Bridge, where you cross Haweswater Beck by the 'new' and fine stone bridge alongside its lovely old packhorse predecessor **27**. Follow the far bank left on a grassy path past Thornthwaite Force and over a wooden bridge, crossing the tributary Naddle Beck, keeping Park Bridge over Haweswater Beck to the left – don't cross that – and continue until a wider track leads up through a gate and stile. A footpath sign then directs you right and up the right-hand side of the field beside the fence and a muddy passage to the right of High Park barn.

From here the path curves left to cross three fields to Rawhead Farm, keeping to the right of the buildings before crossing the metalled farm road. Take the left-most track here over the rough field and through clumps of gorse to an A-stile over the wall to the road at Rosgill Bridge, ignoring tracks to the right which may appear to cut out the hairpin round Fairy Crag but don't. Don't cross Rosgill Bridge but turn right, through a gate waymarked Coast to Coast **F**, then after little more than 100 yards turn right through the gate to Fairy Crag's drive,

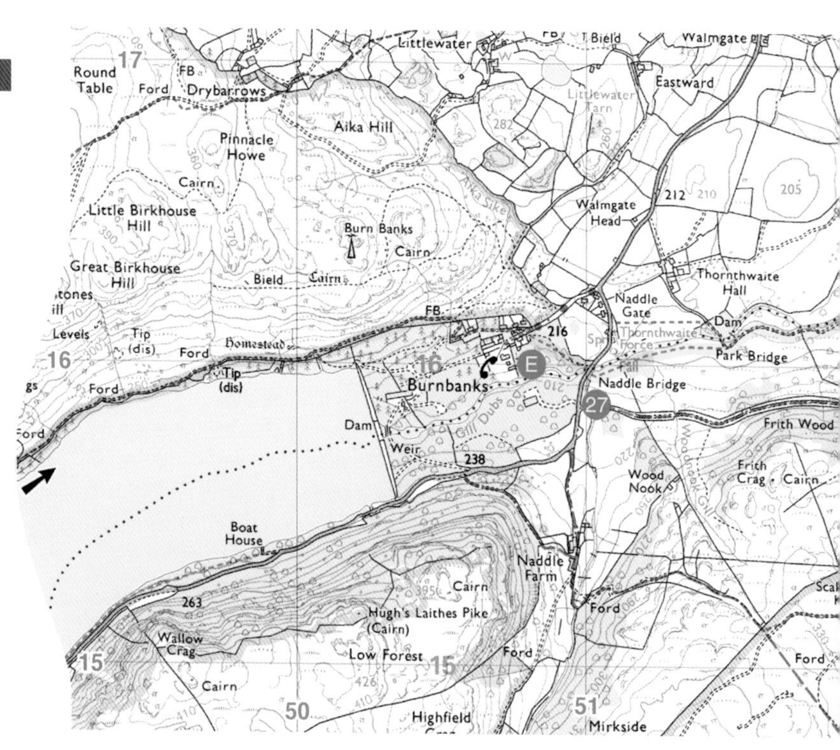

but almost immediately afterwards angle left and follow a path by the wall, well below the drive as it rises to Fair Crag's pretty buildings. Go through a stone stile painted 'C to C' and straight ahead, with a line of straggly hawthorns and Fairy Crag up on your right, until you reach and cross the lovely packhorse bridge over Swindale Beck by Parish Crag.

Climb steeply up from here and angle left across the field to tumbledown farm buildings in the top corner **G**, heading for a stone stile in the north-west corner of the farmyard wall. Cross straight through the old farmyard, noting a fine old metal basin in a stone niche, and when out the far side, walk briefly up to your right to reach a sharp corner in a minor road where you go left. Follow the road uphill for about 150 yards (140 metres) to where a yellow waymarker and sign saying 'Shap' directs the path left and then right to an electricity pylon by a gate and stile. The route continues ahead across an ancient earthwork dyke with the River Lowther down on the left, curves right past another waymark and heads gently left to a small hillock **H**. From the top of this you can see amid trees the ruins of Shap Abbey **28**. A final stile and field lead to the river and Abbey Bridge. That would cut a corner to the long-awaited run-in to Shap itself, but summon up your strength and turn right before crossing it to make a short diversion to the ruins.

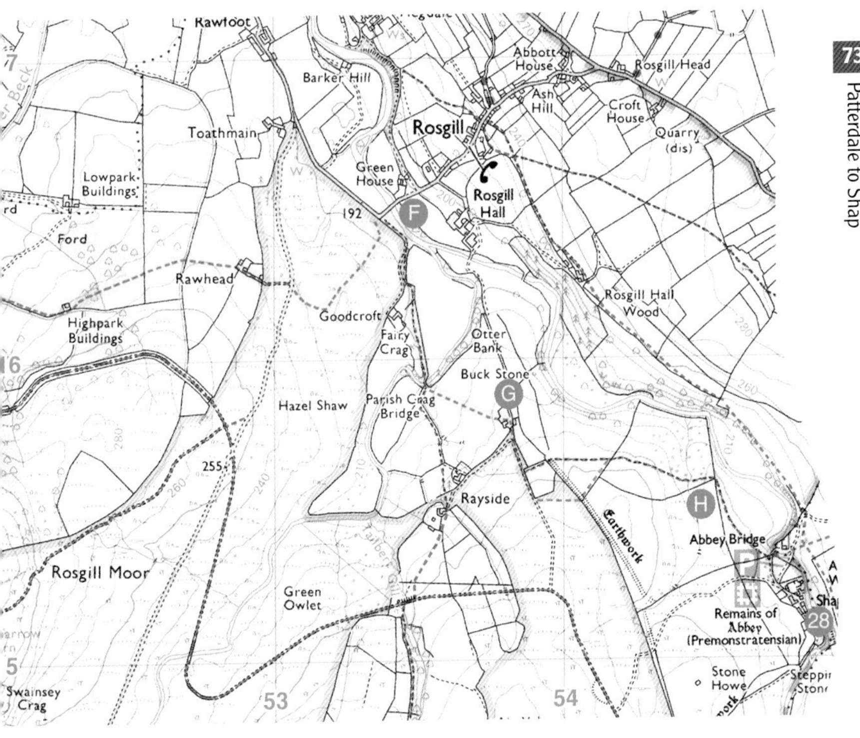

Shap Abbey shares its drive with a busy farm in the quiet valley of the River Lowther, between the Lakeland fells and the West Cumbrian limestone plateau.

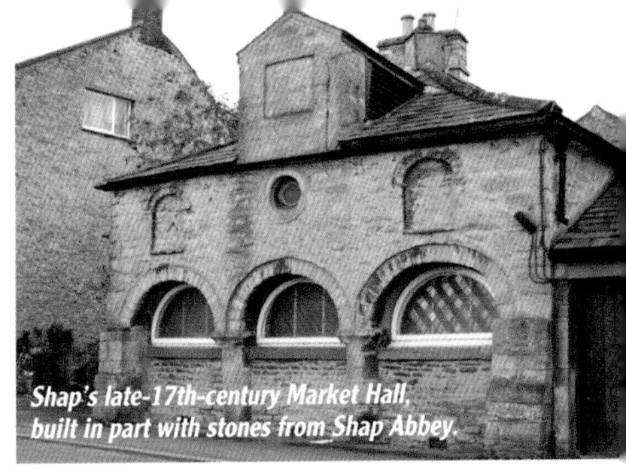
Shap's late-17th-century Market Hall, built in part with stones from Shap Abbey.

The abbey was one of the last of the great medieval foundations to be built in Britain, around 1200, partly using the site of Shap's ancient stone circle, either to benefit from centuries of a different kind of worship or to exorcise any remaining demons. The ruins have much for you to find: stores, an unusually small coffin and communal lavatories as well as the fine West Tower. Like so many monastic settlements, the community found an idyllic site by a well-stocked fishing river, rich in timber and with quarries providing excellent building stone. However, the monks were not tucked-away contemplatives but White Canons whose calling required them to serve the local community as well as the abbey. When Shap was dissolved with the other monasteries by Henry VIII in 1540, its remaining clerics were all given comfortable pensions, although much of their stone was cannibalised for nearby buildings, including the cottage by the ruins and Shap's market hall. From the abbey, the lane leads up to the A6 – a ghost of a road since the nearby M6 motorway arrived – and into the village. On the way, note two things: first an ancient tumulus and huge boulders left over from the stone circle **29**, and then the gleam of limestone in the drystone walls. Both are a foretaste of the walk's next stage.

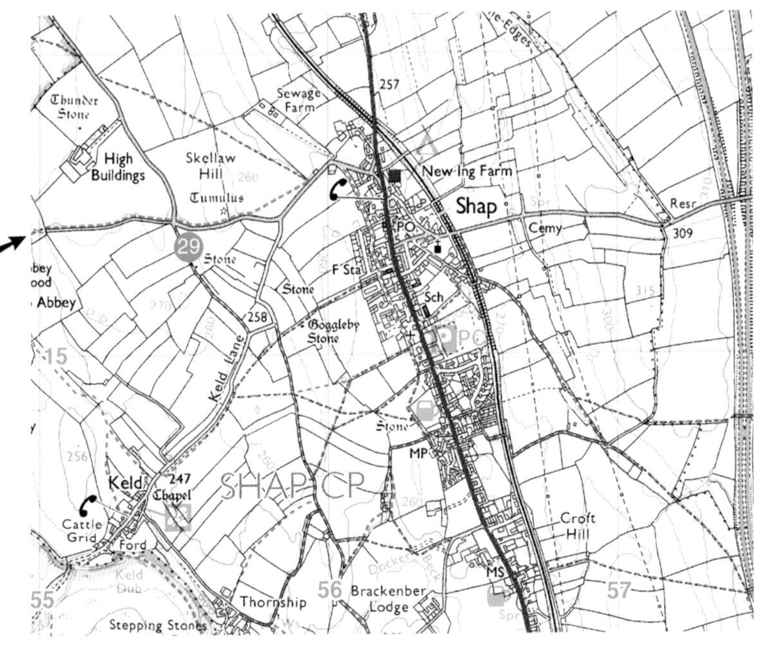

Shadows on the limestone

In 1984 British Gas decided to lay an underground pipeline between Manchester and Carlisle and there was great excitement among archaeologists. The pipe ran across one of the richest areas of prehistoric settlement in the country, the limestone plateau east of Shap. Following behind the free digging equipment, the experts collected a haul of axeheads, arrows, fragments of pottery and seed deposits which added enormously to our vague and fragmentary picture of Britain in the Mesolithic, Neolithic, Bronze Age and pre-Roman era, between 9,000 and 2,000 years ago.

Yet only the sketchiest outline is in our possession. Time and again as you march past the modest little mounds of Severals or Green Riggs settlements, the best a guide can say is: purpose unknown. The highly distinctive 'giants' graves' or pillow mounds by Smardale Bridge may have been animal enclosures, bracken stacks or even medieval artificial rabbit warrens made by monks. No one yet knows.

Still more mysterious are the evocative stone circles at Oddendale and Gamelands, or the tumuli and cairns of stones such as Robin Hood's Grave. There is an abundance of specialised literature on them all, but the academics hedge nervously about which tribe from where did what and when, and there is little certainty about the vegetation – trees, scrub or edible plants – which covered the Coast to Coast's route in ancient times.

Fortunately, much more is known about the antiquaries themselves, the best of them being the indomitable Canon William Greenwell, who holed up in a comfortable berth at Durham Cathedral and lived to the age of 98 after enthusiastic digging around Shap and Orton when a young man. He published details of nearly 200 sites and engaged in the passionate controversy typical of Victorian times. Today's cautious archaeologists, who prefer to leave things buried rather than hurry, criticise him as too speedy and slapdash but acknowledge that he brought a lot of Cumbrian prehistory to light.

Greenwell's interest in buried treasure was triggered by squirming as a boy along Roman sewers below his father's estate near Lancaster. He later invented the Greenwell's Glory fishing fly, encouraged his sister Dora with her poetry and was a famously eccentric magistrate: poachers usually got away with a mild warning but he wanted every errant motorcyclist clapped in gaol. Greenwell died in 1918, contentedly murmuring that he had not attended divine service for 50 years without being well paid for it. He also retained his interest in archaeology and anthropology to the last. When a fellow canon complained that Greenwell never acknowledged his wife, the crusty old bachelor replied that he had indeed noticed her and particularly her very fine skull, which he hoped one day to add to his private museum collection.

A Conservation Triumph

British Rail had £230,000 ready for the demolition of Smardale Gill viaduct after the line's closure in 1962, but gave it instead to help restoration in 1992. In 2010 another £30,000 was needed – and found – to repair ice damage.

Smardale Bridge takes the Coast to Coast over Smardale Beck below Severals settlement, an area hugely rich in archaeological remains.

5 Shap to Kirkby Stephen

via Orton • 9 hours
19.8 miles (31.7 km)

Ascent 1,755 feet (535 metres)
Descent 1,083 feet (330 metres)
Lowest point Kirkby Stephen: 590 feet (180 metres)
Highest point Orton Scar: 1,115 feet (340 metres)

A venture into one of England's few Empty Quarters, traversing a gap on the map via wild moorland, gentle sheep-farming intakes and the dramatic remains of Victorian rail engineering. A long day but with easy gradients and diverting glimpses of the prehistoric past when these lonely tracts were busy with human life.

The path leaves Shap opposite The King's Arms up a narrow street called Moss Grove, turning right after a few houses along a signed track which crosses the West Coast main railway line on a footbridge and then heads up a gentle slope between stone walls. There could scarcely be a less promising start to the lonely natural grandeur which will dominate the day: a housing estate, views of the smoke-plumed cement plant, the railway, the M6 and a huge quarry. All contribute to Shap's straggly, grey bleakness, but they also enable people to live and work in the town. From the walker's point of view, they add to the rich mixture of the Coast to Coast; if you don't buy that, well, they will soon be left behind.

Kidsty Pike's pert summit can be seen all the way to Kirkby Stephen.

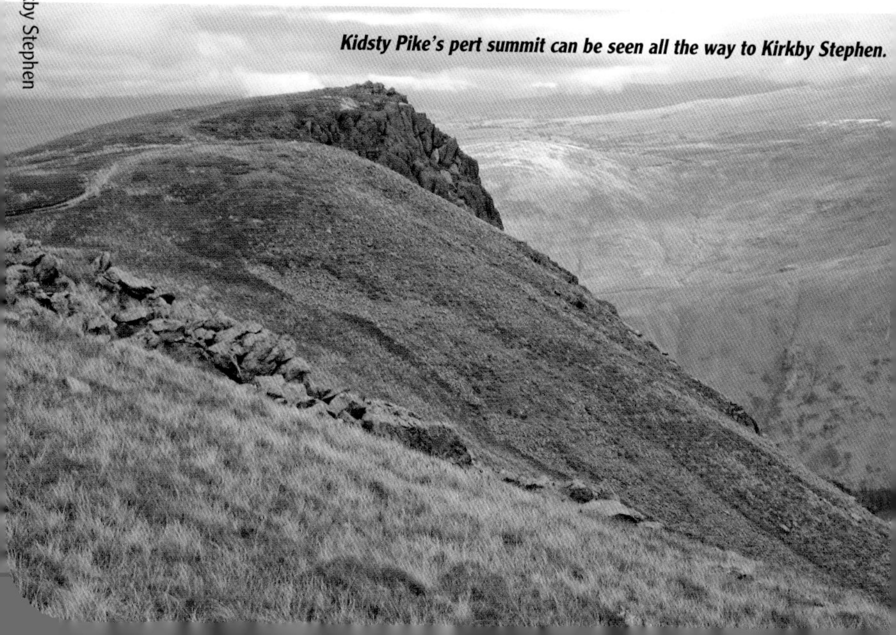

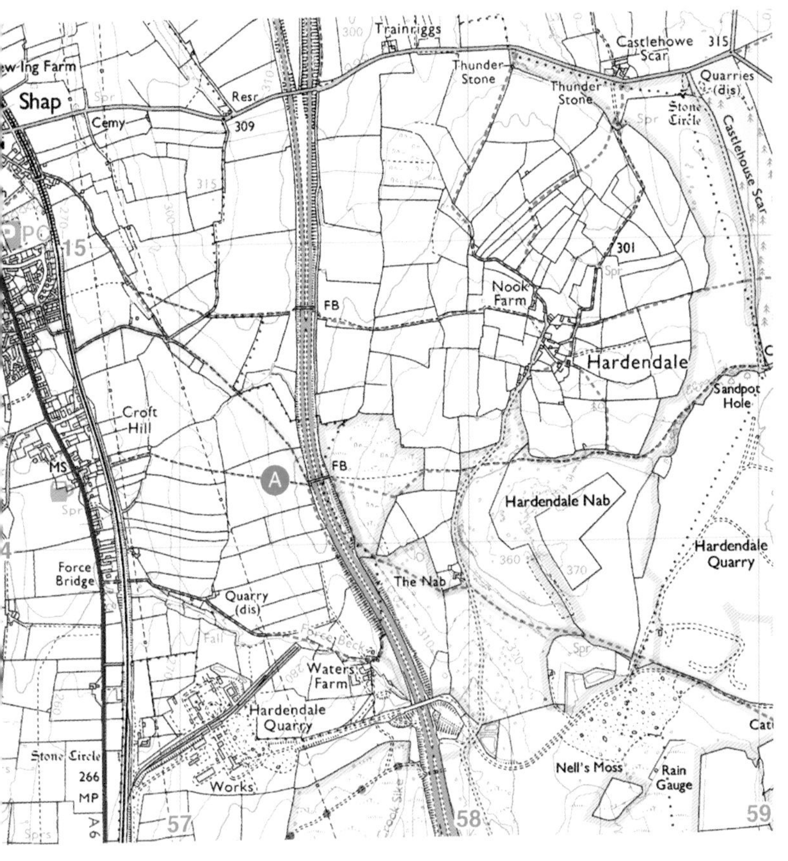

The cement plant actually has an awesomeness of its own and must feature in countless walkers' farewell snaps of the Lakes: a striking foreground for a last panorama of the High Street range and Kidsty Pike's familiar tilting summit. Pressing ahead, the route bears right at a marked stile and crosses a field at an angle straight towards the M6 footbridge, clearly visible. A stone stile **A**, not obvious until you get closer, takes you across the wall in between.

A brief trudge alongside the far side of the motorway provides cheering thoughts about not having to belt along or commute, and then the path climbs left up a pleasant outcrop of limestone rocks and stunted hawthorns, across a meadow and to the right of The Nab farmhouse, whose owners sometimes have a boat stored outside – odd in this aridly stony scene. Cross the minor road to Hardendale, home of John Stuart Mill's great-grandfather, who spent his life translating the New Testament into Greek, and bear slightly right. Follow the wall on the left until Danger notices signal the lunar bowl of Hardendale quarry, which serves the cement plant. Wooden steps drop to the access road (beware large lorries) and up the other side.

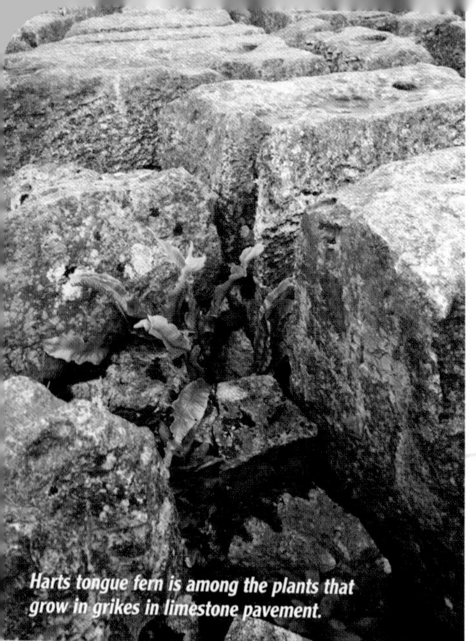

Harts tongue fern is among the plants that grow in grikes in limestone pavement.

A broad, stony track now leads straight ahead to the lovely, notably retiring hamlet of Oddendale, a cluster of farms and cottages hiding behind a communal wall and clumps of trees. The path turns right **B** just before the entrance, passing the first of many limestone pavements on this stretch. Inspection of the clints (eroded 'teeth' of rock) and grikes (narrow fissures in between) may reveal delicate plants unique to this habitat. This is also the first of many places today where you may set up a rabbit or be inspected by sheep mistaking you for their shepherd bringing food.

From this point for the next 10 miles (16 km), much of the route is permissive, that is to say agreed by the local council with landowners who have gone to impressively helpful lengths to mark the way. Because of vulnerable plant life, breeding birds and fragile archaeological remains, walkers are asked to return the kindness by keeping to the track. You lose nothing by doing this; the route is well chosen and the huge, open views allow you to see and enjoy the wilderness in all directions. Ahead are the rounded humps of the Howgills, to the left the summits of the northern Pennines above the aptly named Vale of Eden. Larks rise, breezes blow and if your head needs to be cleared, it will be.

The waymarks, some no more than posts with signs worn off, lead ahead and slightly left on a clear track to a copse which once had a barn called Potrigg **C**. En route, the small Oddendale stone circle **30**, first of several today, is a short detour to the right. After Potrigg you draw level with an evergreen plantation away to your left. A track crosses your path; 200 yards (180 metres) later, slant left to the corner of the plantation **D**, which comes into view as you breast a gentle summit. Beyond the evergreens the path angles very slightly left up a slope where a cairn is just visible on a limestone pavement. Shortly after this you cross the route of the first known road between London and Scotland, engineered by the Romans and invisible now, but still a matter for contemplation **31**.

More history: after an all but invisible tumulus and fragmentary stone circle on the left, a granite boulder left by glacial movement marks the descent through heather to the infant Lyvennet Beck. Look right and glimpse a slender stone column ¼ mile (400 metres) away. This is Black Dub **32**, marking the stream's source and a halt in 1651 by Charles II to refresh his army en route from Scotland to defeat by Cromwell at the Battle of Worcester, followed by his famous hide-and-seek in an oak tree. Please be content with the view from here; there is no legal access from the Coast to Coast Path because erosion by meandering walkers has damaged a sensitive habitat. The path across the flank of Crosby Ravensworth Fell now wiggles somewhat more than the straight line shown on most maps.

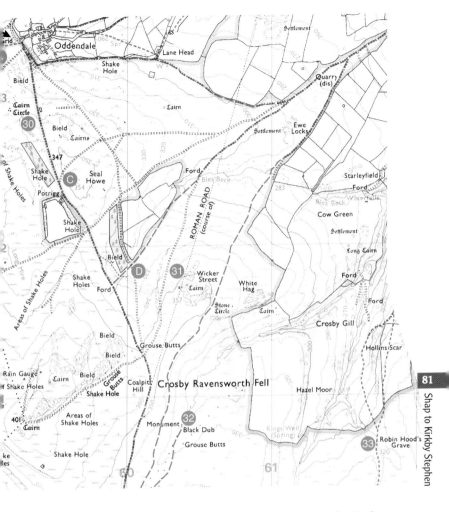

Over the next hill, following excellent wooden waymarks with CC burned into them, plus an arrow showing the exact direction, the path crosses a pretty gorge with a seasonal rivulet and then a small, dry valley. Some 150 yards (135 metres) up this – to the right or south – is a large pile of stones called Robin Hood's Grave **33**. As Wainwright comments drily, this could be anything *except* the grave of Robin Hood, who could not have shot an arrow this far from his deathbed at Kirklees Priory between Huddersfield and Halifax. Where the shaft landed, legend says, bold Robin was buried. Be that as it may, the jumbo cairn is another of the outlaw's persistent links with the long march to Robin Hood's Bay.

After a gentle upwards slope, the path drops to join the minor road to Crosby Ravensworth at a clear stile. Opposite and to the left are the worked-out remains of Blasterfield quarry **34**. Either turn right along the road until its junction with the busier Appleby road, whose hurrying traffic is clearly visible; or reach the same point on indistinct tracks across the grassy triangle between the roads. The clearest goes along the far side of an evergreen plantation, past shake holes (some the remains of primitive quarrying, others natural faults in the limestone) which have become the resting place for much local rubbish, especially fridges **E**.

A good moment now: at the road junction a cattle grid is followed rapidly by an obvious green road bearing off to the left and descending to the cosy panorama of the Lune Valley. The gleaming white limestone tower of Orton church signals facilities – shop, pub, even a chocolate factory – which you may welcome. The track passes two old limekilns **35** on the left, with the fine, tilting limestone sills of Orton Scar beyond, then leads past a mossy wall and tree plantation on the right-hand side of the field to Broadfell Farm. Keep to the right and go straight ahead through a gate, down a sheep meadow with the stream on the left on an indistinct path **F** which soon becomes a pretty bridleway between hedges and walls and leads straight into the village. Turn right between the houses and then left to the George Hotel and the chocolatiers, who run a tearoom. If your pack is full, they do mail order.

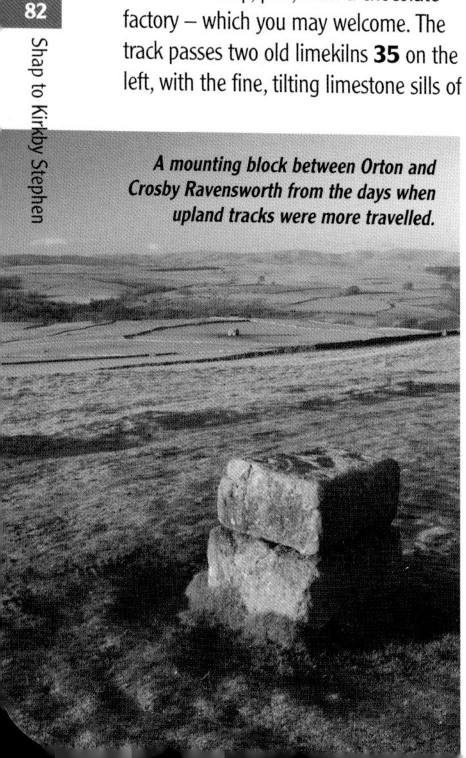

A mounting block between Orton and Crosby Ravensworth from the days when upland tracks were more travelled.

To bypass Orton, follow a clear path from the limekilns. This drops at a gentle angle to Broadfell Farm's track to Street Lane, turns left to Scar Side Farm, then right to Friar Biggins and finally to Scarside. Shortly after, turn left along a bridleway which joins the route from Orton at Knott Lane. This used to be a route for those in a hurry, Spartan in character or equipped with picnics; but now there is a nice tearoom at Scar Side Farm. I'd regret missing Orton, though. It is famed for its longevity – an unusual number of centenarians have lived here – and as the birthplace of George Whitehead, the pioneer Quaker who argued for toleration in person to seven sovereigns. The most sympathetic was Charles II, who perhaps remembered his halt at Black Dub.

Walkers coming from Orton, full of good cheer after their pause in such a lovely spot, reach Knott Lane by leaving the village on the Tebay road (past the pub) then turning left up the road signed to Raisbeck. Leave this, left, at the metalled lane to Scarside, but slant immediately across the field to a stile at the far corner which joins Knotts Lane. Just before this is Gamelands stone circle **36**, much more impressive than the one at Oddendale.

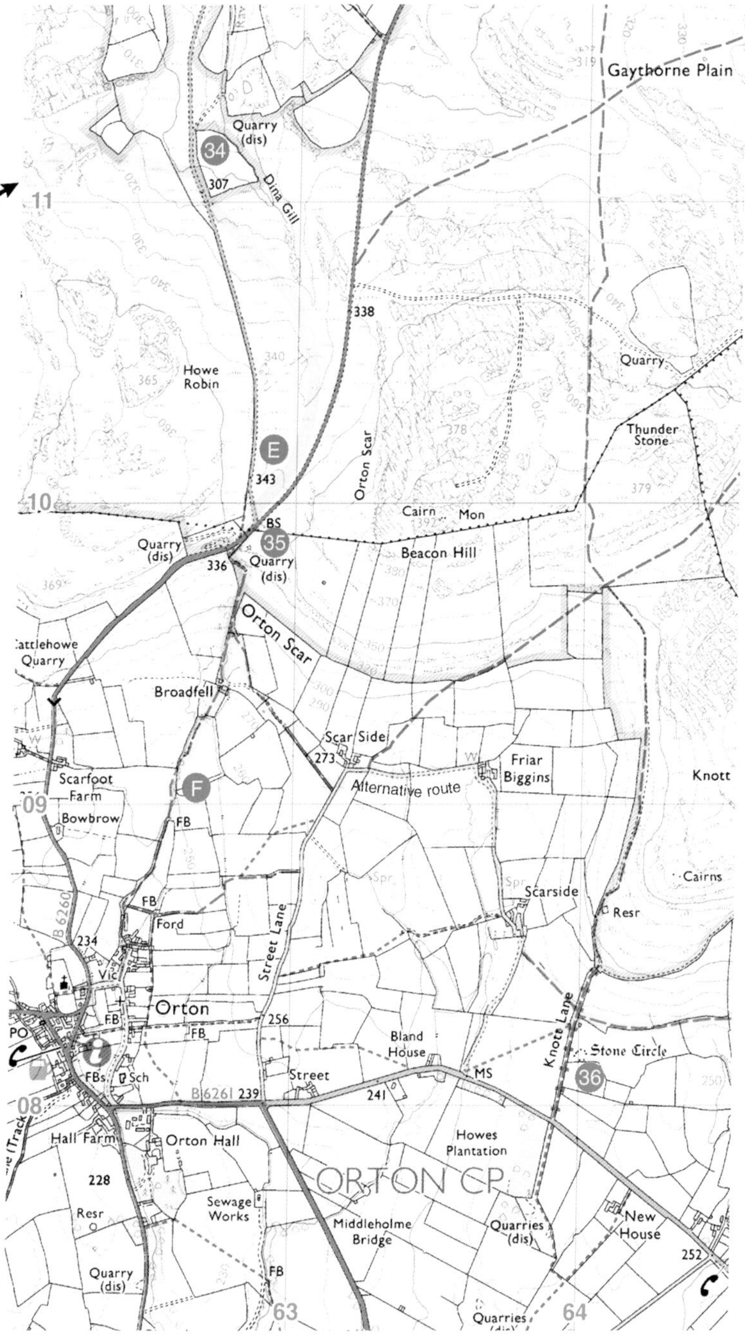
Gaythorne Plain
Quarry (dis)
34
307
Dina Gill
11
Howe Robin
365
338
Quarry
Thunder Stone
E
343
Orton Scar
378
379
10
Cairn
Mon
392
BS
Quarry (dis)
35
336
Quarry (dis)
Beacon Hill
Orton Scar
Cattlehowe Quarry
Broadfell
Scar Side
273
Friar Biggins
Knott
Scarfoot Farm
F
Alternative route
09
Bowbrow
FB
Cairns
FB
Scarside
Resr
Ford
B 6260
234
Street Lane
Vic
Orton
FB
256
FB
PO
Bland House
Knotts Lane
Stone Circle
36
FBs
Sch
Street
MS
08
B6261 239
241
Hall Farm
Orton Hall
Howes Plantation
228
ORTON CP
Resr
Sewage Works
Middleholme Bridge
Quarries (dis)
New House
252
Quarry (dis)
FB
63
Quarries (dis)
64

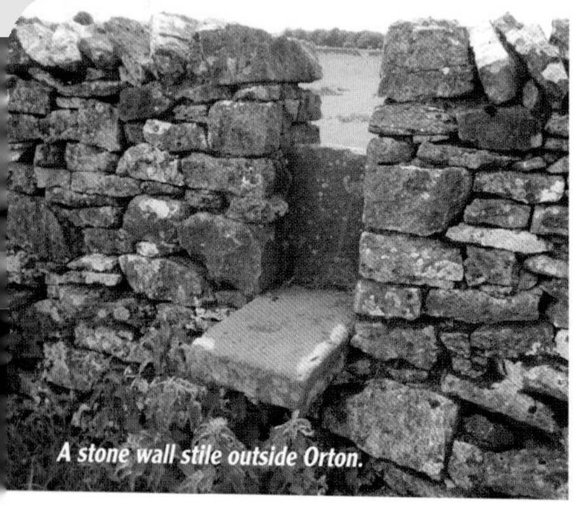

A stone wall stile outside Orton.

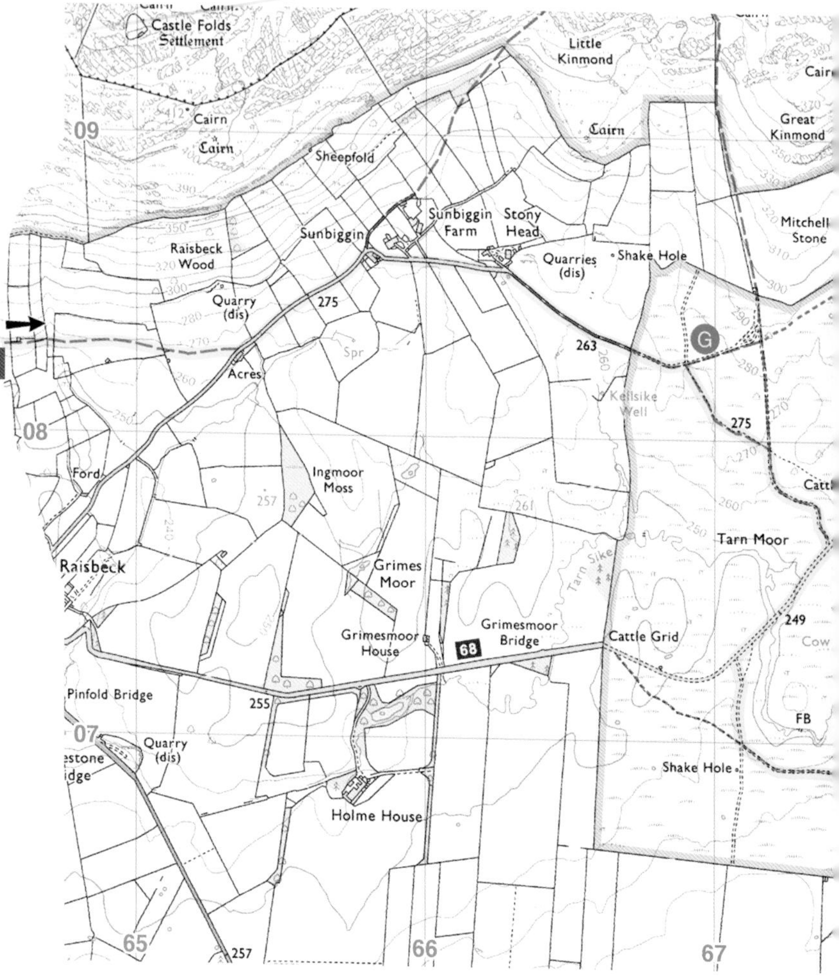

The way ahead now contours for a mile through sheep meadows and a succession of stone wall stiles to Acres Farm. Turn left up the metalled road, then right at Sunbiggin, a busy farm, and past Stoney Head Farm to open heather moor. A short way across this, a path crosses **G**; take it to the right, contouring before dropping down to the minor road to Asby, with Sunbiggin Tarn **37** straight ahead. This is a long-awaited improvement to the route, which previously trudged all the way round to the north and back on a road hairpin through Mazon Wath, the longest stretch of tarmac on the entire crossing and a dreary, instantly forgettable plod. Now, instead, you can enjoy the swans and other waterfowl of Sunbiggin (from a distance; it is a valuable nature reserve) before turning right along the road and then left on a footpath across grassland and moor which curves below Sunbiggin's subsidiary pool, Cow Dub, and up the side of Ravenstonedale Moor, with a line of grouse butts well to the left, to join the Newbiggin-on-Lune road at the top. Turn left and then right up to the obvious mound of an underground reservoir **H**. In recent years an obvious shortcut has developed along the track which cuts out this hairpin and goes straight to join the road opposite the track to **H**

You now march along the contour, keeping a stone wall on your right, past the seasonal tarn at Ewefell Mire, which

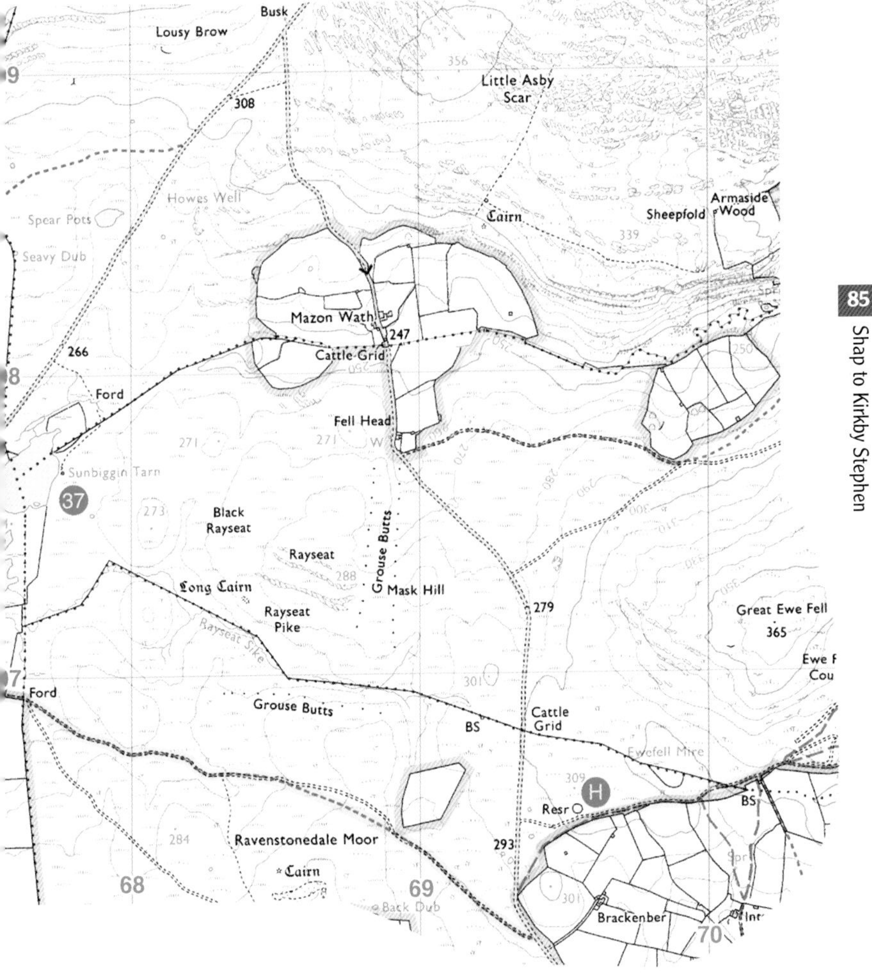

can be quite muddy, and eventually Bents Farm on the right (with a good camping barn which can come in useful if weather or fatigue threaten your plans). On this stretch, which for many walkers from Burnbanks, Bampton or Shap comes at the most tiring and mutiny-prone stage of a long day, resist all temptations to take paths or farm tracks bearing off to the left. Stick with the wall on the right, gently descending into a sheepfold where another wall strikes left uphill, but you go straight on through a gate, keeping the wall to your right for 100 yards to a waymarked post by a stile. Cross this and follow the other side of the wall to a signboard about Severals settlement **I**. As this emphasises, the path clings to the wall (now on your left) to avoid damage to the hillside hummocks and ditches of Severals **38**, which, incredibly, was the Manchester of this region in prehistoric days. There is little for the untrained eye to see, but the bumpy slope is considered one of the most important sites of its kind in Britain, even though, as Wainwright says, 'it still awaits an archaeologist with a spade.' The setting prompts

The Lune Valley's plump, well-cared-for sheep bed down as evening falls on the wildfowl reserve below the Pennines at lonely Sunbiggin Tarn.

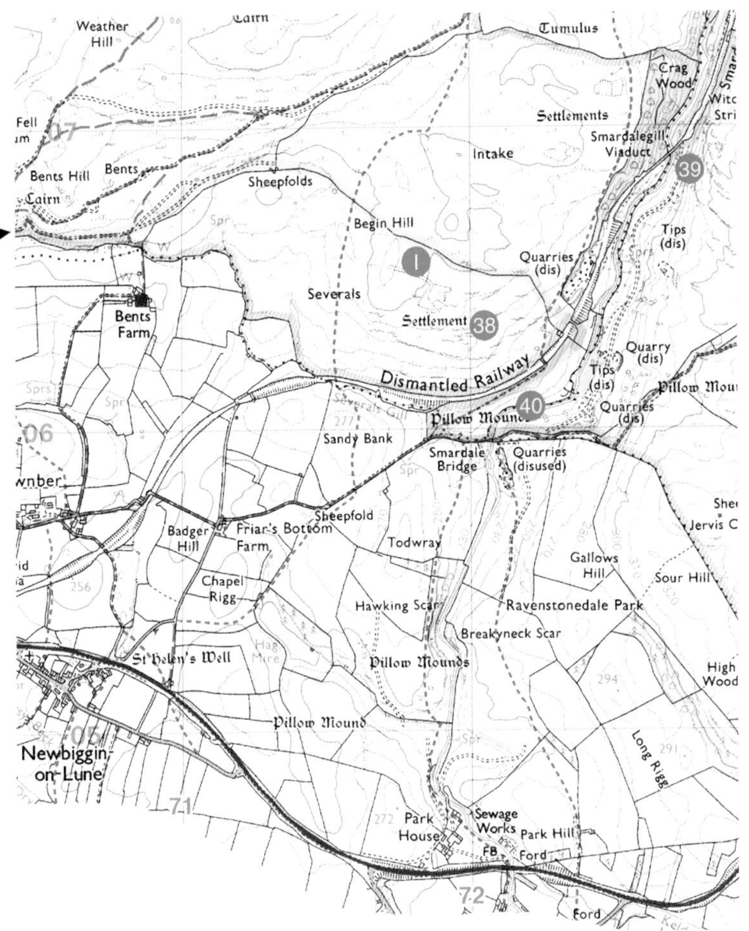

much musing about the dangerous times and different landscape which made a thriving centre of a lonely hillside now visited only by ramblers.

Weariness may be cured by the next stage of the walk. The path drops steeply beside the wall through shallow limestone outcrops to a well-preserved but unused building owned by the railway, whose picturesque route threads below. Smardale Bridge, the path's immediate target, makes a lovely picture, crossing the sinuous loops of Scandal Beck. As you drop to it, look down the valley; the defile is also, and more marvellously, crossed by the distant but still mighty Smardalegill viaduct **39**. Note also, on the steep grassy opposite side of the valley, the rectangular hummocks of two 'giants' graves', as they are called locally, although the map has them as Pillow Mounds **40**. No one knows what they were for. You may set up a hare here, as well as frequent rabbits.

Hills were a challenge for trains on the Settle–Carlisle railway line.

One last push: you must climb the blessedly not too steep path up above the graves and then on a clear, waymarked track for more than a mile, round the shoulder of Smardale Fell, keeping to the right of a very long, narrow intake **41** enclosed by stone walls until this slopes away to the left. A signpost here marks the junction of the Coast to Coast with a bridleway from Ravenstonedale to Smardale Hall **J**.

Keep straight ahead. Passing a well-preserved limekiln, just off the path to the right **42**, dip briefly up and down before the final descent lies clearly ahead, although Kirkby Stephen still hides behind a couple of low hills. The path drops to the Waitby road, turns right and then left down a second road to Waitby, where after 150 yards (135 metres) a stone wall stile leads, right, to a path angling down across a meadow on the edge of yet another prehistoric settlement – more lumps and bumps – to the underpass beneath the working Settle–Carlisle railway line, which has been visible ever since you came round the shoulder of Smardale Fell. A fading but enterprising notice from a Kirkby Stephen restaurant urges walkers with mobiles to ring from here to book a meal with an 'interesting wine list'. Yes please.

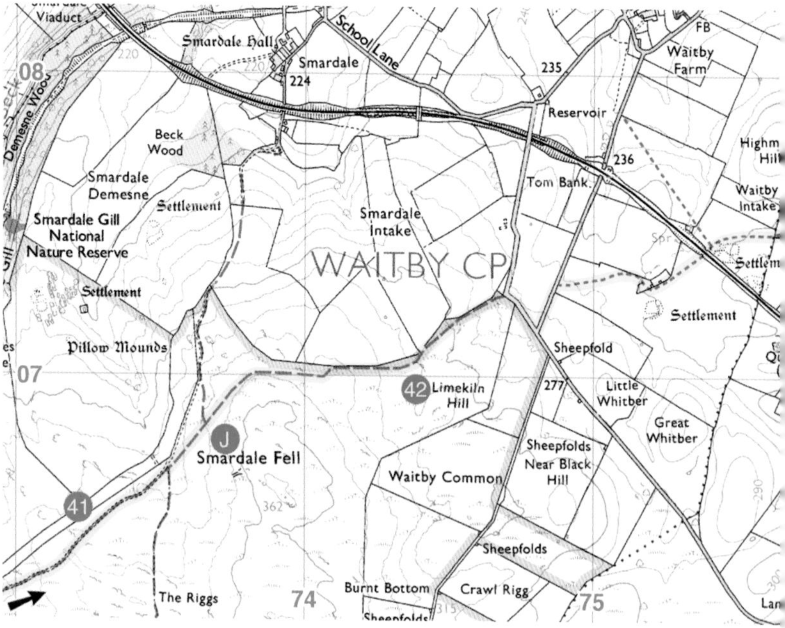

The path after the underpass is initially indistinct but heads down and slightly to the right into an obvious, small valley **K**, which then leads delightfully down to the left. A stile takes you down the right-hand side of a hay meadow to the day's third disused railway line and Greenriggs, a farm with excellent signs through the muddy yard. Another fading advert for exhausted Coast to Coasters commends a local 'holistic healing centre' with the slogan: 'Don't give up until you've tried us.'

The farm lane leads gently into the town, past a very welcome seat in memory of the Greenriggs family's grandparents, surrounded by flowers. Bed, food and, as Wainwright acknowledges after this long day's hike, 'a place for licking wounds' await in this well-set-up little centre. Don't be surprised to meet parrots either: a local enthusiast allows his large and varied flock to fly around town. They particularly favour the two chip shops beside The Black Bull.

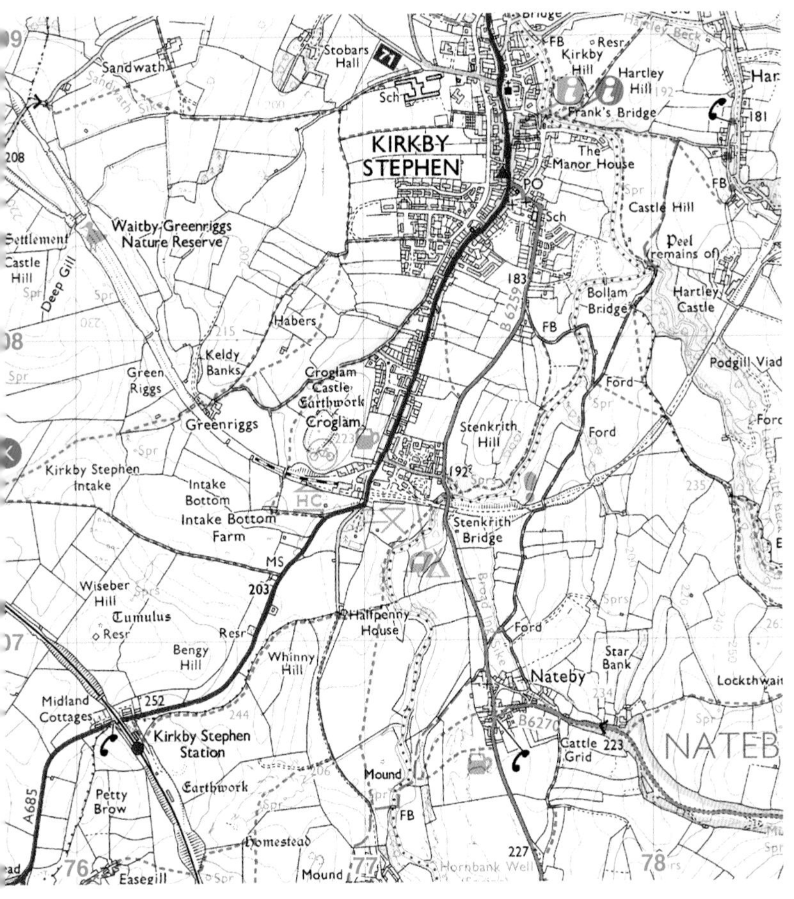

The Pennines crouch behind the Lune Valley, a froth of cow parsley in early summer.

A fine little town

Kirkby Stephen (the second 'k' is silent) has a knack of making you feel fondly towards it. Modest in fame compared to Grasmere behind you, or Richmond ahead, it is full of small-scale interest and has an impressive record of making a living in a rather out-of-the way spot. The most interesting example of this is the number of cafés, a legacy of the town's halfway position on the old charabanc and coach route to Blackpool's illuminations from the North-East. For years, the happy travellers would stop for tea on the way there and supper on the way back. The tradition continues, but more modestly, thanks to rising car ownership and the speed of motorways.

The town has also burrowed into the Pennine fellside to quarry stone and earned a name for miniature housing: for many years gift shops' model cottages were made here. More

recently, a factory has successfully made specialised components for the North Sea oil industry. As well as being welcoming, Kirkby Stepheners are an enterprising lot.

The long, thin straggle of the town has some enjoyable buildings, notably the prominently marked Temperance Hall; and the church of St Stephen is lovely, with a handsome arched gateway leading to the peaceful cloister garden, with a pretty row of cottages on one side. Relics of history going back beyond the building's foundation in 1351 include bread shelves to stack loaves for the deserving poor, an 8th-century Viking stone engraved with Valhalla's practical joker Loki, and the tusk of the last wild boar to be killed in England (at least before their recent reintroduction as part of farm diversification). It was killed appropriately on Wild Boar Fell above the town by Sir Richard Musgrave, who insisted on the other tusk being buried with him when he died in 1464.

6 Kirkby Stephen to Keld

via the Pennine summit • 5–6 hours
15 miles (24 km)

Ascent 1,690 (515 metres)
Descent 1,083 feet (330 metres)
Lowest point Kirkby Stephen: 590 feet (180 metres)
Highest point Nine Standards Rigg: 2,165 feet (660 metres)

An invigorating climb to the watershed of northern England, which is every bit as wet as you might expect. A boggy moorland traverse leads slowly and gently down through the wilderness to the beautiful headwaters of the River Swale.

Leave Kirkby Stephen marketplace down Stoneshot, a lane between narrowing stone walls which once allegedly allowed thieves in a Mini to escape from a police patrol, unfamiliar with the town, whose car got wedged. At the bottom is Frank's

Kirkby Stephen's magnificent church has a Viking carving of the god of mischief, Loki, and an 18th-century cloister

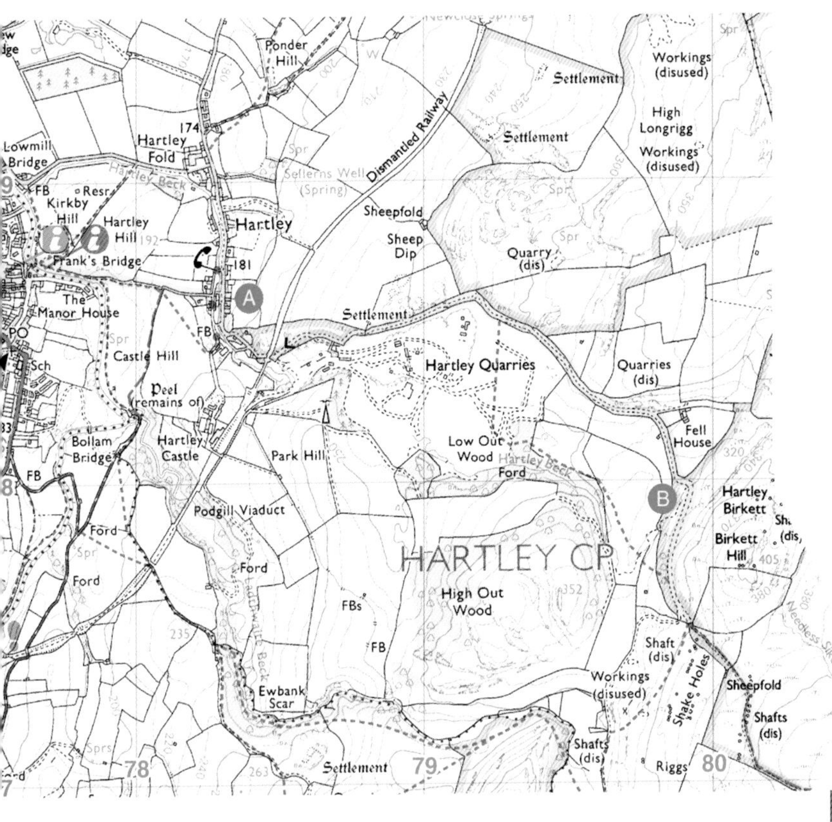

Bridge over the infant, copper-coloured Eden, with many inquisitive and hungry ducks. A metalled path follows the far bank past an impressive array of litter bins, first to the right and then ahead by the hedge of a gradually rising field, as the river bends away. Several gates lead to Hartley hamlet, where the route runs right and then left, waymarked Coast to Coast, via a small dip to an old clapper bridge **A** across Hartley Beck and then up through cow parsley and other wild flowers to join a metalled road climbing gradually left and then round the rim of Hartley quarry, much decorated with Danger notices. The rate of ascent here is well suited to a comfortable morning start, passing isolated Fell House Farm – alpacas are a recent introduction here – and onwards past gorse clumps to a fork where the bridleway on the left leads to the open ground of Hartley Fell. Look back at this point for lovely views of the soft, green fields of Cumbria **B**. A different landscape lies ahead.

The track up the moor is well defined, joining a wall on the right past an old barn, with the escarpment of Wild Boar Fell impressively outlined in the distance. The route climbs with the same pleasant gradient as before, not too steep but making definite progress, with

occasional sightings of the odd little pimples of the Nine Standards **43** (see page 96 and picture page 103), the day's first major goal. Cross Faraday Gill, named after the local family whose members included the pioneer of electricity Michael Faraday (1791–1867), and continue upwards on the right of the wall, ignoring a jeep track to the left. A wide grassy path then leads through a depression back to Faraday Gill's miniature cataracts.

This is the turning-off point **C** for one of the three alternative routes now in use for the next section of the walk, to cope with the worst erosion on the Coast to Coast. The system has been devised by the Yorkshire Dales National Park and is very sensible, even though the Green Route, which strikes off to the right here

Gorse lines the track up to the Nine Standards from Hartley.

between December and April, misses out the Nine Standards. If you are walking in that season and are keen to see them (and they are worth it), it is not a long or difficult detour to hike up to them and then back here. The Green Route is also recommended if the weather is bad, especially if visibility is poor and you have any doubts about compass work. It is the quickest way to the moorland road between Kirkby Stephen and Keld, which provides a safe way down into Swaledale through pleasant surroundings. The only drawback is the jarring of boot on tarmac. The Green Route is described on page 102. The other two, Blue for use between August and November, and Red (much the most used) between May and July, continue directly uphill.

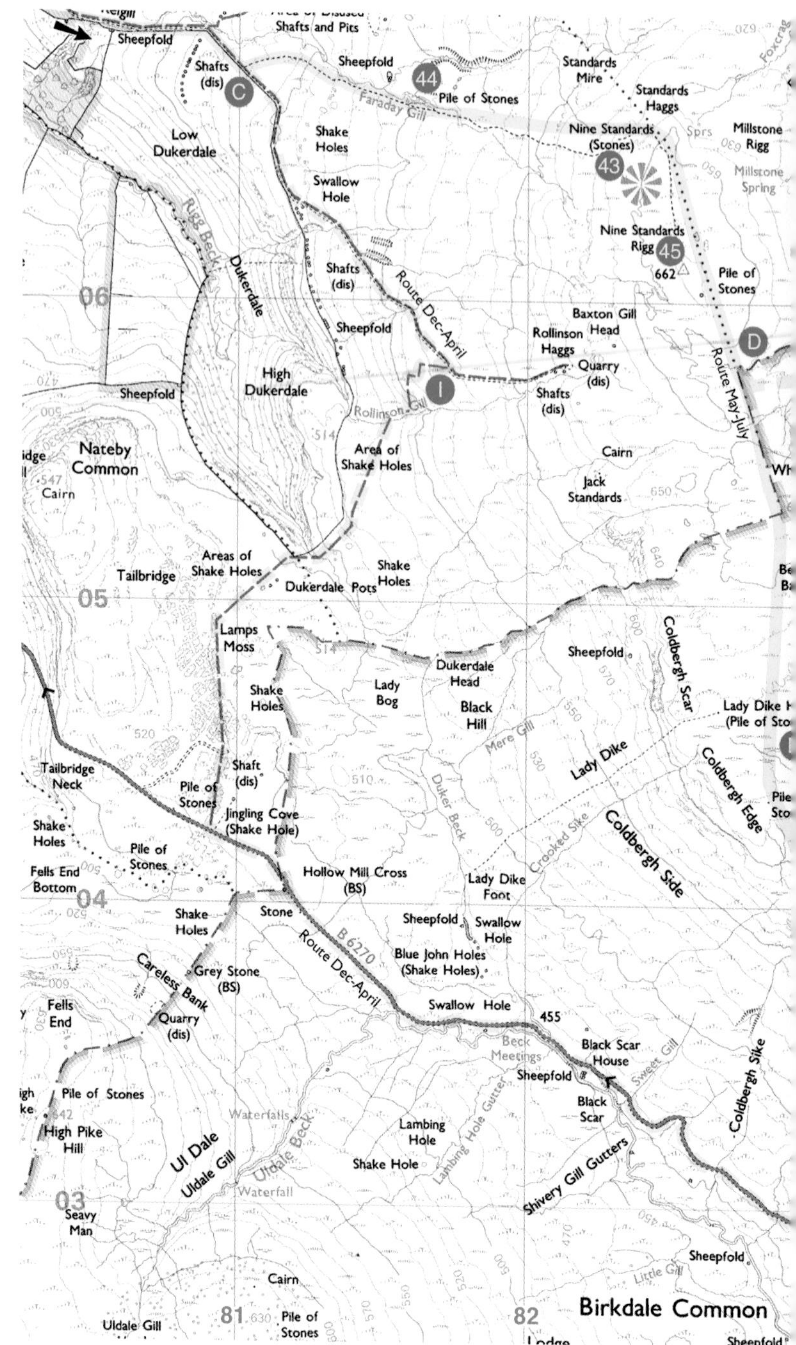
Shafts and Pits
Sheepfold
Shafts (dis)
C
Sheepfold
44
Pile of Stones
Faraday Gill
Standards Mire
Standards Haggs
Foxcrag
Low Dukerdale
Shake Holes
Nine Standards (Stones)
Sprs
Millstone Rigg
43
Millstone Spring
Swallow Hole
Rigg Beck
Nine Standards Rigg
45
662
Dukerdale
Shafts (dis)
Route Dec-April
Pile of Stones
06
Sheepfold
Baxton Gill Head
Rollinson Haggs
D
High Dukerdale
Quarry (dis)
Sheepfold
I
Shafts (dis)
Route May-July
Rollinson Gill
514
Nateby Common
547
Cairn
Area of Shake Holes
Cairn
Jack Standards
650
Areas of Shake Holes
Tailbridge
Shake Holes
Dukerdale Pots
640
05
Lamps Moss
514
Sheepfold
Dukerdale Head
Coldbergh Scar
Shake Holes
Lady Bog
Black Hill
Lady Dike
Mere Gill
520
Shaft (dis)
Tailbridge Neck
Pile of Stones
510
Duker Beck
Coldbergh Edge
Shake Holes
Jingling Cove (Shake Hole)
Crooked Sike
Coldbergh Side
Pile of Stones
Fells End Bottom
Hollow Mill Cross (BS)
Lady Dike Foot
04
Stone
Shake Holes
Sheepfold
Swallow Hole
B 6270
Careless Bank
Grey Stone (BS)
Route Dec-April
Blue John Holes (Shake Holes)
Fells End
Quarry (dis)
Swallow Hole
455
Beck Meetings
Black Scar House
Sweet Gill
Sheepfold
Coldbergh Sike
Pile of Stones
642
High Pike Hill
Waterfalls
Black Scar
Lambing Hole
Lambing Hole Gutter
Ul Dale
Uldale Gill
Uldale Beck
Shake Hole
Shivery Gill Gutters
Waterfall
03
Seavy Man
Sheepfold
Little Gill
Cairn
Birkdale Common
Uldale Gill
81
630
Pile of Stones
82
Sheepfold

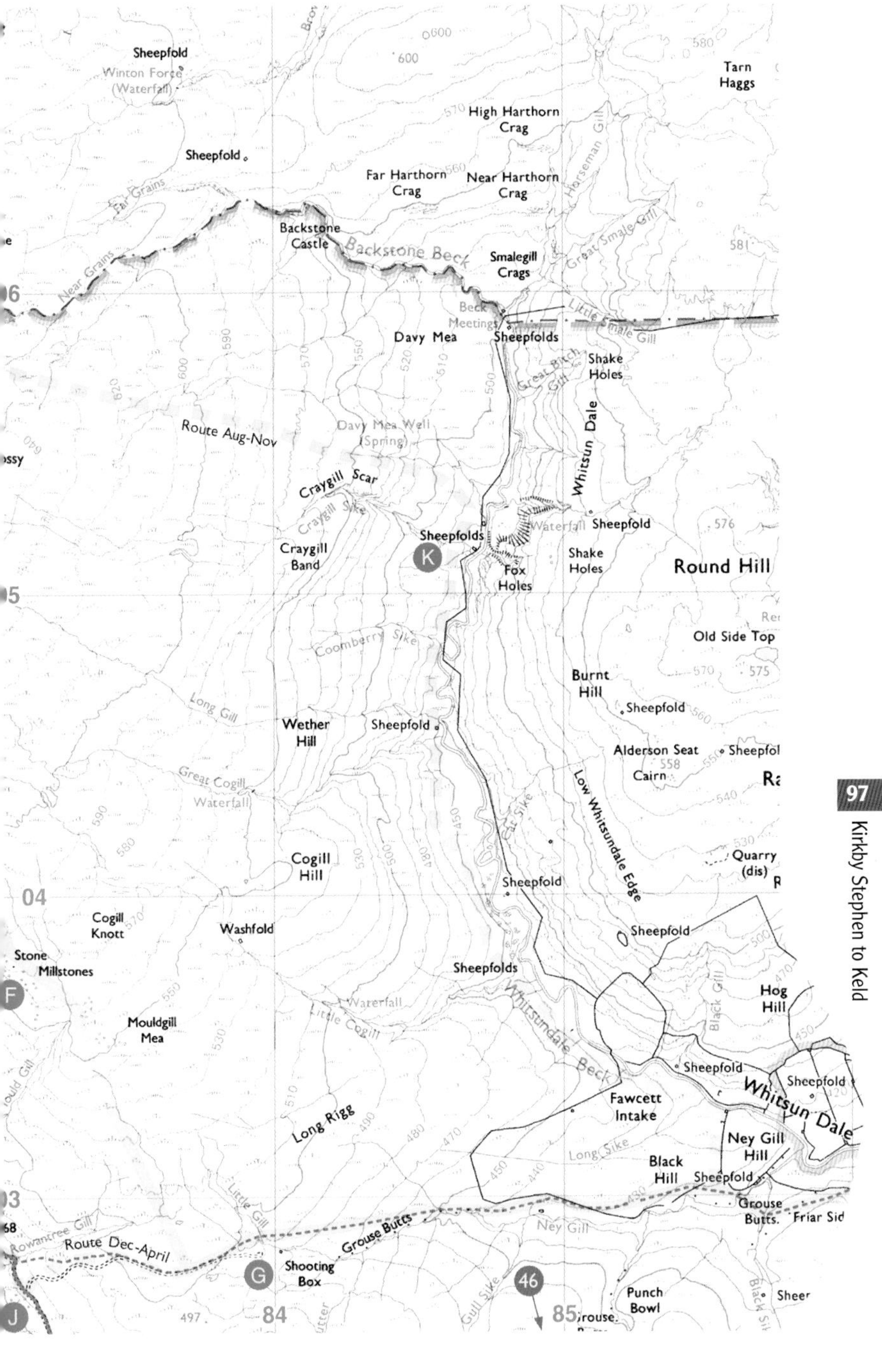
Sheepfold
Winton Force (Waterfall)
Sheepfold
Far Grains
Near Grains
Backstone Castle
Backstone Beck
High Harthorn Crag
Far Harthorn Crag
Near Harthorn Crag
Horseman Gill
Great Smale Gill
Smalegill Crags
Tarn Haggs
600
580
570
560
581
Beck Meetings
Little Smale Gill
Davy Mea
Sheepfolds
Great Bitch Gill
Shake Holes
Whitsun Dale
Route Aug-Nov
Davy Mea Well (Spring)
Craygill Scar
Craygill Sike
Craygill Band
Sheepfolds
K
Waterfall
Sheepfold
Shake Holes
Fox Holes
Round Hill
576
Old Side Top
570
575
Coomberry Sike
Burnt Hill
Sheepfold
Long Gill
Wether Hill
Sheepfold
Alderson Seat
558
Cairn
Sheepfol
Great Cogill Waterfall
Low Whitsundale Edge
Cat Sike
540
530
Quarry (dis)
Cogill Hill
Sheepfold
04
Cogill Knott
Washfold
Stone
Millstones
F
Sheepfold
Sheepfolds
Hog Hill
Black Gill
Mouldgill Mea
Waterfall
Little Cogill
Whitsundale Beck
Sheepfold
Sheepfold
Whitsun Dale
Fawcett Intake
Long Rigg
Long Sike
Ney Gill Hill
Black Hill
Sheepfold
03
Grouse Butts
Rowantree Gill
Route Dec-April
Little Gill
Grouse Butts
Ney Gill
G
Shooting Box
46
Gull Sike
Punch Bowl
Black Sike
J
497
84
85
06
05

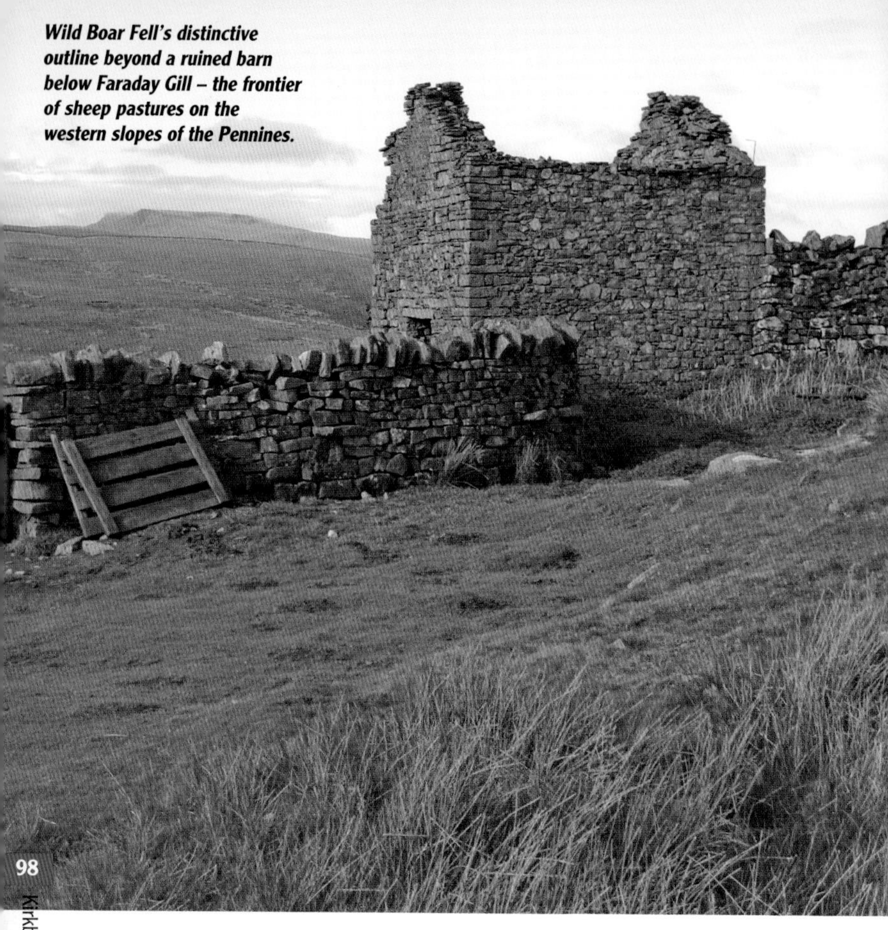

Wild Boar Fell's distinctive outline beyond a ruined barn below Faraday Gill – the frontier of sheep pastures on the western slopes of the Pennines.

The track shrinks to a footpath at the ever-eroding pile of stones which mark the former site of Faraday Hall **44**, a Wuthering Heights if ever there was one. Silvery with water in the dark peat, the route continues straight up the Standards past a couple of large but deceitful cairns which are outriders and not the real thing.

The beautifully laid drystone Standards may be exuberant county boundary markers, but the theory that they were a decoy to worry the army of Bonnie Prince Charlie is credible. They are carefully positioned to be seen from the north–south highway far below. The view backwards from here is very fine, with the blue remembered hills of Lakeland drawn up beyond the green valleys of the Lune and Eden, and the limestone plateau between them. North and south, the western scarp of the Pennines marches away in a series of bastions jutting out into Cumbria.

The way ahead is a rather different matter. This is the border between Eden and God's Own County, Yorkshire. On the face of it, God got the worse deal. Dark moorland hags of peat bog, topped with heather – black and scratchy for much of the year – and tired-looking, long, dun-coloured grass, stretch away, seemingly for ever. Rainwater divides here, going west to the Atlantic or east to the North Sea, but a great deal of it doesn't seem to want to go anywhere. Squelch, squelch. At all costs bring waterproof boots or socks for this stretch.

Strike off south from the Standards, taking a slight rise past a useful orientation disc, erected by Kirkby Stephen Fell Rescue, to the trig. point **45** and then on in a straight line to the undistinguished hummock of White Mossy Hill. About halfway **D** a signpost with removable arms, depending on which coloured route is in use, points the Blue Route off to the left (see page 103) and the Red onwards on a path which in clear weather can usually be made out without difficulty – a smear of blurred bootprints and crushed vegetation across the gluey terrain. It crosses a drainage channel and two or three short but horrible bits of unavoidable bog, where stones and planks help prevent you sinking into the gloopy mess. Spying out hummocks and moving quickly are also useful ways of avoiding knee-deep, or even higher, immersion. But there is nothing higher than the trig. point between here and Robin Hood's Bay and you are also about to cross the walk's halfway mark, so be of good cheer.

From White Mossy Hill, the route turns gently right and then curves left towards a rocky outcrop, like a pile of ruins **E**. Reaching this, you can see the next target, a slender cairn which becomes more obvious as you approach **F**. Ahead the waters of Birkdale Tarn **46** also shimmer in the distance beyond the shallow pass which carries the road from Kirkby Stephen to Keld. Green, grassy sheep intakes on either side of this make a welcome contrast to the moors. Before you reach the road, a gamekeeper's track takes you left (and also reunites the path with the Green Route, which meets the track earlier and well to the right after its contour round the fell lower down).

There is now that heartening sense of downhill all the way, with glimpses of narrow green cloughs (valleys) ahead after the long, slow traverse of the high moor. As you stride along, you may want to debate the accuracy or otherwise of Tom Bradley's description of the path you have taken in his 1891 book on Yorkshire's rivers: 'There is absolutely nothing of interest beyond

Michael Faraday's father, James, was a blacksmith near Kirkby Stephen before moving to London, where the pioneer of electricity was born.

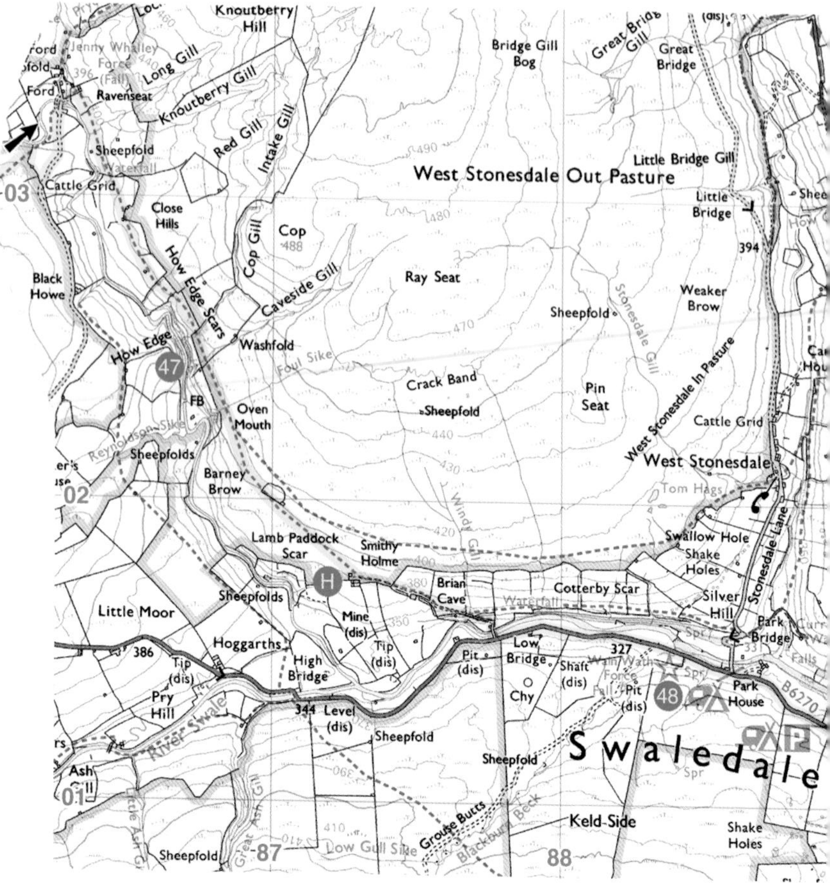

the wild mountains. An uninviting path that for 11 weary miles winds its treacherous way across the blustering moors.' If you are tired, in a hurry or enduring bad weather as you descend to Ney Gill, you will agree.

The track now passes a shooters' hut and an almost suburban gravel parking area for their 4x4s **G**, and then a line of butts strung down a narrow valley above Ney Gill. Keep on, ahead and downhill, crossing the stream twice until the way is blocked by walls on either bank, with wiring strung between them over the water. The stream forges through but you must go right, a careful wobble across Ney Gill on large stones then up a brief slope and down to the farm road to Ravenseat by the cattle grid. The Blue Route rejoins the main path at the crossing of Ney Gill.

Turn left at the cattle grid, and before plodding down to the farm take in the lovely view: the cosy dwellings of many generations amid their carefully-tended fields, in spring and summer ablaze with kingcups. Circling behind and above them lowers the great wilderness which you have crossed. It is a fine image of civilisation holding back the wild. and the delightful family here is justly famous for excellent tea and scones. One reader writes cheerfully of 'oystercatchers calling by the stream while the farm children run around with water pistols' The path crosses the pretty old bridge (one of several in this small but excellently engineered huddle of buildings) amid excited barks from the farm dogs. It then heads right across a smaller stream and along the far bank of Whitsundale Beck, a pleasant route through fields and stiles and up to the left of a barn to How Edge Scars above Oven Mouth **47**. Keep up to the left to stay well above this dramatic ravine, although you can venture safely to the edge at several places to enjoy the precipitous view below. If you have plenty of time, there is a lower path down to the beck and its defile, and a steep scramble back up.

On the main path, a gate in a fence above Oven Mouth leads to a fork where the path on the right drops past Eddy Fold to Smithy Holme Farm **H**, sadly empty, and a steepish descent to the Kirkby Stephen–Keld road at Low Bridge. Turn left on the road for the final stretch into Keld, stopping at Wain Wath Force **48** with the limestone cliffs of Cotterby Scar rising picturesquely behind. A gated path leads to grassy picnic spots on the edge of the Swale, where canoeists often gather before shooting the wide, straight curtain of tumbling water. Back on the road, Keld is just up the hill with the centre of the hamlet – café and well-kept public lavatories – a short step down the first turning left.

At Smithy Holme farm, you can postpone the tarmac a little longer — albeit at the considerable expense of bypassing Wain Wath Force — by taking a path which heads left above a largely fallen-down wall. This contours along the top of Cotterby Scar to the Tan Hill road, where a right turn either crosses Park Bridge to the main road (then left into Keld), or you can drop down left before the bridge and accompany the Swale to a footbridge which leads you back on a hairpin into the village.

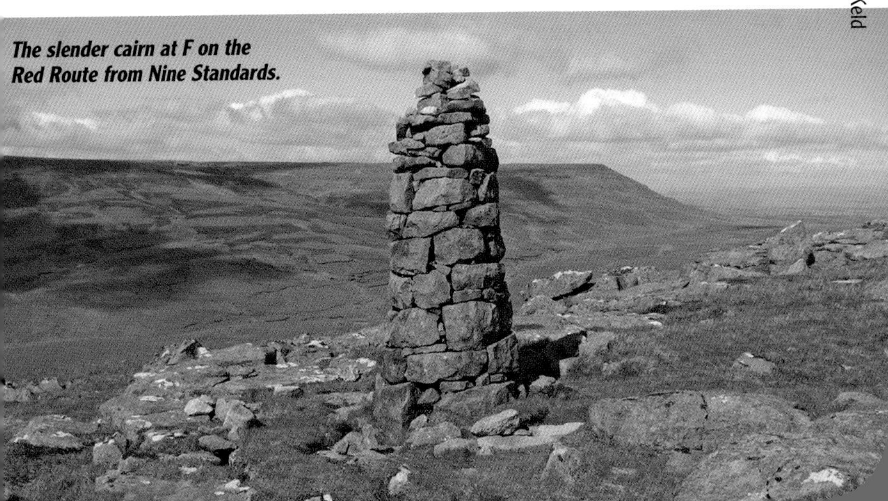
The slender cairn at F on the Red Route from Nine Standards.

Water seeps from the peat hags on Nine Standards into the ravine of Faraday Gill, once home of the family of Michael Faraday the inventor.

The Green Route – December to April

This is the lowest and easiest way across the summit from Kirkby Stephen and makes a safe option in bad weather, especially mist, when navigation from Nine Standards Rigg is a demanding exercise. It leaves the main path at Faraday Gill **C**, a junction marked by a sign, and follows a bridleway initially by the wall. The path climbs 200 feet (60 metres), where another sign at a junction points you, right, to a wind shelter **I**. From here the path drops towards the wall again, crosses the boggy patch of Rollinson Gill, and then follows the wall gently down and across moorland, with Tailbrigg Pots swallets or potholes on the left, to the B6270 Kirkby Stephen to Keld road. If the weather is really grim or you just want reassurance and don't mind tarmac, this quiet road makes its way safely through the wild landscape to Keld.

The Green Route follows it left, with another gateway to the underworld at Jingling Pot on the right, and continues through a landscape of evocative names – Shivery Gill Gutters, Blue John Holes – until just after Rowantree Gill a clear shooters' track heads left **J** and is soon reunited with the Red Route above the line of grouse butts which slopes down to Ney Gill.

The Blue Route – August to November

This stays with the main path after Nine Standards until, shortly after a rapidly vanishing ruin on the left, the sign with removable arms **D**, lettered in blue or red depending on the time of the year, directs you left and straight down the boggy fellside, helped by a line of posts, to a final curve to the right which meets Craygill Sike just before its junction with Whitsundale Beck **K**. Keeping the latter always on your left, descend through this great wilderness until, soon after the fences of Fawcett Intake, a wall heads off right. Follow this to join the other two paths at a ruined barn just above Ney Gill.

Masterpieces of drystone walling, the Nine Standards crown the western escarpment of the Pennines, some tall and slender, others short and fat.

A very different dale

Stand by Wain Wath Force and look down the valley of Swaledale. It is hard to imagine that this lovely landscape was once the Rotherham or Gateshead of its day, a teeming industrial anthill producing much of the world's lead. Hugely in demand for bullets, roofs and waterpipes, the seams – which slant almost vertically upwards, unlike horizontal coal levels – were first mined by the Romans; their word for lead, *plumbum*, gives us 'plumbing'. An ingot from Hurst survives at the Yorkshire Museum in York, stamped with the Emperor Hadrian's name.

Lead from Swaledale roofed the Tower of London in the 12th century and for the next 600 years the hugely destructive system of 'hushing' laid waste to the valley, especially the narrow ghylls along its flanks. Their becks were dammed and then torrents of water released, stripping away soil and stones to reveal traces of the precious grey-black veins. Hushing reached its peak in the mid-18th century but then dropped away as the Industrial Revolution made alternative techniques available.

Rails were laid in adits, or side-tunnels, that were bored into the hillsides, striking the veins at several points.

Crackpot Hall: Lord Wharton's gamekeeper enjoyed one of England's best views.

Extremely dangerous work followed, with men on ladders hacking out the ore. Women and children hauled tubs along the rails to daylight where they hand-hammered the rock until crushing machinery was introduced. By 1820 more than 40 smelt mills blackened the sky between the valley and Arkengarthdale. Millions of tonnes of lead rumbled off to the railhead at Richmond in ponycarts. Add the regular presence of long, slow droving parties – some 10,000 cattle a year passed this way until refrigeration allowed cheap imported meat from the 1890s – and marvel at the noise, filth and turmoil which reigned in this peaceful haven.

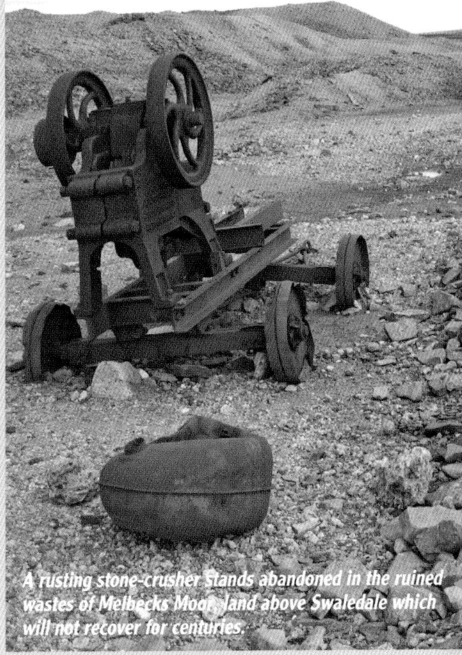

A rusting stone-crusher stands abandoned in the ruined wastes of Melbecks Moor, land above Swaledale which will not recover for centuries.

On the high path from Keld, the pandemonium is easier to conceive. Between Crackpot Hall and Gunnerside, the felltop and sides have many years to wait before their scars heal. The scene can be bleak, especially on a dull day, but the almost lunar dereliction means that the bones of the once great industry are clearly and fascinatingly displayed. Surviving shells of buildings at Old Gang and Surrender Bridge show the scale of things; even more striking are the flues which snake ½ mile (800 metres) up the hillside from both mines, in effect enormous chimneys laid at an angle up the slope. Small boys had to crawl through these, scraping off lead or its oxide which condensed in the tunnel and was worth its weight in cash. If they survived, their life expectancy as an adult lead miner in 1850 was 46, compared to a national average of 61.

The profits went to distant shareholders, but some of them were spent by firms such as the London Lead Company on improving the Yorkshire workers' lot. Swaledale miners were encouraged to take smallholdings and to spend spare time in the open air, away from the labyrinth whose tunnels at Gunnerside allowed a 7-mile (11-km) crawl to Arkengarthdale. One result is an excellent network of footpaths which have become rights-of-way, including much of the Coast to Coast's route along Swaledale. Another memorial to the industrial age is the roll-call of evocative names: Crackpot, the pothole of the crows; North, Bunton and Old Field Hushes (the last the scene of fistfights between the rival miners of the Parkes brothers and Lord Pomfret in the mid-18th century); and Surrender, named after the Surrender Mining Company, which was one of the most prosperous in the dale.

7 Keld to Reeth

via the mines or the River Swale • 5 hours
10.5 miles (17 km)

Ascent 1,790 feet (545 metres)
Descent 1,673 feet (510 metres)
Lowest point Reeth: 656 feet (200 metres)
Highest point Swinner Gill: 1,837 feet (560 metres)

A fascinating meander among the ruins of Swaledale's lead industry, reached and left by beautiful stretches of riverside, rich in flowers, wildlife and waterfalls. An alternative route follows the river all the way through some of the finest landscape in the Yorkshire Dales.

Some people toss a coin when they leave Keld, because the choice between the moors and mines and the grand march down the riverbank is such a tough one. Both walks are richly rewarding, but for the first-timer I would definitely plump for the mines unless the weather is miserable or path-finding potentially a problem because of mist. The remains of smelters, tunnels, forges and flues are both fascinating and completely different from any other stretch of the Coast to Coast, and there is plenty of riverbank later on. Once again, Wainwright's genius for variety earns a respectful bow.

Time has also made some of the skeletal remains very beautiful, especially the first you encounter in the narrow cloughs of Swinner Gill. The path leaves Keld by an unmade lane signed to Kidston Force and Muker, branching off left to cross the Swale by a footbridge just before Kidston Falls tumble impressively down on the far bank. The route climbs to the left of the falls and then across their feeder beck before heading up and left at a fork **A** to the ruins of Crackpot Hall **49**. This is an idyllic place with a sensational view of the narrow valley of Kidston Gorge **50** down to Muker and the distant sweep of the main dale. Far from being a madhouse, the handsome hall was built in the 17th century for Lord Wharton's red-deer keeper and belonged in turn to prosperous farmers, gamekeepers and mining officials. Finally abandoned to mining subsidence in the 1950s, it would once have rung to the shouts and laughs of children, as an eloquent historical plaque on one wall describes (if there; it has been removed and replaced several times). Its memorable name is one of a grand roll-call in Swaledale: Wavery Gill, Blackberry Beck, Oxnop and many more.

Here the way divides, down to the river route (see page 114) or left and up past Crackpot's former smithy and along the increasingly steep side of

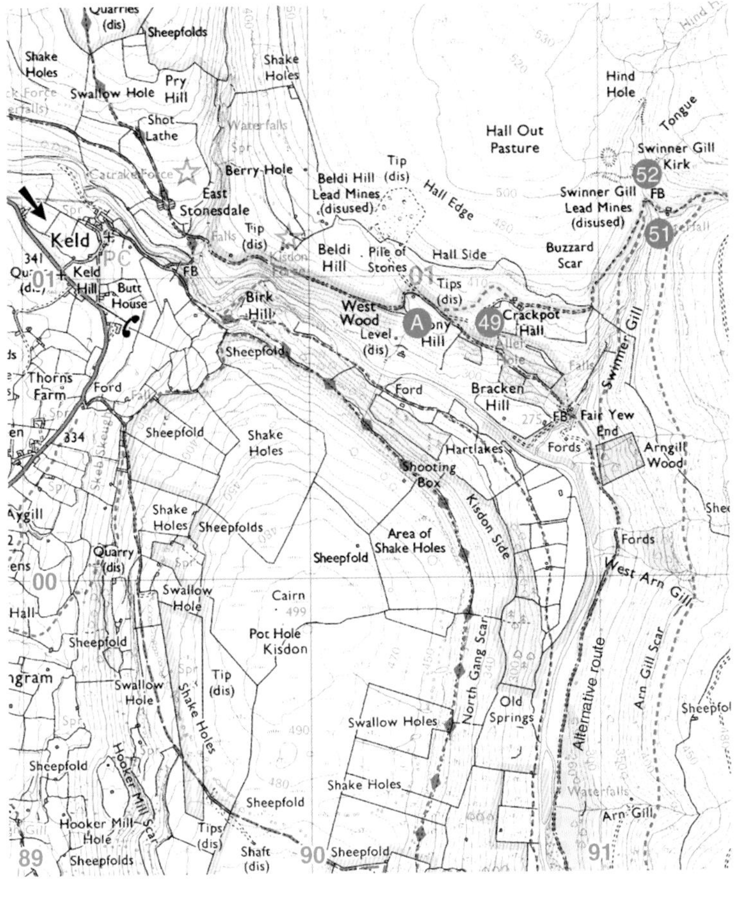

Swinner Gill below Buzzard Scar. At a fork in the great gorge, smelt mill ruins **51** sit snugly above a tunnel from which the coppery water of one beck emerges. The other tumbles wildly down the right-hand fork, East Grain, which takes the path up to the moor, keeping to the rocky slope on the left of the waterfalls. Before tackling this, you may want to prospect a little up the west fork to Swinner Gill Kirk **52**, a cave used by Catholics and Nonconformists in troubled religious times. Superficially, this area is a stony wasteland, but closer inspection reveals all manner of plants: herb Robert, maidenhair fern, green spleenwort, New Zealand willowherb and many more. Pottering round the dramatic landscape helps an understanding of how the steeply falling becks which gash the northern side of Swaledale encouraged mining by exposing the seams of lead. Dammed and released, the streams were then used to 'hush' or sweep away great slices of soil and stone to expose the ore. The devastated aftermath still remains.

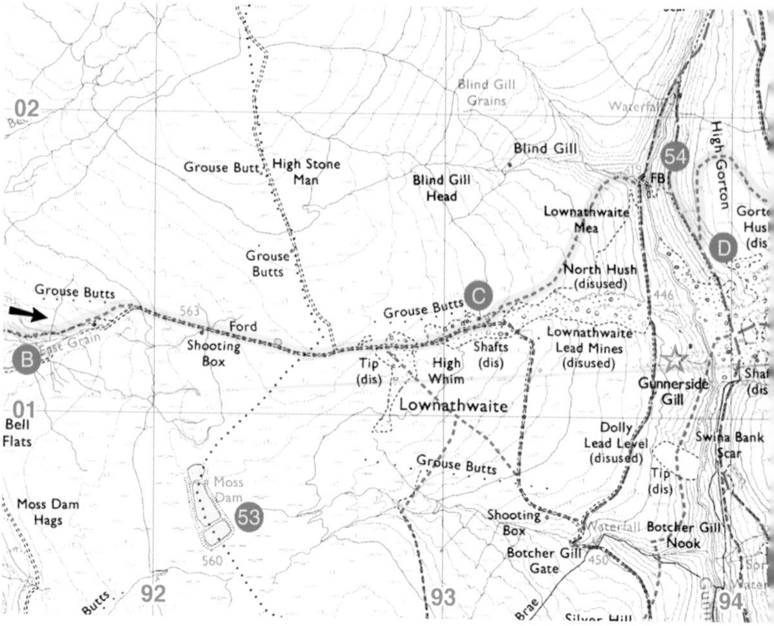

After an initially steep haul up East Grain, the gradient eases and takes a deeply channelled route to a grouse-shooters' jeep track **B** which curves up to the left and then gently right. This leads the route to the moortop just after a fence and a path signed left to Rogan's Seat, which you can explore some other time. More accessible to the right is Moss Dam, crossed by a little causeway, and used for hushing and other mining work **53**. The Coast to Coast heads onwards on the main track, past a corrugated iron and stone enclosure. Keep a good eye out here for two small cairns on the left **C** which mark an initially indistinct path leading off at an angle to the left. A larger cairn soon follows and the track becomes clear, running along the top of North Hush above Gunnerside Gill, then doubling back and dropping steeply down in a big zig-zag to Blind Gill and the substantial cloister-like ruins of Blakethwaite mine **54**. While still above Blakethwaite, scope out the path **D** on the other side of the valley; it is your route after the ruined mill and is easier to see from here. Cross the stream on a

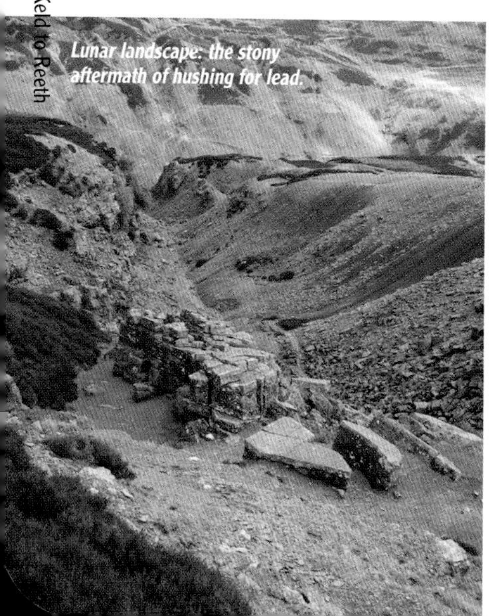
Lunar landscape: the stony aftermath of hushing for lead.

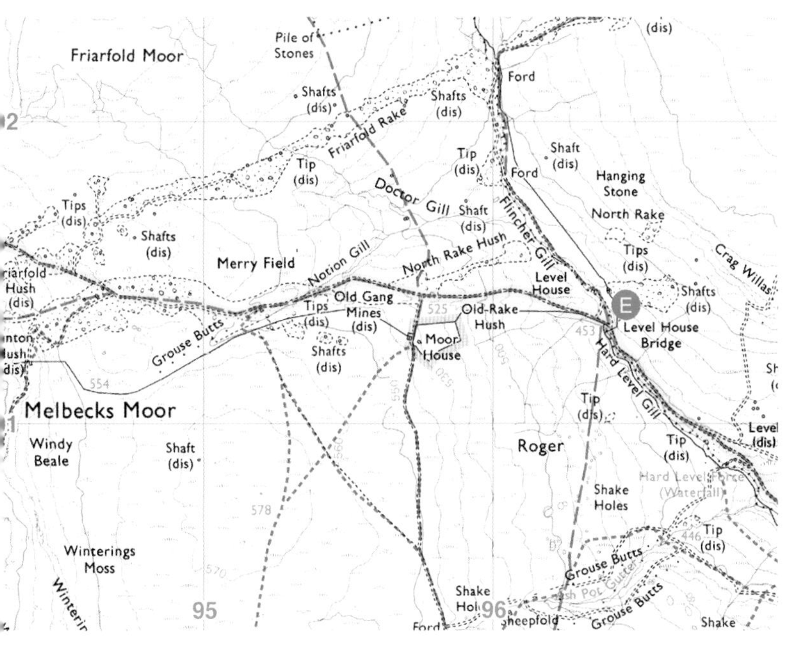

simple but large stone-slab bridge and have a good potter around, before mounting the steep zig-zags on the far side and turning right on to a level green track which once took miners, ponies and their carts. A little further down the valley towards Gunnerside, more large and tempting remains are visible, which may be inspected as a detour. But look out carefully for a path **D** angling back up the valley below a broken cliff more or less directly above the Blakethwaite ruins. Its progress across a scree of large rocks can be seen by discolorations from the passage of boots, but it is easy to miss. Failure to find it is not disastrous; many walkers have gone on Friarfold and Bunton Hushes or the lower mine ruins and then taken a variety of steep, stony scrambles up the valley side, which all eventually hit the route onwards over the moor. But the path across the rocks is much easier and gentler, ending in a line of modest cairns up a grassy ridge.

This quickly changes into a landscape straight from the moon: land stripped bare by hushing and then subjected to the further ravages of stone crushing by quarrymen. They have left one rust-red crushing machine as a sort of memorial to the wholesale exploitation of the plateau which will not recover for centuries. In good weather, the track across an initially largely featureless half-mile is clear, but in mist follow your compass due east. Be prepared, too, whatever the weather, for a long, long but gentle descent in a broad sweep down to Old Gang mines.

At last, after crossing Level House Bridge **E** on a handsome stone bridge and, later, Flitcher Gill about three-quarters of the way down the valley, the mines' distinctive chimney appears, with impressive ruins at its base and up the fellside **55**. These include one of the flues distinctive to this area, which reached a great height and created a fearsome draught for the smelting furnaces by snaking up the hill. Each is both a stone tunnel and an enormous chimney lying on its side. Beyond Old Gang, the gravelly road continues to the road and beck at Surrender Bridge.

Stay your side of the bridge and follow a waymarked sign above Surrender smelt mill **56** through heathery intakes to a nasty surprise. This is the sudden, very steep ravine of Cringley Bottom **F**, a Noel Edmonds sound-alike which ambushes walkers just when Reeth seems within easy reach. It is over quickly, though, after a wobbly crossing of its beck and an equally steep scramble up the other side. The initial apparent absence of a way out at the top, through a formidable-looking drystone wall, is resolved as you scramble down to the beck. About halfway, look up and you will see a stile on the skyline. Make a note of its whereabouts because it cannot be seen for most of the climb up.

Roman 'Pigs'

Among the earliest relics of Roman lead-mining in Swaledale were two ingots or 'pigs', now lost. One was stamped HADRIAN and the other TRAJAN – ideal teaching aids for local schools' history lessons.

Beyond the stile, a pleasant path runs across several heather and grass fields to Thirns Farm, where it angles up left

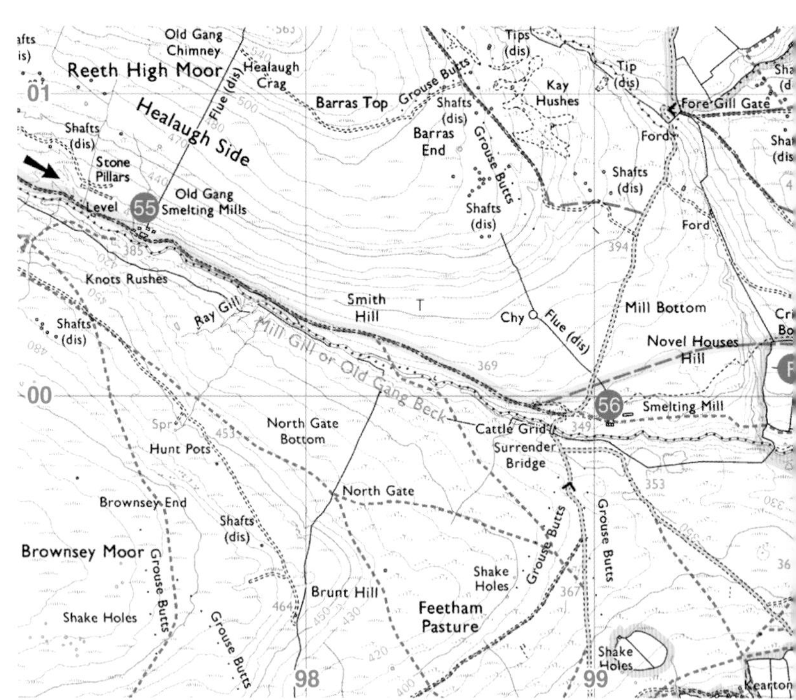

he monastery-like
nave' of Blakethwaite
ead mine, with the beck
umbling beneath a simple slab
ridge and the trail angling up behind.

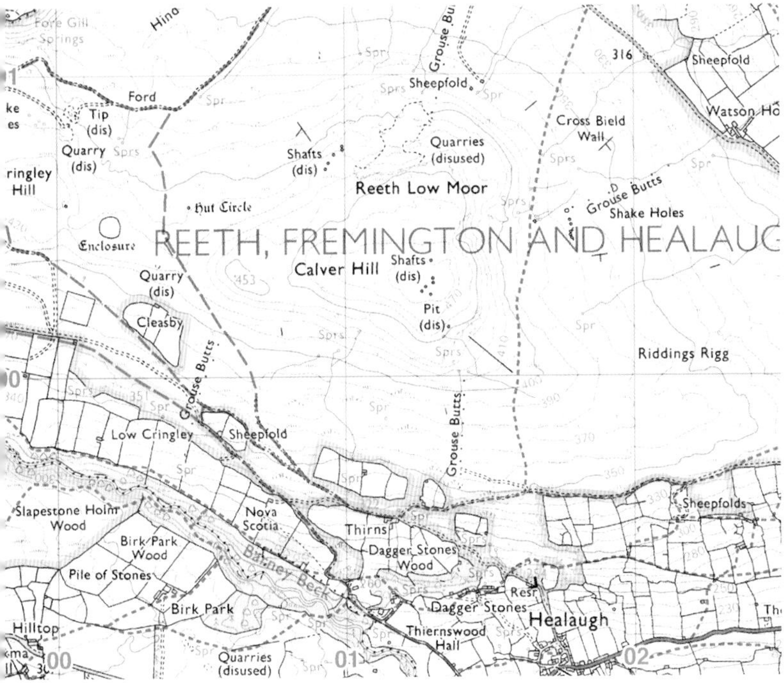

to Moorcock Cottage and on through more sheep enclosures on the flank of Calver Hill. When Riddings Farm appears ahead and slightly below the route, the path runs slightly left above the buildings and across a field to the right-hand corner and a gate in the wall **G**. This leads to a delightfully hidden (albeit sometimes midgy in summer) green lane called Skelgate, often partly awash with a small beck, which runs in a series of twists and turns to the main dale road. Turn left and within five minutes you are among the plentiful cafés and pubs of Swaledale's little capital, Reeth.

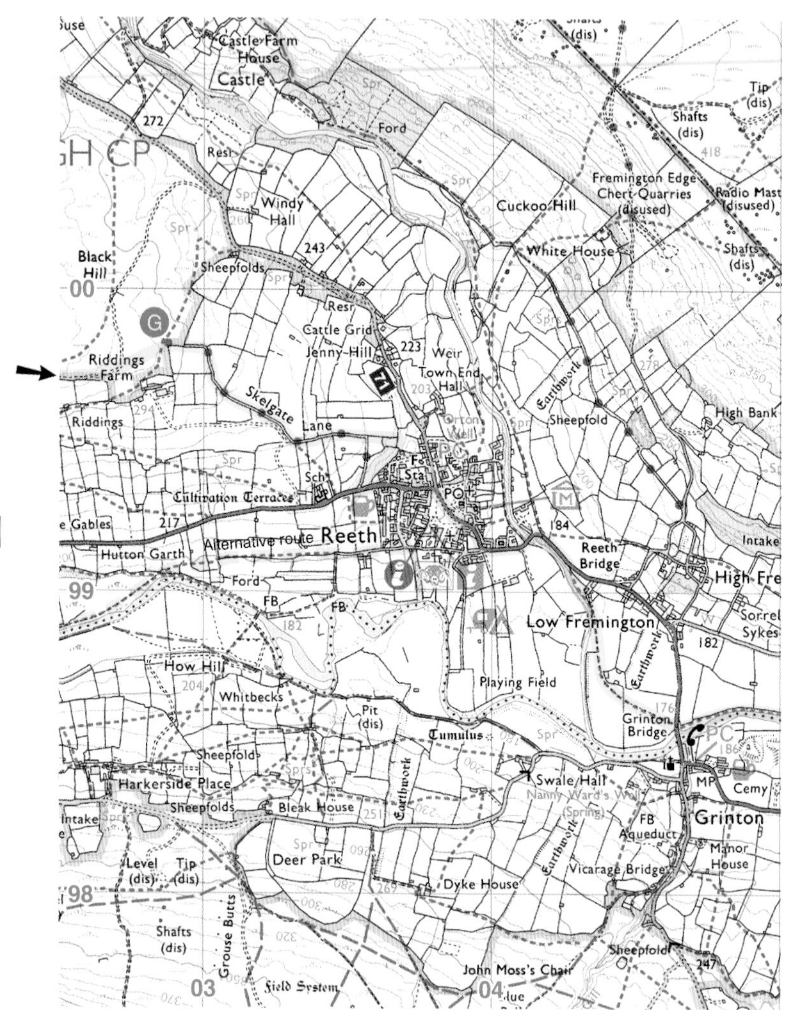

A classic Dales farmhouse beneath quarried cliffs in the rich farmland by the Swale, which marks the approach to the local 'capital', Reeth.

The riverside alternative

Wainwright called this beautiful walk 'the royal road from Keld to Reeth', but rejected it in favour of the moorland industrial relics. I'm with him on that, but another great pedestrian chose to follow the Swale instead. In 1789, as France descended into revolutionary chaos, the first Methodist minister of Keld, a Rev. Stillman, set out along the river on one of Britain's first recorded sponsored walks, to raise funds to make a chapel out of the village's abandoned Anglican church. His route? To London and back, a real epic which he managed in three months. There is a note of his expenses in the chapel's papers: an invoice for 6 old pence (2½ p). He raised over £200.

The riverside alternative starts just before Crackpot Hall, where the clear track forks right **A** and down to the sweeping curve of the Swale, which forms such an outstanding view from the ruined house (don't miss the chance to poke about the picturesque remains; it's a very small diversion) **49**. The riverside path marches along steep-sided Kidson Gorge **50** over springy stretches of cropped turf, abounding in rabbits and occasionally their predator the stoat, to Muker, which is worth another diversion over the bridge at the end of Ivelet Wood.

Judging Swaledale sheep at the annual Muker Show..

The name doesn't sound instantly attractive, but Muker is a thriving community as well as a pretty one, with a lovely church, once thatched with heather. After the collapse of mining, which in its heyday kept three pubs thriving in this tiny place, the economy was revived by the Morris family, who set up Swaledale Woollens, a hand-knitting co-operative using the high-quality wool of the 'Swardels' – Swaledale's own sturdy breed of hill sheep which nibble the grass in all directions. Next door to the Woollens' shop, a plaque records the village's famous sons, the brothers Richard and Cherry Kearton, outstanding naturalists whose pioneer wildlife photography was achieved by such devices as making artificial cows and standing patiently inside them with a camera. In May and June the wild flower meadows around Muker are delightful, and the first Wednesday in September sees Muker Show, a thoroughly Yorkshire occasion down to the oompahing silver band. The Farmer's Arms is a welcome survivor of the three pubs.

Back on the track, the path sticks with the Swale, allowing lots of opportunities to enjoy the wagtails, dippers and other river birds which abound. If you are lucky you will see a kingfisher streak past or a sandpiper stalking about. At a fork **H**, with

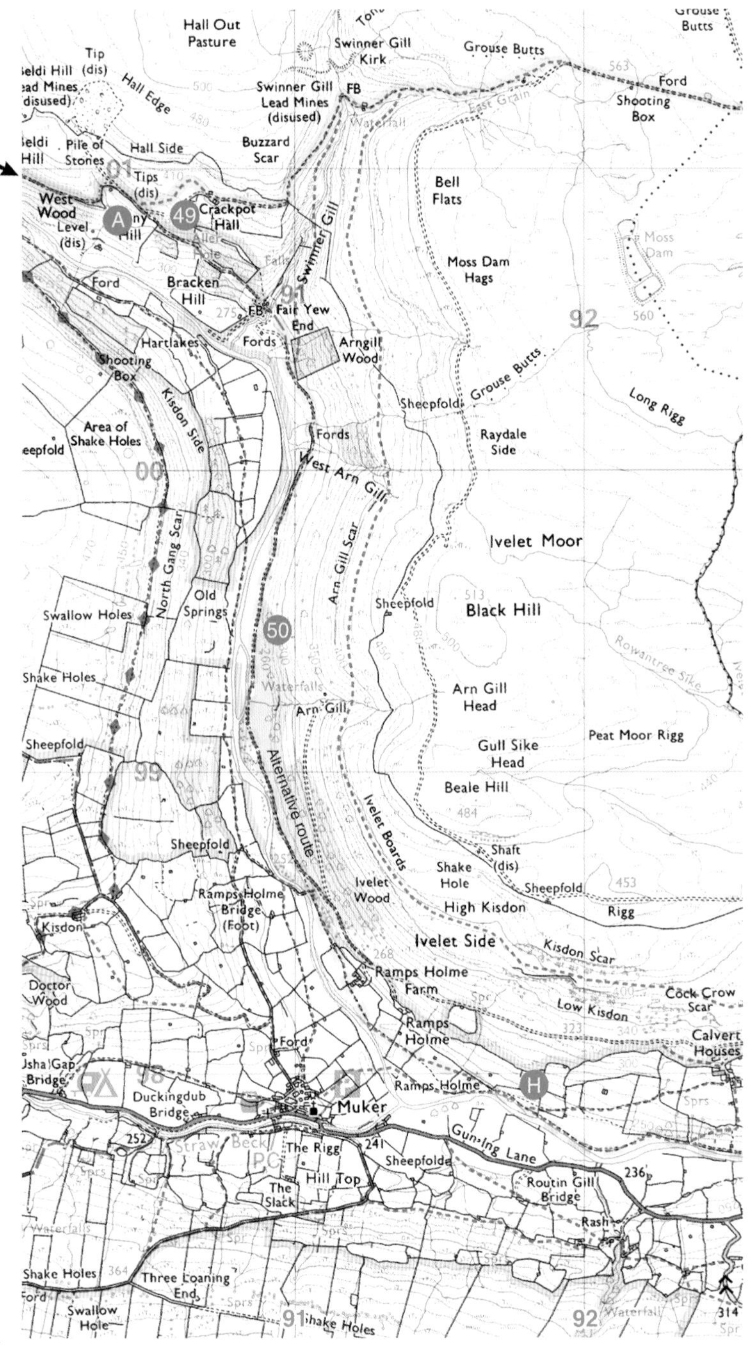
Hall Out Pasture
Swinner Gill Kirk
Grouse Butts
Tip (dis)
Hall Edge
Swinner Gill Lead Mines (disused)
FB
Ford
Shooting Box
Pile of Stones
Hall Side
Buzzard Scar
East Grain
Tips (dis)
West Wood
Level (dis)
Crackpot Hall
Bell Flats
Swinner Gill
Moss Dam
Moss Dam Hags
Ford
Bracken Hill
Fair Yew End
Fords
Arngill Wood
Hartlakes
Shooting Box
Grouse Butts
Sheepfold
Long Rigg
Kisdon Side
Area of Shake Holes
Fords
Raydale Side
West Arn Gill
North Gang Scar
Arn Gill Scar
Ivelet Moor
Old Springs
Swallow Holes
Sheepfold
Black Hill
Rowantree Sike
Shake Holes
Waterfalls
Arn Gill
Arn Gill Head
Peat Moor Rigg
Sheepfold
Alternative route
Gull Sike Head
Ivelet Boards
Beale Hill
Sheepfold
Shaft (dis)
Shake Hole
Ramps Holme Bridge (Foot)
Ivelet Wood
Sheepfold
High Kisdon
Rigg
Kisdon
Ivelet Side
Kisdon Scar
Ramps Holme Farm
Doctor Wood
Cock Crow Scar
Low Kisdon
Ramps Holme
Calvert Houses
Ford
Usha Gap Bridge
Ramps Holme
Duckingdub Bridge
Muker
Straw Beck
The Rigg
Gunnerside Lane
Sheepfolds
Hill Top
The Slack
Routin Gill Bridge
Rash
Waterfalls
Shake Holes
Three Loaning End
Swallow Hole
Shake Holes
Waterfall

Gunnerside signed in both directions, keep right past a barn and continue through an entrancing world of meadows, drystone walls, the dancing river and some stiles designed for whippet-lean local farmers rather than ramblers with large backpacks. The flowers here are plentiful in season: yellow rattle, pignut, wood cranesbill and the melancholy thistle. Avoiding all diversions to the left, stay with the river until steeply humpbacked Ivelet Bridge, where you turn left on to the metalled lane which bends right into the hamlet. Go right at the phone box to rejoin the footpath to Gunnerside, briefly using a lane and a gravelly path between a cottage and a barn to reach a footbridge over Shore Gill **I**, just after a pretty descent through trees. More meadows, stiles, fleeing rabbits and the river lead on to a briefly more dramatic stretch where the path creeps above a high, steep section of bank before more fields lead to Flatlands estate, a 20th-century introduction to Gunnerside.

Ivelet Bridge.

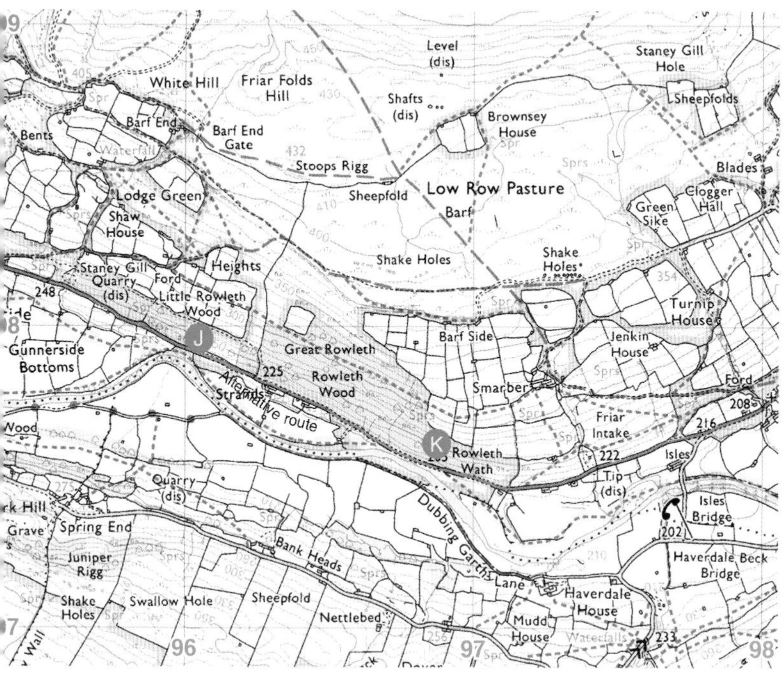

Don't miss the wider views along the valley: the broad shoulders of the fells, the nibbling marks of quarrymen and, over to the right, beyond Gunnerside, another Crackpot, where satellite navigation systems have notoriously led unwitting drivers on to a fearsome unmade road surrounded by precipices. The distinctive Swaledale barns, almost one to every field, housed up to four cattle through the winter – often very harsh – with their hay feed above them in the byre. A few have piles of fresh cowpats outside, showing that they are still in use. Gunnerside village was the miniature capital of this area in lead-mining days but has shrunk back to a population of a couple of hundred, which trebles when all the holiday homes are in use. It has a strong Methodist tradition but also a Shortest Day Festival in December with undoubted pagan origins. Tearooms and a pub will add to your general sense of joy.

Reluctantly perhaps, take your leave by turning right in front of The King's Head down a snicket (to the pub lavatories), then left and back on to the meadow, stile, rabbit and wild flowers. The Swale was left behind at Flatlands but now it returns and remains your companion past Feetham and Healaugh to Reeth. The path seeks refuge on the dale's main road a couple of times, when the river's high banks cut off any room for a separate way ahead, but returns via a slippery slope **J** and, on the second occasion, a gate **K**. From here the path crosses meadows a little further inland before rejoining the Swale at Isles Bridge, reached by a flight of stone steps.

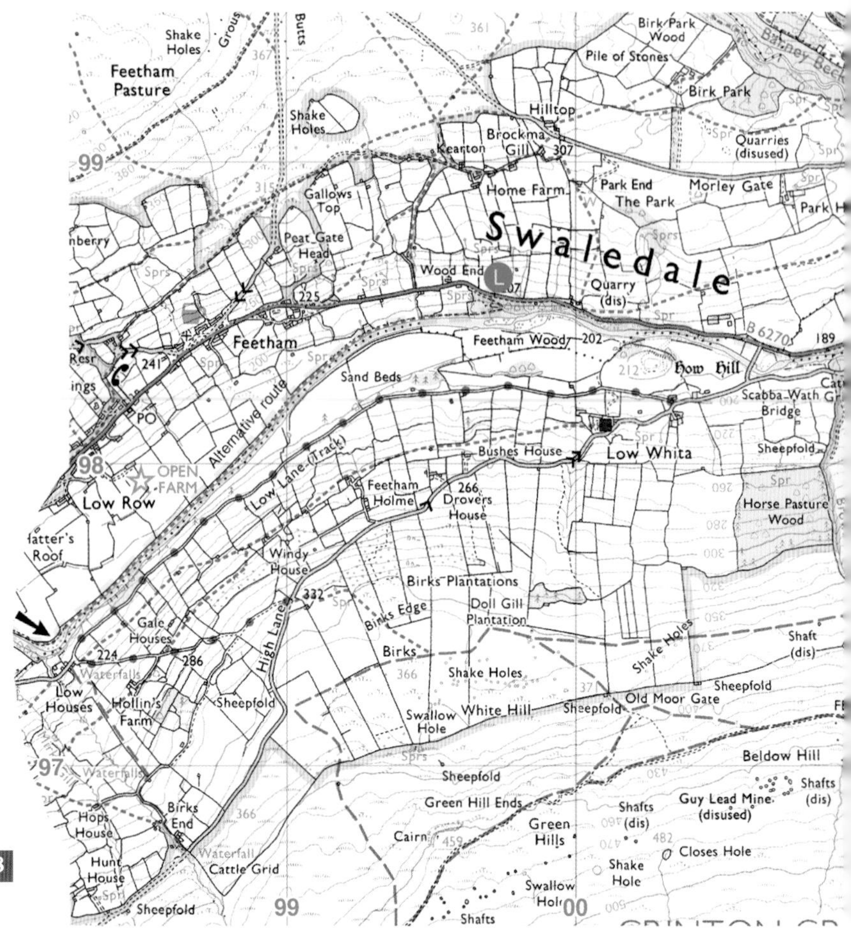

Turn left and then right along a path, now signposted for the journey's end, Reeth, and pick your way along a succession of walls and flood defence banks to more meadows, before joining the main dale road again just after Feetham via steep zig-zags through the wood **L**. After about a mile of tarmac (unless you decide to divert left along a footpath into Healaugh), turn right at a public footpath sign near a roadside parking bay **M**, following the path with a fence on the left and the river on the right, jumping nimbly over stones to ford Barney Beck and then onwards along the riverbank, shaded by trees. Where the Swale bends away to the right, continue ahead to the first, welcome, houses of Reeth.

Poetic Names

'Swale' is a fine onomatopoeic word meaning 'swirling, whirling, swallowing', while 'Keld' is from the Norse *kelda*, meaning a spring.

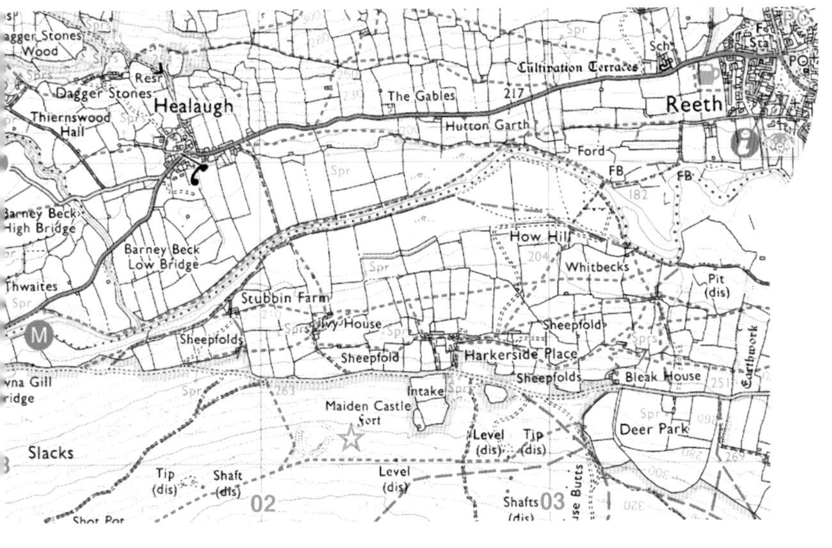

Potters and knitters

Reeth is the capital of upper Swaledale, with a handsome line of pubs and other solid stone buildings to prove it. Its life has always been bound up with the river; indeed its name comes from the Old English for 'riverside'. The Swaledale Folk Museum tells the story of an economy where farming was matched for many years by mining and knitting, and more recently, as at Kirkby Stephen, by all manner of other imaginative enterprise. Housed in the old Methodist school on the edge of the green, it tells the story of the extraordinary dispersal of Reeth's population, all over the world, when mining collapsed. Its exhibits also cover a fascinating range of crafts. Do you know what a Spoke Dog is? Or a Stickle Pricker? This is the place to find out. Chert for pottery was mined locally, as well as lead, while barytes, used in paint-making, were reclaimed from mine spoil. Television regulars will also know the place as a backdrop to the vet James Herriot's tales. Brass-banding and an annual show (the last Wednesday in August) are part of life here, as in the other dale villages, and the Swaledale Music Festival grows in scope and enterprise every year. The small shelter on the green is known as the Reeth Parliament, because locals sit and sort out the world's problems here. At the top of the green an unusual Community Orchard has opened recently, behind delicately forged iron gates.

Yarn spun and dyed at the Swaledale Folk Museum.

Swaledale widens out into a broad valley dotted with stone barns as the river flows over gravelly banks towards Marrick Priory and Steps Wood.

8 Reeth to Richmond

via Marske and the 'Costa Applegarth' • 4–5 hours
10.3 miles (16.5 km)

Ascent 1,100 feet (335 metres)
Descent 820 feet (250 metres)
Lowest point Richmond: 426 feet (130 metres)
Highest point Marrick: 1,050 feet (320 metres)

A pleasant, short stretch up ancient nuns' steps and through a semi-feudal village to peaceful hillside woods above the steep valley of the lower Swale.

The way ahead starts at the southern end of the green in Reeth, with a fond look back to all those pubs. Cross the road bridge over the Swale and turn right at a small wooden gate **A** on to a broad water meadow, golden with buttercups in early summer, which leads to Grinton Bridge. This is reached by some solid stone steps which assert the walker's right-of-way in no uncertain terms. Cross the road and into the meadow opposite. Pipe-laying has recently caused diversions here, but the route is marked along the river and up to the lane; cross and take a field path which leads to Marrick Priory **57**, whose tower has been a landmark since leaving Reeth. You can take either the lane or the path across the sloping grass-land to the left, shown as a green dotted line on the map.

Founded in 1154 for Benedictine nuns by a conscience-stricken baron, this has the grave of a local ancient called Thomas Peacock, who lived to be 102 (a record which will hold only until the next stage of the

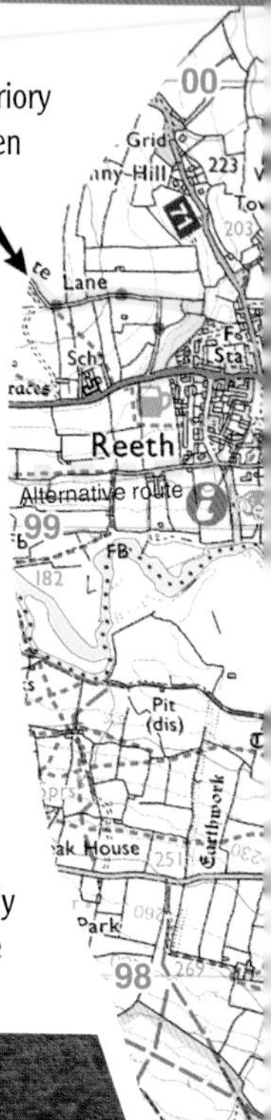

Marrick Priory's tower, ruins and farm beside the Swale.

walk). It was also the scene of a romantic episode when a beautiful pageboy arrived in a storm in 1535 and was given shelter by the nuns, who soon discovered that he was actually Isabella Beaufort, a Court favourite. She had attracted Henry VIII's lascivious interest but had no wish to become yet another of his wives, and so fled London in disguise. Isabella later married a sound local noble and lived happily ever after, unlike the priory, which was dissolved by Henry in 1540. It is now

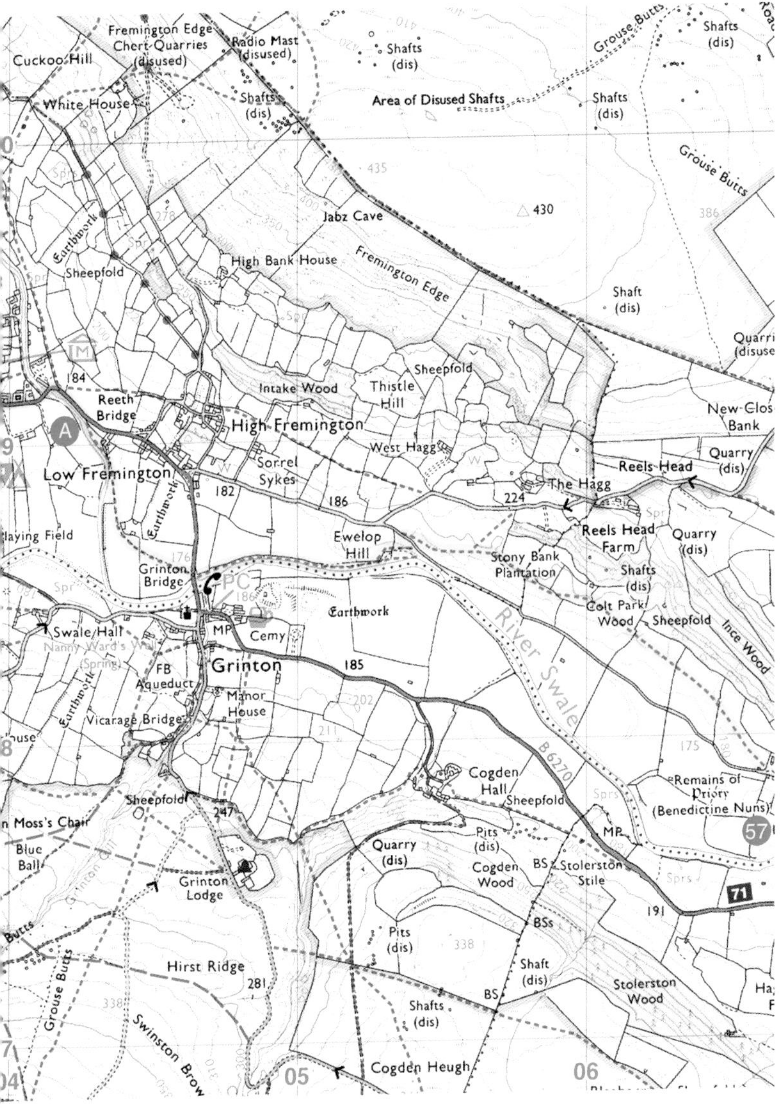

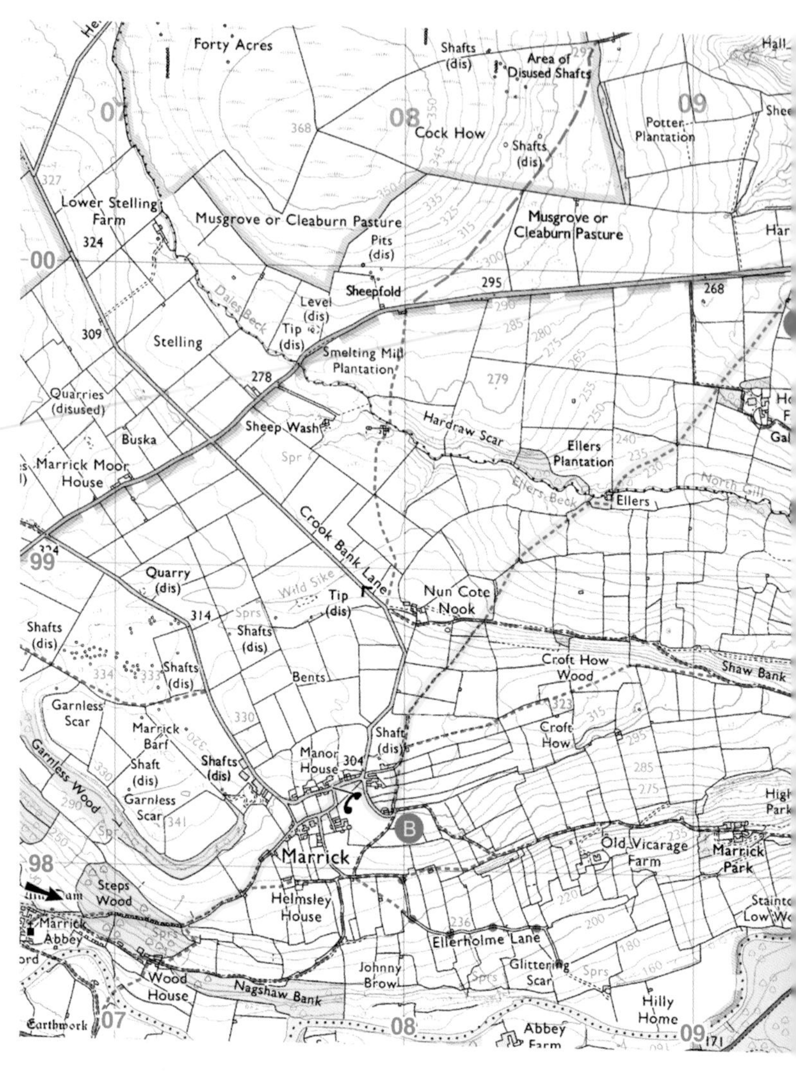

an outdoor activities centre; you can't look round, but they are used to walkers taking a discreet peep. The artist Turner was one of your predecessors on this stage of the walk, and left a drawing of the ancient buildings to prove it.

A lovely section of the path now tempts you away: the Nuns' Causey (or causeway) climbs a generally agreed estimate of 375 sometimes wonky steps to Marrick hamlet through Steps Wood. This is an excellent place for birds: green and great-spotted woodpeckers, pied and spotted flycatchers and three warblers, including the garden warbler, which has a sweet song and a habit of stuffing itself with blackberries (but allegedly preferring cherries in Yorkshire) before emigrating in late autumn to North Africa. Leave the trees and follow the path along the edge of a couple of fields until you reach the old Methodist chapel, these days a house, and the lane through the village. Turn right at the phone box and then right again past the former village school to a green lane **B**. This leads to a series of stiles across fields, descending to the track to Nun Cote Nook Farm (a 200-yard/180-metre diversion for teas, when open), where you jink right through a gate and then left at a waymark. Cross more fields dotted with yellow rattle and yellow vetchling (useful to farmers because it fixes nitrogen in the soil, and cattle like it too) to Ellers, a lonely outpost in a lovely spot by Ellers Beck. This is often bright with water crowfoot.

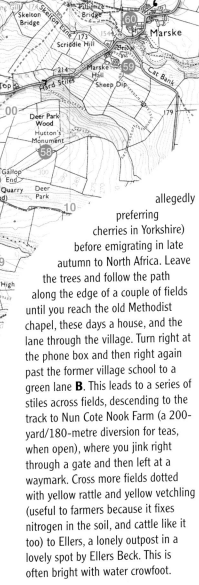

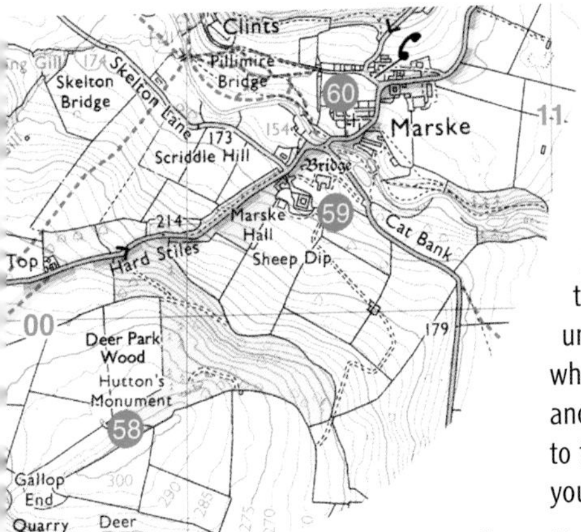

Cross it on the footbridge and continue over two fields to the access road to Hollins Farm. Up ahead is the Hutton obelisk **58**, which marks the former presence in this area of a powerful family, based at Marske Hall and numbering two Archbishops of Canterbury among their many illustrious progeny. Cross over and skirt around to the north of the farm road and through a stile with a copse on your right, to a wall. Turn left up the slope with the wall on your right until just before a hedged path, where a gate on the right leads to another field **C**. Cross this diagonally to the road from Reeth, which takes you steeply down into Marske.

Alas, no pub. There was one once, with the delightful name of The Dormouse, but it was anything but sleepy. Ructions reached a peak one Bonfire Night before the First World War when a party of carters got hopelessly drunk and made a bonfire of everything wooden in the village that they could find. The Huttons cracked down, getting The Dormouse's licence revoked and turning it into a temperance hotel (because of lack of demand, perhaps, this has long since become Temperance Farm). The village is pretty, in a slightly estate-dominated way, although the hall **59** – a fine building which you can examine through the big iron gates – is now flats. St Edmund's Church **60** has the interesting hierarchy typical to such places of socially graded seating, culminating in box pews, with a specially big one for the Huttons. A grave in the churchyard recalls the drowning in November 1771 of two brothers in Chapgate beck. You will be crossing this shortly, but it seldom looks remotely lethal and may easily be jumped in summer.

The wealthy Hutton dynasty has long abandoned Marske Hall, but the neatly raked gravel drive to the mansion's flat conversions must please their ghosts.

Go left over Marske Bridge and right at the T-junction, where you continue, right, along the tarmac for about 500 yards (450 metres) to a stile on the right with a waymark often hidden by the hedge **D**. Follow the narrow path across fields, through gaps and a stile in hedges and gradually down to Clapgate Beck, then up, quite steeply, to a cairn on the track to West Applegarth Farm. This is the start of the 'Applegarth Riviera' – a series of farms which works through every variation of the name Applegarth; in the spirit of the thing, a sign at West Applegarth directs Coast to Coasters ahead to the Costa del Sol and back to the Costa Brava. Let's hope the sun shines on this section of your crossing.

The stretch winds below the fine limestone outcrop of Applegarth Scar **61**, skirts West Applegarth Farm and crosses a field to the track for Low Applegarth Farm. Cross this and a stile to a field which passes High Applegarth and reaches the road to East Applegarth Farm. You are getting the Applegarth point? Soon after this, take a stile left to cross another field, and via a further stile meet a track coming up from East Applegarth below. Follow this through a scrubby patch to Whitcliffe Wood, a lovely haven for abundant wildlife. The effect is continued on emerging at High Leases Farm which liberally allows its hens to roam. This prolonged march through Applegarth-land takes place below the crags of Whitcliffe Scar, the site of Willance's Leap **62**. Robert Willance was a Richmond draper who got so carried away in a hunt in 1606 that he followed his quarry over the lip of the scar, killing his horse but miraculously emerging with only a broken leg. This had to be amputated, but Willance was so grateful for still being alive that he donated a silver chalice to Richmond, which still has it, and erected three stones at the site of the catastrophe, engraved with the date. These were joined in 1906 by another, commemorating the 300th anniversary. Willance had his leg solemnly buried in St Mary's churchyard and was eventually reunited with its remains after a long and useful life. You can pay your respects at his tomb shortly when you reach Richmond, because we are nearly there.

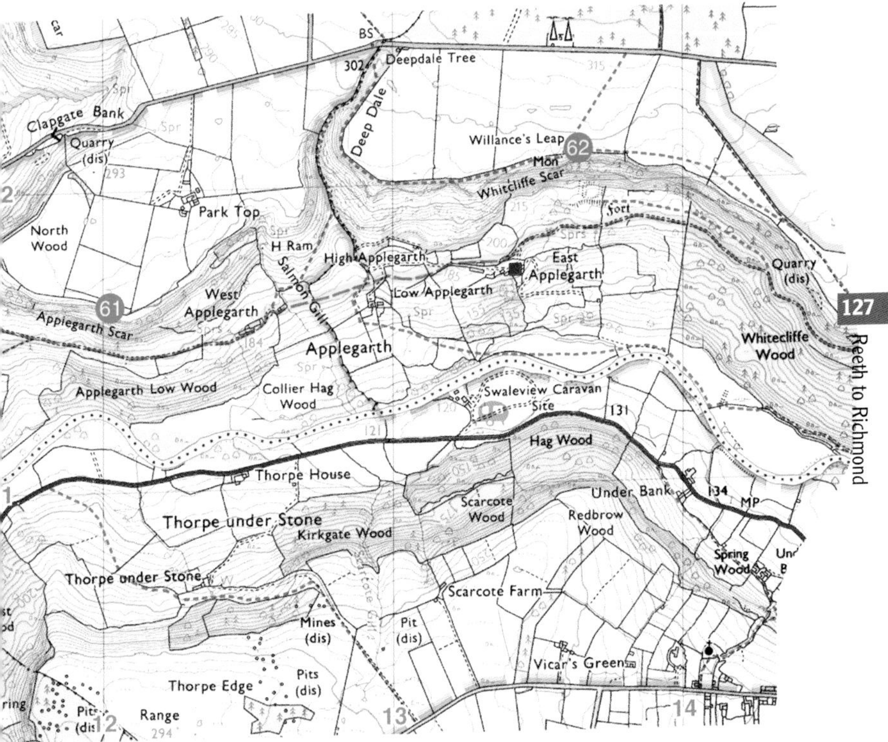

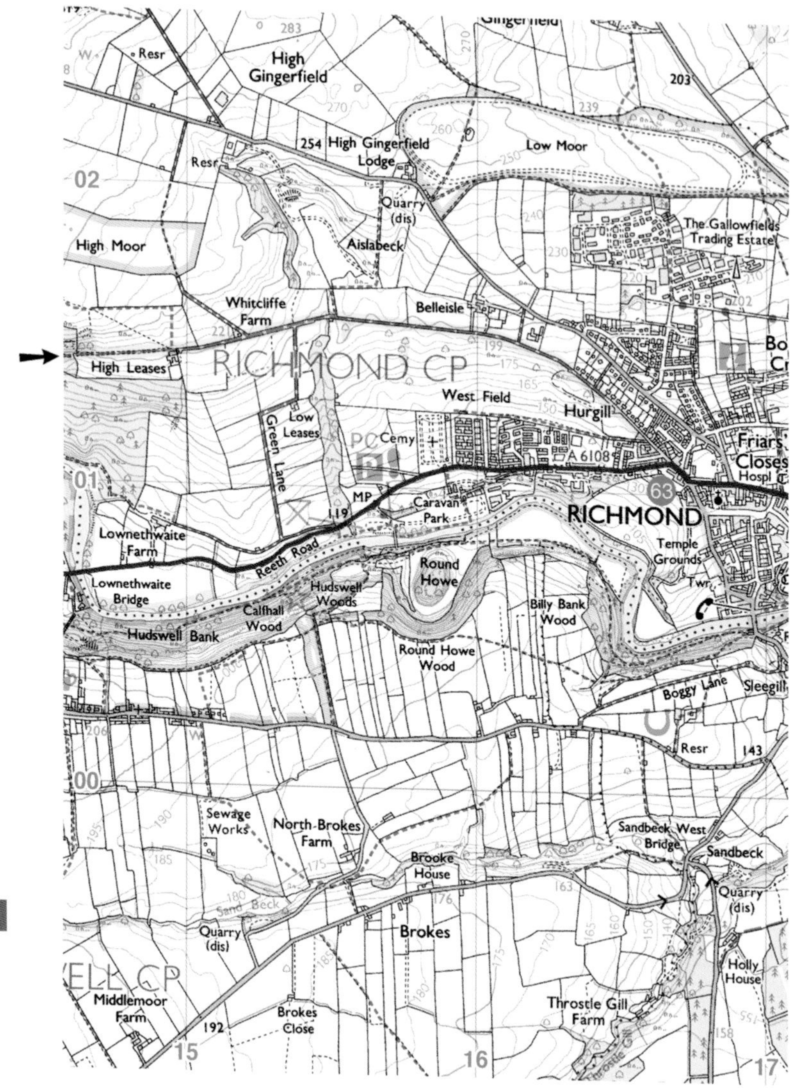

From High Leases join the tarmac of Westfields, a lane which runs gently down to the town's outskirts, with an alternative, parallel footpath through fields on the right which is easier on tired feet. At the bottom, an ancient AA wall plaque records that this spot, otherwise significant only because it reintroduces you to the world of food, drink and a bed for the night, was the centre of totality during the June 1927 solar eclipse **63**.

Home of the Lass

Don't let them kid you down in Surrey that the Sweet Lass of Richmond Hill had anything to do with the Thameside borough. She was definitely from up here. A romantic young Irishman, Leonard McNally (1752–1820), wrote the words in honour of a Miss Frances L'Anson, who lived between Richmond and Leyburn and was so touched that she became Mrs McNally. Leonard was exposed after his death as a double agent used by the British government against the United Irishmen, rebels whose ranks unusually included many Protestants as well as Catholics. But his love lyrics, set to music by James Hook, became so popular that King George IV was credited with writing them, when Prince of Wales, in honour of his unfortunate first wife Mrs Fitzherbert, whose marriage was annulled so that he could marry a proper princess, Caroline of Brunswick. That was when Surrey started sticking its oar in.

Yorkshire's Richmond is every bit as elegant as its southern counterpart. As well as local sheep farmers going to market, the town has been a military centre since Alan the Red started building the mighty castle in the 11th century. As officers came to live in the town, so did the gentry, and the Georgian period, when the Green Howards regiment was stationed here, has left a particularly grand legacy. There are many fine houses, the splendidly preserved Georgian theatre and the Green Howards Museum. The town was considered the smartest place in Britain to buy fine, locally made furniture in Georgian times, a tradition which survives in the concentration of hand-made businesses between here and the North York Moors escarpment – your next goal. The military tradition also flourishes. Although invisible from the town, the largest army base in Europe is just a couple of miles away at Catterick Camp, a child of Richmond which has outgrown its parent.

The castle is well worth a visit, with a very informative exhibition, including unusual material on conscientious objectors who were imprisoned here during the First World War. Amid the convivial elegance of the town, they stood out as people of exceptionally strong moral principle. Many were 'absolutists' who refused to do anything at all which might help the country wage war. The original carvings on cell walls are too delicate for public display, but a tranquil garden also honours the men. They were hated by many at the time and their health was broken by ill-treatment, but supporters such as the Liberal MP for York, Arnold Rowntree of the chocolate dynasty, ensured that they were not buried away and forgotten.

Richmond saw all manner of parties and celebrations during the 1927 eclipse.

9 Richmond to Ingleby Cross

via Danby Wiske and the lowest point in the walk • 9 hours
22.65 miles (32.2 km)

Ascent 560 feet (170 metres)
Descent 328 feet (100 metres)
Lowest point Danby Wiske: 131 feet (40 metres)
Highest point Richmond: 426 feet (130 metres)

An ingenious traverse of heavily farmed, flat land with much in the way of history and wildlife to enliven route-finding and a calm, placid atmosphere unique to this stretch of the walk.

A choice of quaint, steep streets drops down from the Market Place to Richmond Bridge, which the path crosses before turning left into playing fields past a pavilion whose public lavatories deserve a national 'well-kept' award. The castle towers above the far bank of the Swale, which runs smoothly over broad stone slabs interspersed with rapids and sandy beaches good for paddling in warm weather. Follow the field edge to woods filled with wild flowers in season, where an obvious path threads up to a stile and a buttercup meadow. Cross to a couple of farm sheds and on past a row of Victorian houses (Priory Villas, although the sign is not obvious), with a lovely view of the town **64** over a field where you may set up pheasants. At the end turn right along the busy A6136 for ½ mile (800 metres) until the road bends sharply right after crossing Sand Beck. Turn left here along a metalled road signed to the sewage works. A less busy alternative, especially if you have spent the night in the lower part of the town and leave by the A6136, is to walk along the track from the old station – now a marvellous hive of crafts, food and entertainment created by local community enterprise – as far as the sewage works. You can also take this diversion from the busy main road if you left Richmond from the Market Place as described above; when you reach the A6136, just turn left for the short walk to the old station.

Skirt the filter beds by crossing the field to their right. The path runs beside the works, but if you climb up, right, to the gorse bushes **A** there's a good view of ruined Easby Abbey **65** on the other side of the Swale (and a better chance of dodging the niff). In the far distance, you can also see today's goal, the North York Moors escarpment above another of Yorkshire's many monastic relics, Mount Grace Priory. Then drop down to the corner of the field, where a stile leads into pretty woodland with the river dancing along on your left. A mass of wood anemones in spring, the wood has dells and miniature waterfalls and a footbridge before the path climbs up, mud-clarty after wet weather, to a field with the ruins of Hagg Farm, now little more than a heap of stones, ahead up the slope. Pass just below them, then climb gently across the field beyond to a stile in the

corner, then over a further field to cross another stile in the hedge. Turn left along the field edge, favoured by butterflies in summer, down to woodland and a third stile half-hidden a few yards into the trees **B**. Follow the left bank of a woodland stream, which emerges from boggy ground full of interesting plants, on to a metalled lane where you continue your direction of travel down into Colburn.

It is hard to imagine that this delectable spot, with its manor house **66** and usually drowsy Hildyard Arms pub, is only a mile away from Europe's largest army base at Catterick and the sprawling estates of modern Colburn which service the barracks. They remain unseen as the path turns right at the

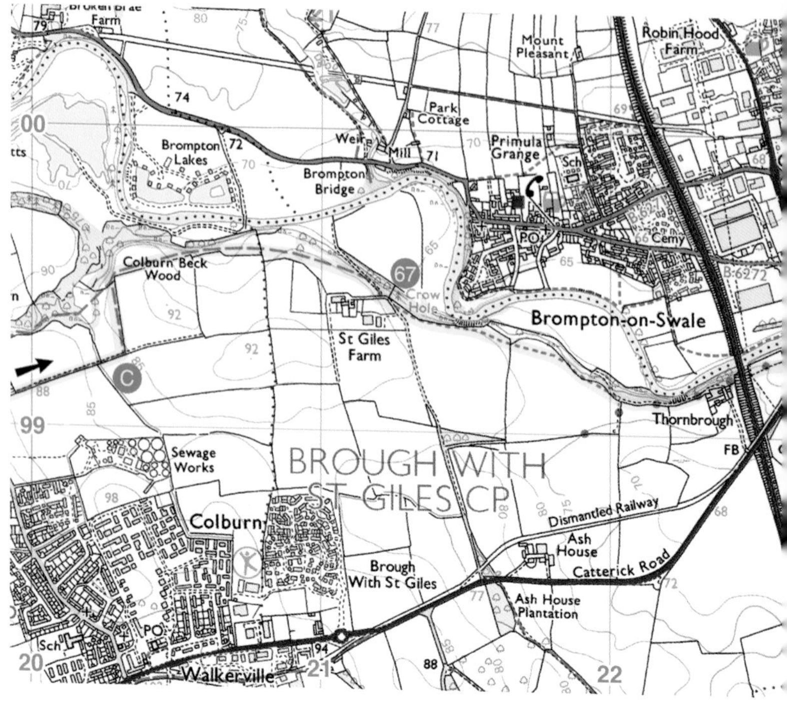

end of the hamlet, then left into a farm drive, waymarked at both points, and crosses two fields before turning left down the edge of a third **C**. At the end, a stile leads to a short descending track, which then bears right and slopes up to become a fine green lane along the top of the high bank above the Swale. If you go down to the river, you will have to clamber steeply up again before long, so best keep to the high ground and enjoy the views northwards beyond Brompton-on-Swale. Opposite Brompton Bridge, there once stood St Giles' Hospital **67**, where archaeologists unearthed a pile of skeletons in 1990 which have greatly added to our knowledge of medieval health, or lack of it, but nothing remains. Continue along the increasingly high bank-top and field edges towards St Giles Farm, bearing right to pass in front of the buildings and join their drive at a stile. The path continues along the edge of two fields, still clinging to the top of the Swale bank, until Thornbrough Farm, where suddenly, below you, the source of the hum which has been growing in your ears since leaving Colburn is revealed: the endless traffic of the A1 Great North Road, for centuries the nation's main highway. Drop steeply down to an underpass, then follow the riverbank under a disused railway bridge before slanting half-right across a field to a stile opposite Catterick racecourse **68**.

A brief return to the everyday world takes you across the A6136 – a tricky junction which needs care – with an optional stop at the big hotel. Go over Catterick Bridge and take a metalled path slanting down, right, to a squeeze-stile with a crude iron swing-gate, leading into a pasture. For the first time since Richmond, you are back on the north side of the Swale. Keep to the riverbank, alongside a wall thought to be partly Roman, and watch for herons and kingfishers as you pass reclaimed gravel pits until the path slopes up left to the B6271 or, just before the hedge, a permissive path which stays at one remove from the traffic. Turn right and then right again at **D** on to a track to Bolton on Swale whose St Mary's Church is visible ahead to the left. Turn left into unmade Flat Lane, which leads with one zig-zag to meet the B6271 again, a short walk, right, from the proverbial village pump where you turn left to the church **69**.

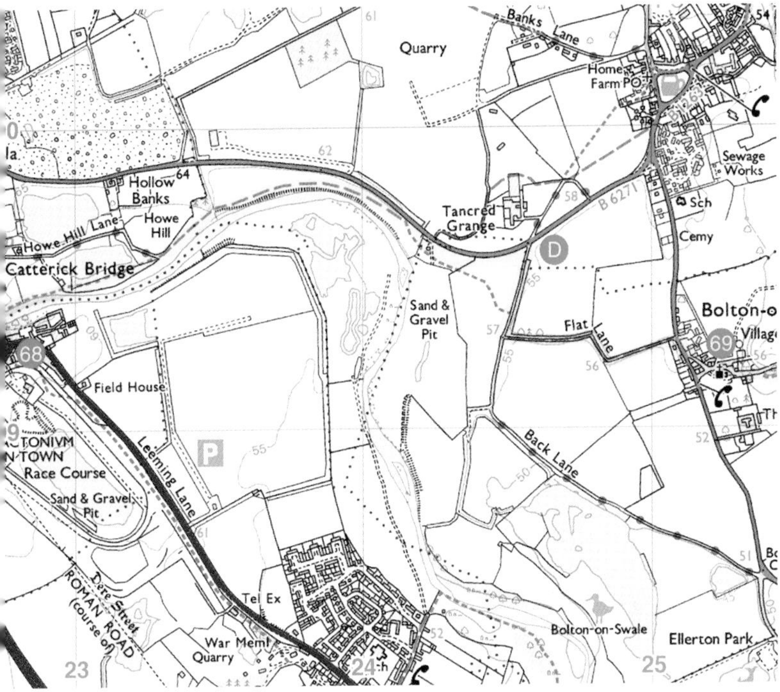

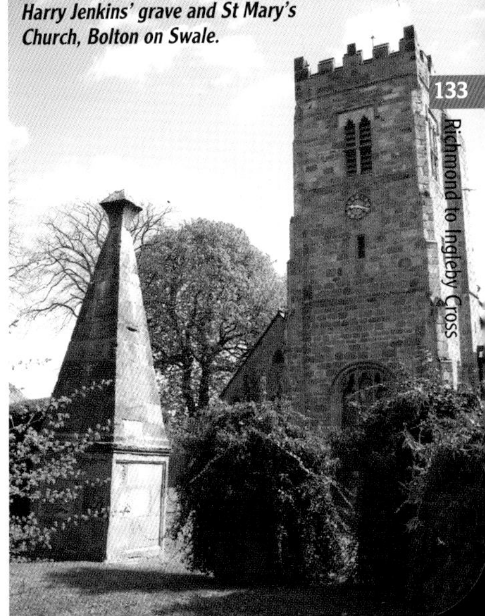

Harry Jenkins' grave and St Mary's Church, Bolton on Swale.

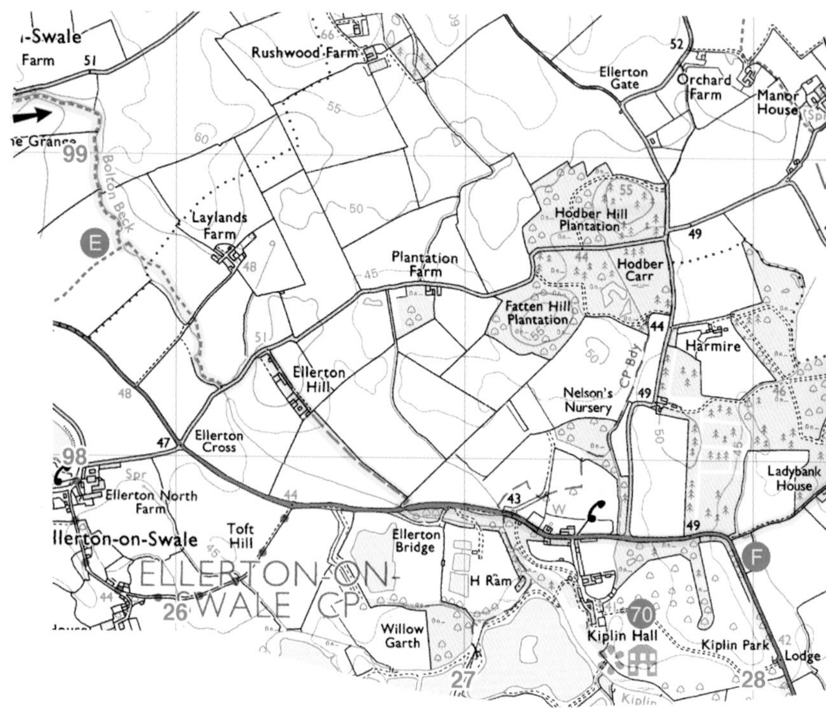

This is a lovely spot for a rest and the chance to get to know Henry Jenkins, a salmon fisher in the Swale and part-time thatcher who supposedly lived to be 169, making Marrick Priory's Thomas Peacock a mere child by comparison. Jenkins died in 1670, still reminiscing about the Dissolution of all the local monasteries in 1539. You are bound to be sceptical, but court records show that he was much in demand in land disputes after the Civil War as an unrivalled witness of who had previously owned what. His quaintly etched monument is the biggest in the churchyard, but don't miss the fulsome plaque in the church. Bolton is a village of strong characters; two of the Gunpowder Plotters, John and Kit Wright, were born here.

Leave the churchyard and its rabbits by the east gate and follow the lane briefly before crossing a stile on the right immediately after the fine Old Hall with its pele tower, the medieval equivalent of a nuclear fall-out bunker in a region often ravaged by Scots. Turn left along the meandering course of Bolton Brook, prettily framed by mature trees, and keep with the stream via fields, stiles, over a dilapidated stone bridge **E**

Green Tax

Gravel pits such as those by the Swale provide huge resources for 'green' projects through the Aggregates Levy of £2 per tonne imposed by the government. Between 2008 and 2011 Natural England spent £10 million a year from the tax.

(see photo page 139) and across the drive to Laylands Farm, all the way to a metalled lane. Turn left and up to Ellerton Hill, where the path goes right and passes in front of red-brick cottages and newly developed outbuildings before sloping down, following the left field boundary through a couple of gates to your old friend the B6271. A short walk, left on poor verges, reaches Kiplin Hall **70**, an interesting stop for food, drink and, if time allows, a tour of the house and grounds.

Onwards past the stove-wall of the Kiplin glasshouse, which once produced exotic fruits, the road turns sharp right **F** between wooded areas, where a bridlepath takes the Coast to Coast off left and past The Smallholding, a house on the right whose barn, when I passed by in 2006, housed a handy-looking light aircraft which could have ferried me to Ingleby Cross in five minutes. More recent walkers have been invited in to see the owner's newer model. Just after this, an enclosed stretch of track ends at two gates where you turn right,

Bolton Brook meanders quietly through a spinney in the Vale of Mowbray below the pele tower of the Old Hall at Bolton-on-Swale.

following the field edge to a gate just after a small stream, where the hedge swaps from your right side to the left. The path leads straight ahead to ruined Stanhowe Cottages, but just before them note a significant little board in the hedge: on it, the farmer at Stanhowe, across the field, tells walkers about the estate's excellent environmental and access improvements, invites your views in a logbook with working ballpoint pens attached, and even leaves his mobile phone number for further comments. Wainwright would be in rhapsodies. He abandoned repeated efforts to negotiate this stretch on footpaths after encountering barbed wire, bulls and other obstacles, and ended up walking on the road all 8 miles (13 km) from Ellerton Hill to just beyond Danby Wiske. Coast to Coasters owe a debt of thanks to today's farmers and North Yorkshire County Council's countryside access staff. The beck crossed soon after the notice is bright pink in July with Himalayan balsam flowers – Policeman's Helmet or Bobby Tops.

The path is now in the great, flat heart of the Vale of Mowbray. The walker becomes a ship on a rolling sea of crops, mostly barley, with successive farms standing out like islands on the top of rises, which makes them invaluable aides to navigation. An increasing number offer walkers welcome home produce and drinks, alongside honesty boxes for payment. Dropping gently down from Stanhowe

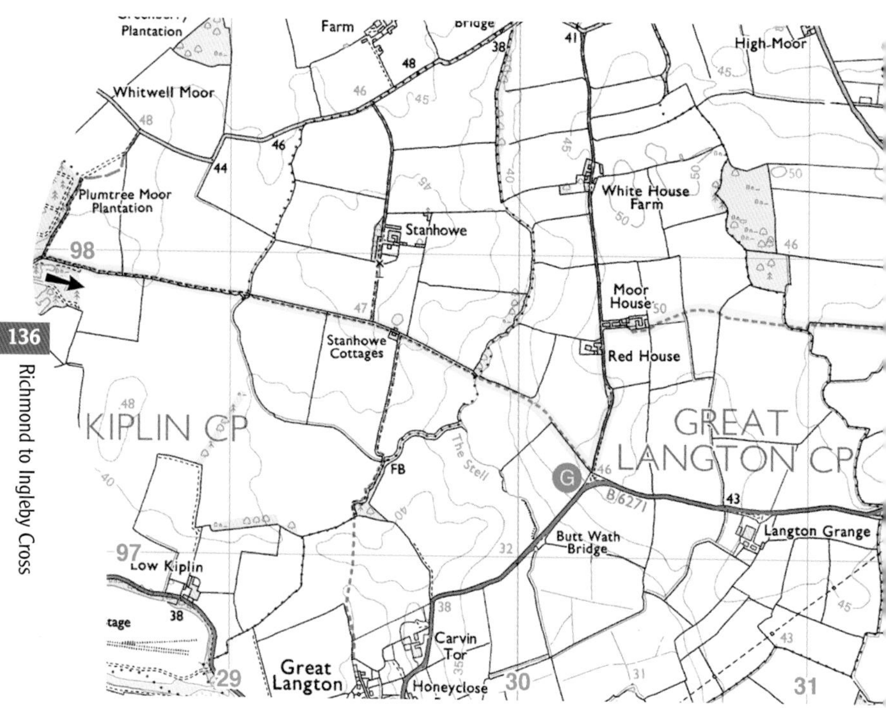

Cottages to the Stell Beck, the route breasts the next swell to cross a field at a slight angle to the right (often helpfully marked with bamboo sticks), making for a conspicuous lone tree, then a left turn at the bridleway **G** to Red House and Moor House Farms. Go right in front of Moor House and follow round to the right of the buildings over an often muddy patch and into the next meadow, where you turn left at the rear of the buildings and immediately right through the gate into the next meadow. Cross this, sometimes amid cows, to a stile and railway sleeper bridge over a beck in the hedge on the far side.

Continue over several more fields and stiles, one with a tall white marker post, heading all the time for Brockholme Farm. At the road just before the farm turn right, then left after about 400 yards (365 metres) on to a clear track which passes the turning to High Brockholme (right) and heads on through a series of gates.

This is an unfrequented area where it pays to walk quietly. I got within a few yards of a big red dog fox before he heard a rustle and shot off. After a gentle leftwards curve, go through another gate and turn left, then promptly right, and keep the field hedge on your left until the path enters a spinney **H** and makes its easy way to a final field before the road, where you turn left into Danby Wiske. The church, one of very few in Britain with no dedication, has been visible for some time, well south of the rest of the

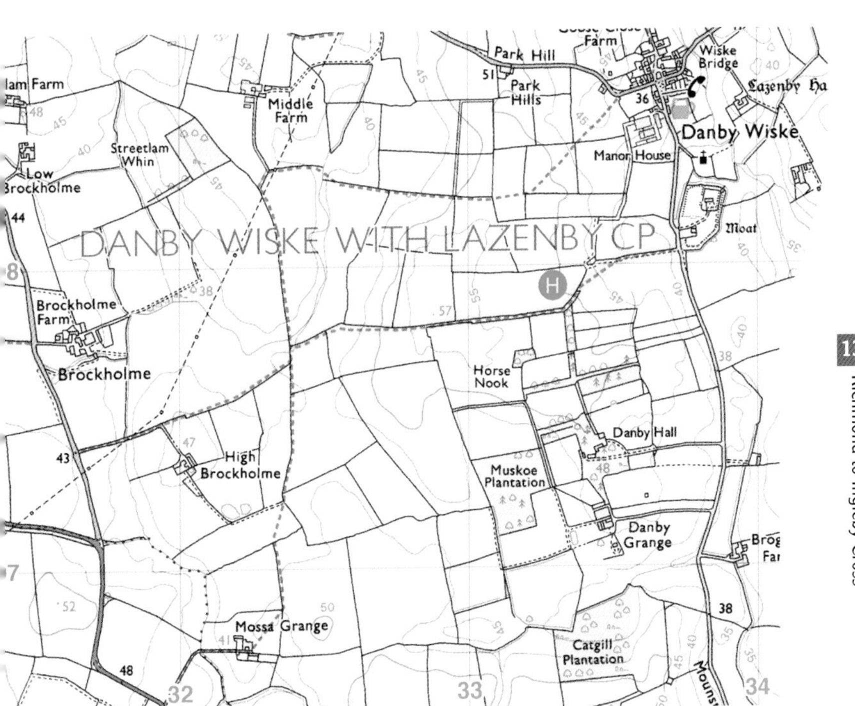

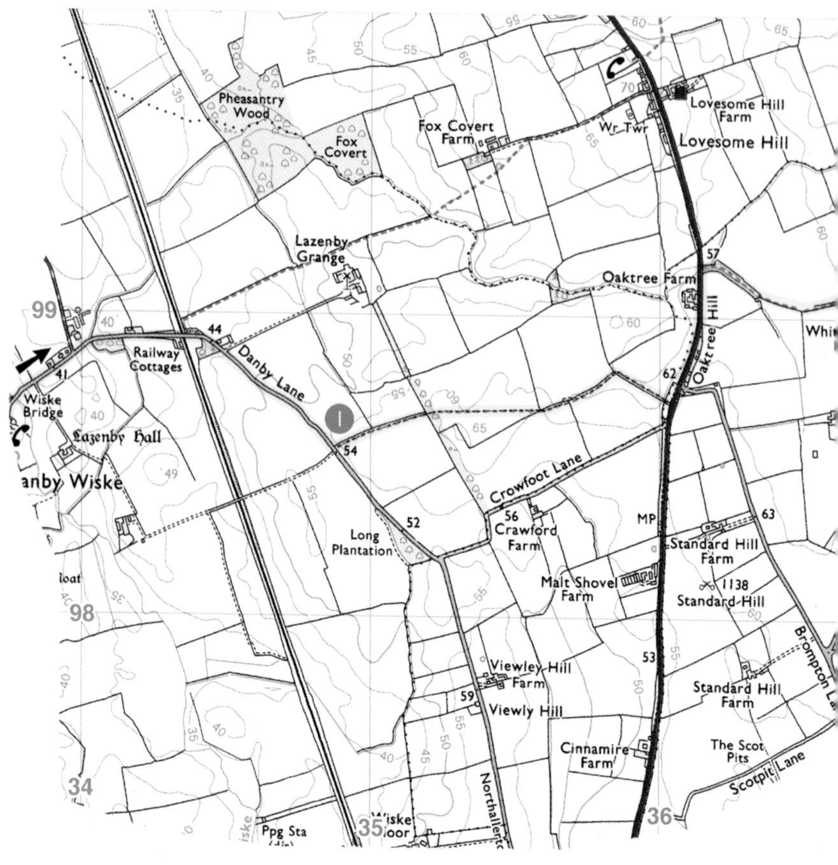

village, which was moved in its entirety after the Black Death. The White (formerly Grey) Swan pub is a welcome sight, but check opening hours in advance.

Danby Wiske has little else to delay you, apart from the thought that it is the lowest point above sea level on the entire walk. Leave by Danby Lane over the insignificant River Wiske and the contrastingly vital East Coast main line with its hurtling London–Edinburgh trains. Bear right on the road until a footpath sign in the left-hand hedge points left **I** along the edge of the field. The path skirts a second field to a straggle of woodland and then strikes at a bold angle straight across crops, with the route helpfully weed-killered by the farmer – in spring a striking slash of yellow through the green shoots. Keep the hedge to your left in the next field, then bear right, now with the hedge on your right, to the A167 at a car-repair workshop on Oaktree Hill, actually the gentlest of inclines in this pancake-flat part of the world.

Follow the road uphill past Oaktree Farm on the left, then take a clear track right and head past White House Farm (which is red, not white) to Deighton Lane. Cross a wide corner verge left, then turn right down the drive to Moor House, keeping the farm buildings on your right (well waymarked) **J** and following a grassy strip to a stile. Keep to a small stream on the field edge to a simple bridge, which takes you left past a couple of small barns and on to Northfield House, where you keep the buildings on your left and join the farm drive leading to Long Lane. Turn right on this former Roman road, then after 200 yards (180 metres) left on to the signed drive to Wray House. Keep the buildings to your left and make for an obvious crossing of the York–Middlesbrough railway, but turn left before reaching it and then, a little further on, go over a stile and a foot-crossing of the line, watching out for trains **K**. Cross the field on the other side to a metalled footbridge due east, followed very shortly by a sleeper bridge across a ditch, then go left and right round the edge of the next field to Low

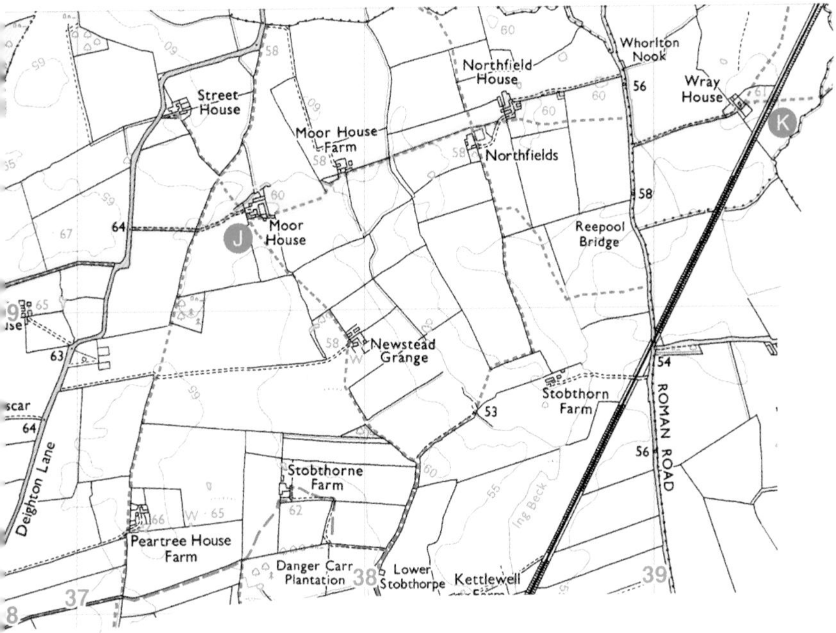

he dilapidated stone ridge over Bolton rook, before aylands Farm.

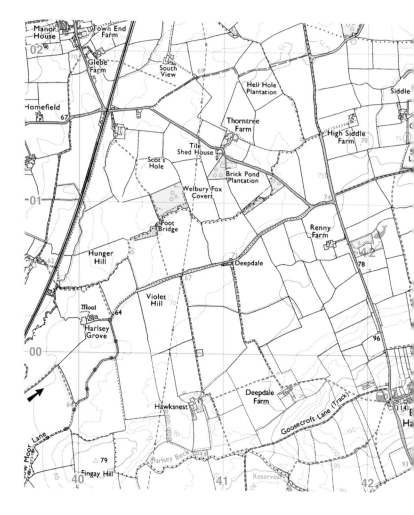

Moor Lane, a metalled road which heads north past Harlsey Grove Farm, then bears right on a short stretch of rough track to rejoin a metalled surface all the way – and at this stage of the day it can seem a very long way – past Violet Hill and Deepdale to a minor road which leads rapidly, right, to a T-junction. Go left and immediately right between the handsome gateposts of Sydal Lodge, a fine house whose humbler – and more

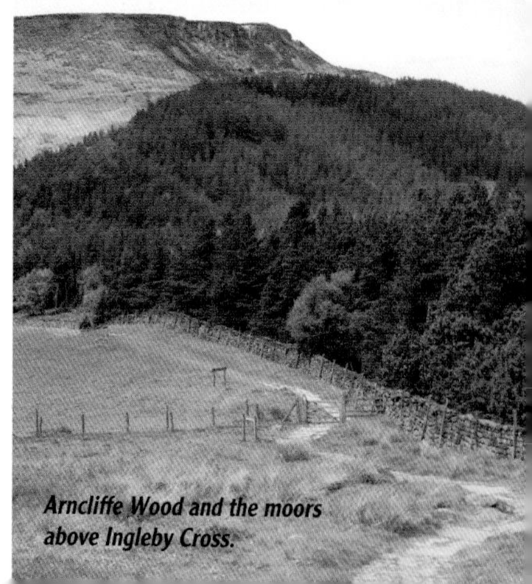

Arncliffe Wood and the moors above Ingleby Cross.

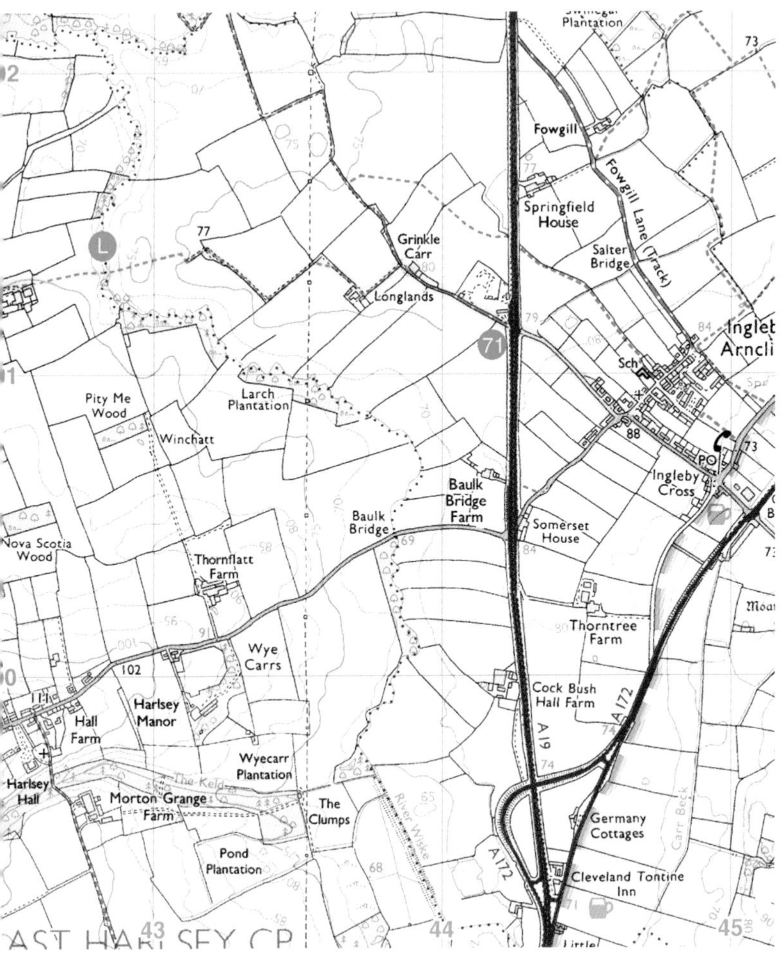

humbly spelt – relative Siddle Grange is a field away to the left. March past the Lodge and as you descend to the Wiske, often amid plump sheep, veer diagonally right to a footbridge **L** directly in line with the farm buildings. Cross the dawdling little river for the last time and climb the other side in a straight line to the ruins of Brecken Hill Farm. Decaying fruit trees may feed you in summer at Brecken Hill, which also has a sinister pond overgrown with trees like a mangrove swamp. From here descend on a gentle zig-zag by field edges to Longlands and Grinkle Carr Farms and a filling station on the A19 **71**, which is the last shop for a very long time. Cross the extremely fast dual carriageway with great care; this is much more dangerous than Striding Edge and a footbridge would be most welcome. A pretty lane directly opposite leads into Ingleby Arncliffe and via a quick left and right to The Blue Bell inn at Ingleby Cross.

Kiplin Hall.

An ancient vale

The Vale of Mowbray, which Coast to Coasters cross on their way from the Pennines to the North York Moors, owes its name to the Norman baron Robert de Mowbray, who got the earldom of Northumberland in the division of spoils after the Norman Conquest. Thus began a mighty dynasty which was eventually to unite two dukedoms, Northumberland and Norfolk, and create the premier barony of England, an archaic but impressive-sounding feudal title which once gave its holders precedence in debates in the House of Lords. Robert, whose name was anglicised from the French Montbrai, was an effective warrior whose private army defended England's northern frontier. His troops killed King Malcolm III of Scotland in 1093, earning even more respect, and rewards, from the Conqueror's son and successor, William Rufus. This was the same Malcolm who ends the bloody usurpation of Macbeth in Shakespeare's play.

Mowbray's vale may not look much from a distance. Flat and farm-filled, it includes the lowest point on the normally height-hugging Coast to Coast, where the path sinks to only 110 feet (35 metres) above sea level at Danby Wiske. But the soil is extremely fertile and the wide plain has always been prosperous. Mowbray set about defending it with a stronghold of thousands of timber pillars and planks on an earthen mound at Thirsk. Other lordly figures later followed him to this area, including the first Earl of Baltimore, George Calvert of Kiplin Hall, who founded Maryland in the United States and gave his name to its capital.

Although aristocratic, these great figures were wary of too much royal power, and one of the sights at Kiplin is a piece of the block used in the execution of King Charles I. The hall is a good place for an afternoon stop if your timing works that way, open Sunday–Wednesday between Easter and the end of October, but check for changes on www.kiplinhall.co.uk. The Mowbray family still lives nearby in the grounds of their Adams Family Victorian Gothick mansion at Allerton Park, on the A1 near Boroughbridge. The house, however, has been sold to an American computer multimillionaire.

Farming dominates the vale, but is not the only way of making a living. Fine furniture-making is a tradition and other enterprises include an international coach firm, Atkinson's, based at Ingleby Arncliffe, which runs into Ingleby Cross. If you are fed up with the Coast to Coast, they can take you to Rome or Paris.

atterick has been a crossing point since pre-Roman
mes, with the old road's stone bridge flanking the
'sused railway over the Swale and the A1 beyond.

10 Ingleby Cross to Clay Bank Top

via the Cleveland escarpment • 6 hours
11 miles (18.4 km)

Ascent 2,545 feet (775 metres)
Descent 1,870 feet (570 metres)
Lowest point Ingleby Cross: 230 feet (70 metres)
Highest point Cringle Moor: 1,378 feet (420 metres)

An exhilarating switchback along the Cleveland escarpment, dipping down to quiet villages before striding back up to the heather moors and panoramic views, including the first glimpse of your second sea.

A last saunter through quiet farmland lies beyond the A172, crossed by taking the road out of Ingleby Cross by the north side of The Blue Bell. Directly opposite, at the junction with the main road, a metalled lane leads gently up to a cattle grid and more steeply past the church and Arncliffe Hall **72**, handsome in a severe way. This was the home of the Mauleverer family, companions of the Conqueror, who endowed the fine church with its three-decker pulpit and purple-coloured pews. Past a few cottages, the path climbs to a waymarked gate and across a field to a second gate into Arncliffe Wood and an immediate T-junction with the broad forest trail. Turn right, dropping gradually and then rising into the pleasantly mixed trees, rich with birdsong in season and wild flowers at the track's edge.

Pheasants and rabbits greet the quiet walker here before you pass Park House **73**, known to thousands from school or youth group trips. On the right, a path leads to Mount Grace Priory **74**, a lovely and interesting diversion. The gardens are beautiful, including patches of herbs used in medieval times, and one of the monks' cells – number 8 – has been painstakingly restored. The monastery's well-preserved drains also excite historians.

The way ahead stays left and climbs more steeply before going right at a junction and – ignore an earlier wide track on the left – reaching the edge of the wood at a gate **A** where a much-used footpath heads down the fields to the pretty village of Osmotherly. This is off the route, but often serves as an overnight base for Coast to Coasters and is notable for the only pub in the country named after Catherine of Aragon, the first of Henry VIII's six wives. Ironically, she is remembered all over the place by Elephant and Castles, a crude rendering of her royal title, Infanta de Castile. Back on the path, turn left, in a gentle hairpin back into the trees and up through South Wood on a pretty meander over knobbly tree roots. The first of many signs saying 'Cleveland Way' at the gate marks the fact that you are now joining

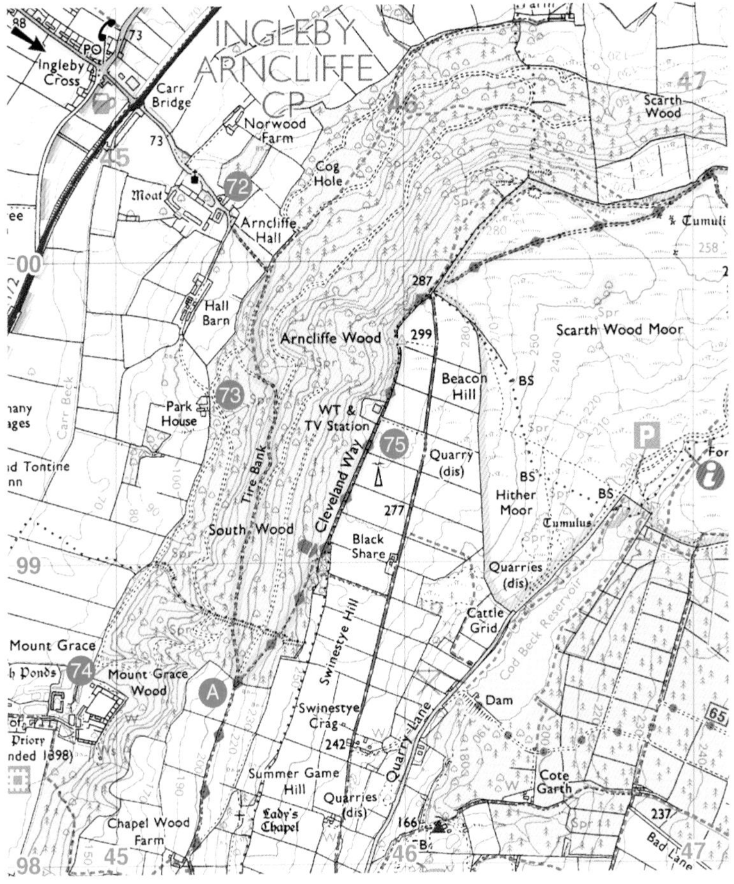

a sort of motorway among long-distance treks. Three unite for the next 13 miles (21 km): your own, the Cleveland Way and the Lyke Wake Walk, which takes sturdy souls 42 miles (67 km) from Osmotherly to Ravenscar on the coast within a deadline of 24 hours if they want to win a coffin badge and the title of Dirger of the Lyke Wake Club (see also page 152).

It is no coincidence that so many route-planners lighted on the rolling escarpment with its wonderful views in clear weather, moors to the right, soft green fields to the left, leading away to the miniature Matterhorn of Roseberry Topping and smoky glimpses of Teesside beyond. One result is that the path is clear and well maintained throughout; almost too obvious if you enjoy an element of exploration, but a relief after the intricacies of navigation across the farms from Richmond.

The track up through South Wood comes to a wall on the right and an incongruous mini-forest of telecom

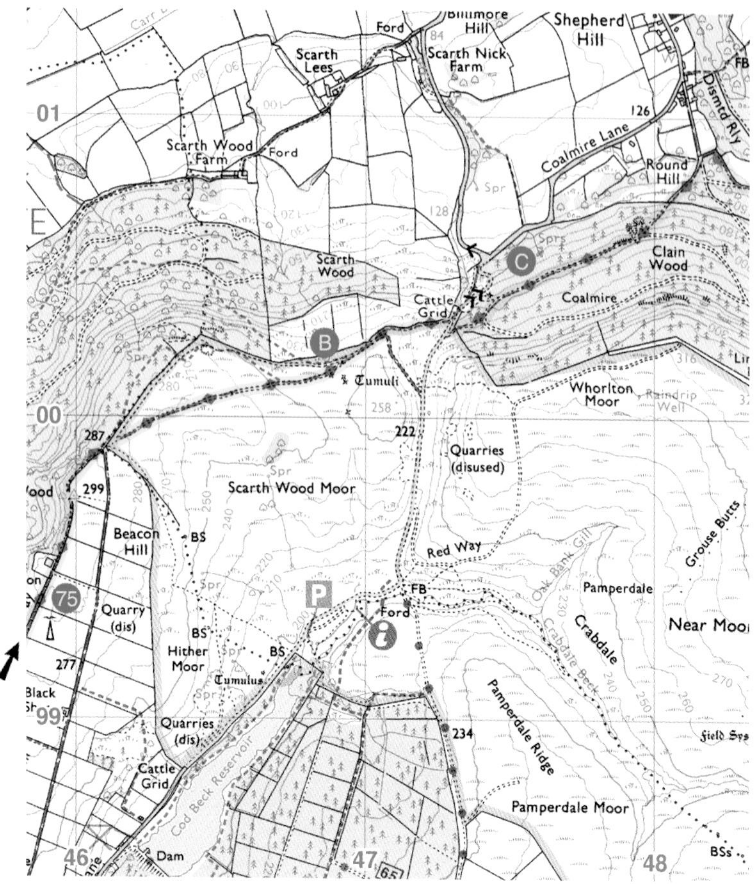

masts **75**, berated by Wainwright but at least prepared to explain itself with information panels. The spikes and dishes have been kept as low as practicable, but our mobile phones and government communications need a clear line of sight to the next such station, so staff have to come and do regular tree-pruning.

A new type of easy-to-use latch gate makes its first appearance here as the path is corralled behind the station to reach the summit of Beacon Hill and emerge from the trees through a gate on to Scarth Wood Moor. After the shade of the wood, this is an inviting taster of clear air, big skies and much moorland to come, with the path angling downhill and restored almost to the standard of a medieval packhorse route with neatly laid stone slabs. For the first time since leaving Ingleby Cross, the constant surfing noise of traffic along the busy A19 also disappears, shielded by the route's gradual turning-away towards the east.

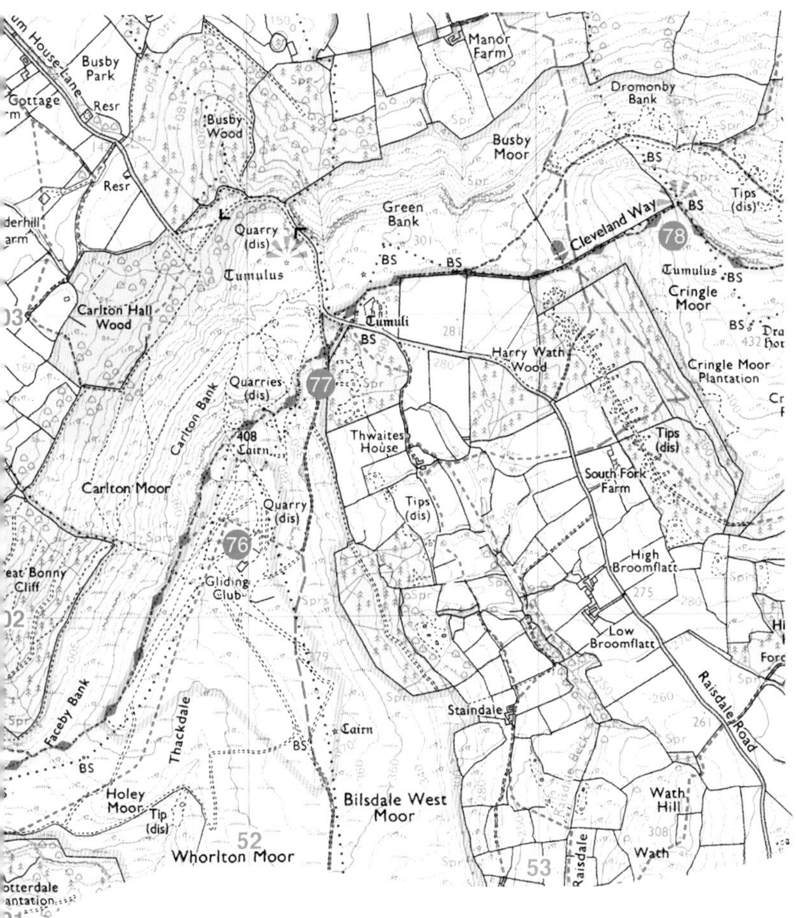

beautifully engraved with 18th-century landowners' initials. The bold summit of Carlton Moor – the highest of the escarpment's series of rounded shoulders – rises ahead, coming encouragingly closer. An easy drop down leads to another climb along the edges of Gold Hill and Faceby Bank, before a longish haul up Carlton itself, with the glider hangar **76** looming surprisingly large and solid in the otherwise wild landscape. Signs underline the obvious danger of straying on to the rough-and-ready runways and the path has recently been re-routed closer to the escarpment edge – an advantage because you can savour the views. The land drops thrillingly and the comfortable-looking farms and hamlets seem like another world. This is how eagles and ravens must feel in their refuges on mountain crags. After the summit trig. pillar, the route drops down in a clear succession of twists and turns – note remains of jet and alum workings – to a green valley and the Promised Land of the Lord Stones Café **77**.

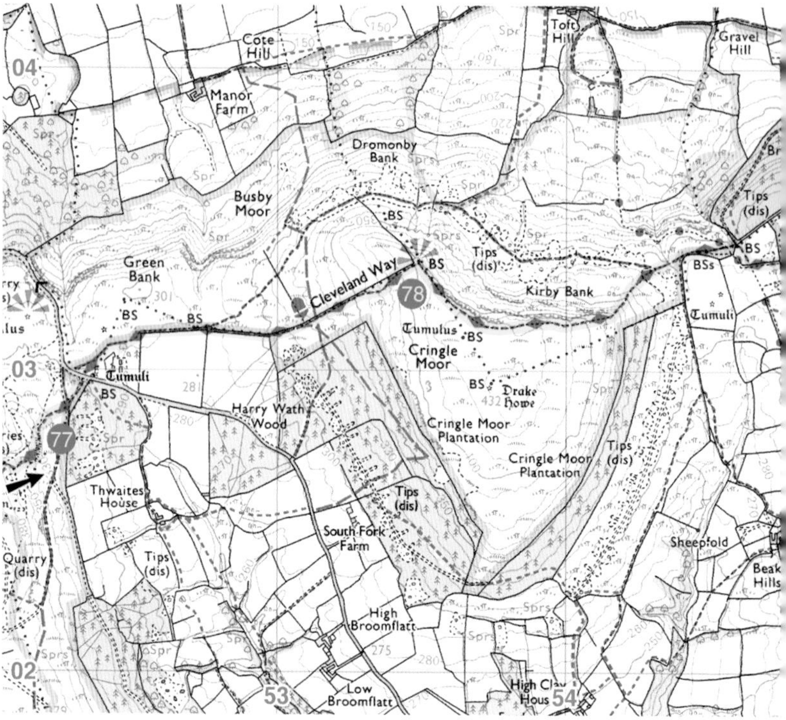

Can there really be such a timely place? It isn't on the map and gives no hints of its existence as you approach, skirting forestry plantations to the metalled road, turning right briefly and then crossing over to a stile and a wide grassy path through a patch which is almost like parkland – and can be as busy as a park at weekends. Turn right and you see why: a hidden car park and the café tucked into the side of the hill. It is an excellent place, with an opinionated and entertaining proprietor who will start a political discussion while serving you a black pudding in a warm bun, and much else to eat and drink. There are lavatories where swallows return to nest in the eaves every year, and you will often find other Coast to Coasters and the chance to compare notes.

The Wainstones, rising like a ruined fortress across the route.

The path from Arncliffe Wood has been clear almost all the way and this

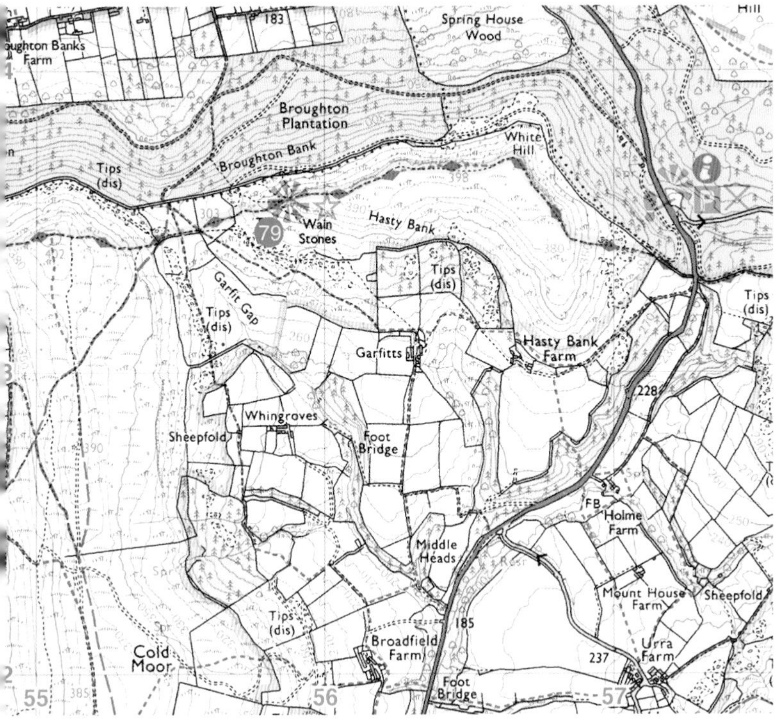

continues, leading ahead up the next switchback to Cringle Moor. A gate at the wall corner after more trees heralds the march up to Cringle End and the fine stone seat and view plaque **78** which honour the inventor of the Cleveland Way, Alec Falconer, who sadly died the year before that trail was opened. Give him thanks before striding along the escarpment edge, enjoying more ravishing views of the cosy Hobbitland at the foot of Rosebery Topping. Then head down steeply past more mining debris to a jeep track and flatter ground. Go right just before the stream bed at a gate and stile and follow the wall ahead and then left, through a gate and up to the top of Cold Moor. Up . . . and down again along the familiar escarpment edge and a gate at Garfit Gap, and so to the final switchback, which has a sight to lift flagging spirits.

Tumbled and jumbled, with one great monolith poking up like a velociraptor's snout, the Wainstones **79** crown the ascent, reached through gaps in criss-crossing drystone walls. The dramatic outcrop is an irresistible place to explore, rest, picnic and see if you can find a carved 18th-century 'I love you', which for years was thought to be prehistoric code. And so to the short stretch across the flat top of Hasty Bank and the final steep drop to trees, bluebells in spring and a kissing gate at the corner of a wall which runs down to the B1257 at Clay Bank Top.

George Cayley's magnificent steam-powered flying machine.

Ghosts on the moors

The North York Moors are perhaps the most numinous landscapes of the British Isles, haunted by the ghosts of vanished tribesmen, wrecked industry and abandoned creeds. Between their relics – mounds, kilns and crosses – flourish mile after mile of heather uplands, gloriously purple and honey scented in August and divided by cosy green valleys whose stone houses are topped with red pantile roofs. If you watch TV's *Heartbeat*, you will feel at home.

On the undulating tops there is a feeling of real wilderness, but this is actually a place which has been put to productive use for centuries. In prehistoric days the moors were a refuge from the jungly, malarial lowlands with their danger of invaders. The inhabitants could see to the far horizon, a role now taken by the Star Wars listening post at RAF Fylingdales, a dumpy pyramid which replaced three evocative giant golf balls in the 1990s. The tumuli are the tribesmen's fragile signature on the landscape.

The moorland crosses date from the heyday of Celtic Christianity, the simple, democratic version overthrown at nearby Whitby in AD 667 when St Wilfrid's subtle theology persuaded the Anglo-Saxons to opt for centralised, hierarchical Rome. Many of the tracks originated at the same time, including much of the famous Lyke Wake Walk, a 42-mile (67-km) hike based loosely on an ancient coffin-carrying path. You qualify as a Dirger of the LWW Club if you take less than 24 hours to do the route, which shares the path of the Coast to Coast for 16 miles (26 km).

Later riches lay deep: the ironstone of Rosedale, which made the fortunes of Middlesbrough, indeed effectively built the entire town. Industrial relics reminiscent of Swaledale's lead mines lie a little off our track, but the bed of the ironstone railway takes the path in a gentle curve round the head of Farndale between Urra Moor and The Lion inn at Blakey.

Today, farming and shooting are secondary to tourism, with the National

Park particularly imaginative about getting visitors out of their cars, on to the Moorsbus or for a walk. There are characters aplenty to discover in the many books and internet sites about the moors: Sir George Cayley, the Flying Yorkshireman who pioneered manned aircraft, is one; another was the curate of Lastingham, the Rev. Jeremiah Carter, who supplemented his meagre clergyman's stipend by becoming landlord of The Blacksmith's Arms, where he also played the fiddle in the evenings.

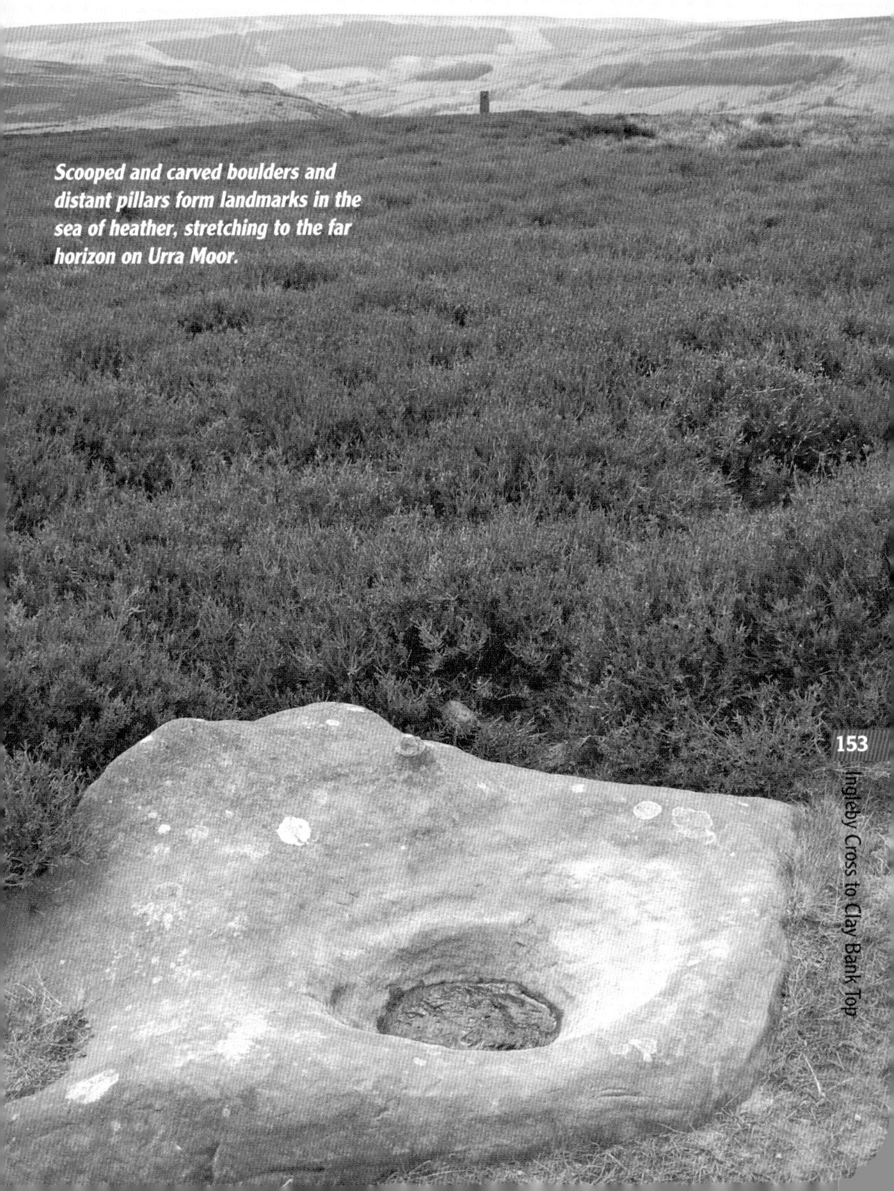

Scooped and carved boulders and distant pillars form landmarks in the sea of heather, stretching to the far horizon on Urra Moor.

The path switchbacks through bilberries and heather on the dramatic escarpment edge between Cold Moor and the Wainstones on the edge of Hasty Bank.

11 Clay Bank Top to Glaisdale

via Blakey Ridge • 6 hours
18 miles (28.9 km)

Ascent 984 feet (300 metres)
Descent 1,148 feet (350 metres)
Lowest point Glaisdale: 328 feet (100 metres)
Highest point Urra Moor: 1,476 feet (450 metres)

The classic moors and a lost railway line, with marvellous views of green valleys and a rich heritage of carved stones.

A surprisingly large amount of traffic hurries through Clay Bank Top, making it an easy place to leave for the peace of the moors. The path climbs straight up and away from the pass, through a gate and along an old packhorse track which hugs the stone wall, keeping it to the left. A narrow gap leads through an outcrop of rocks at the top of the pasture, where another gate marks the way to the open moor **A**. This is Carr Ridge, the start of a vast purple world in August, scrubby brown and black for much of the rest of the year: heather land. The track across is clear and widens as you plod up the edge of Urra Moor, doubling as a firebreak in these highly inflammable surroundings. Lighting casual fires is absolutely forbidden but deliberate burning by the landowners is part of the intensive, though largely invisible, management which maintains this apparent wilderness. To succour the red grouse, whose presence keeps the upland

The Face Stone grimaces at travellers on the summit of Urra Moor.

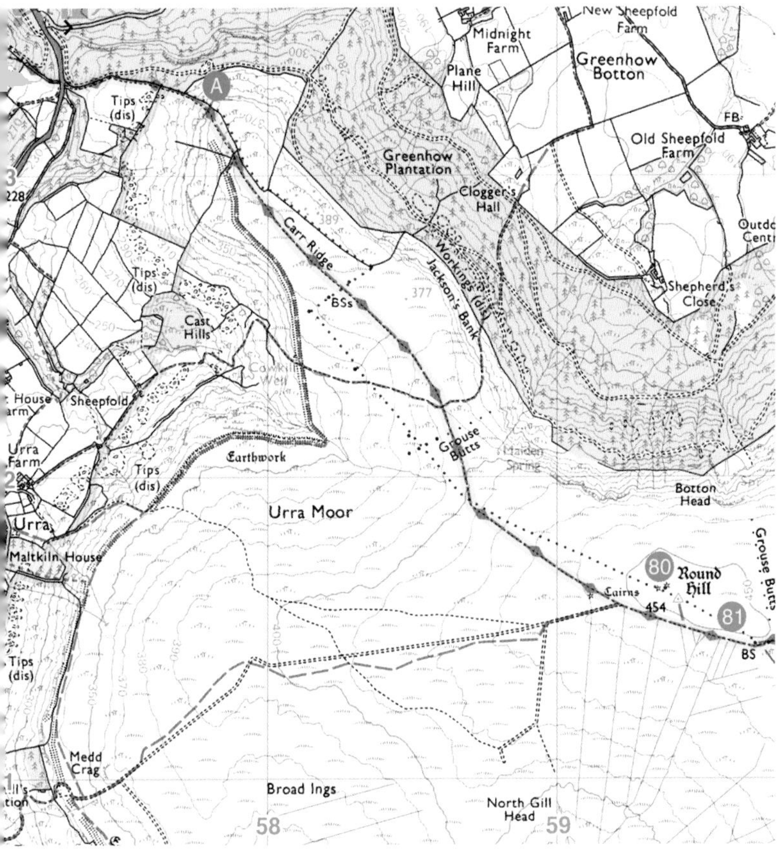

economy viable, heather must be constantly rejuvenated. The birds nibble the fresh green shoots. They are mostly well away from the path, however. During my long, leisurely crossing from Urra to Glaisdale, I set up and enjoyed the 'Go-back, go-back' call of a grand total of three.

Urra Moor's dinky little summit is Round Hill **80**, a prehistoric tumulus just off the route to the left, with its trig. point clearly visible and reached by a narrow path. A little further along the main track, two carved pillars are a foretaste of the larger moorland crosses which lie ahead. One has crude and barely decipherable lettering, but the other, unsurprisingly known as the Face Stone **81**, has clearly cut and rather cheerful eyes, nose and grin. These are ancient direction posts and markers, like the serif-lettered boundary stones encountered earlier on Round Hill. They were practical objects in their day, but time has made them part of the mysterious, age-old atmosphere of the North York Moors which strikes so many visitors and can send a shiver up your spine.

The way ahead trudges on past some grouse butts and a faint grassy path going off to the left, then across a shallow bowl in the middle of nowhere. Although you are in the very heart of hill country, the flat plateau has something of the atmosphere of East Anglia, a level plate under an enormous sky. Then, just when you may be getting fed up with quite so much heather, the landscape dips ahead to one of the great surprises of the moors. Sinuously engineered across the wild countryside, the trackbed of the Victorian mineral railway **82** between Rosedale ironstone quarries and Teesside provides the route for the walk's next stage: comfortable, contoured travel for 5 miles (8 km), with no chance whatever of getting lost.

Ignoring an earlier path which right-angles off right, take the right-hand path at the obvious fork to continue straight ahead and climb the railway embankment at Bloworth Crossing **B**, a grassy slash across the dark arena of heather, and march happily off to the right. At a lonely junction before a long straight stretch of trackway banked high above the bogs, the Cleveland Way finally heads off north **C**. It deserves thanks, as an unfailing guide all the way from Arncliffe Wood, but the railway efficiently takes its place. Alternating embankments with cuttings, it loops around the head of Farndale **83** and along a succession of ridges which flank the dale's eastern side.

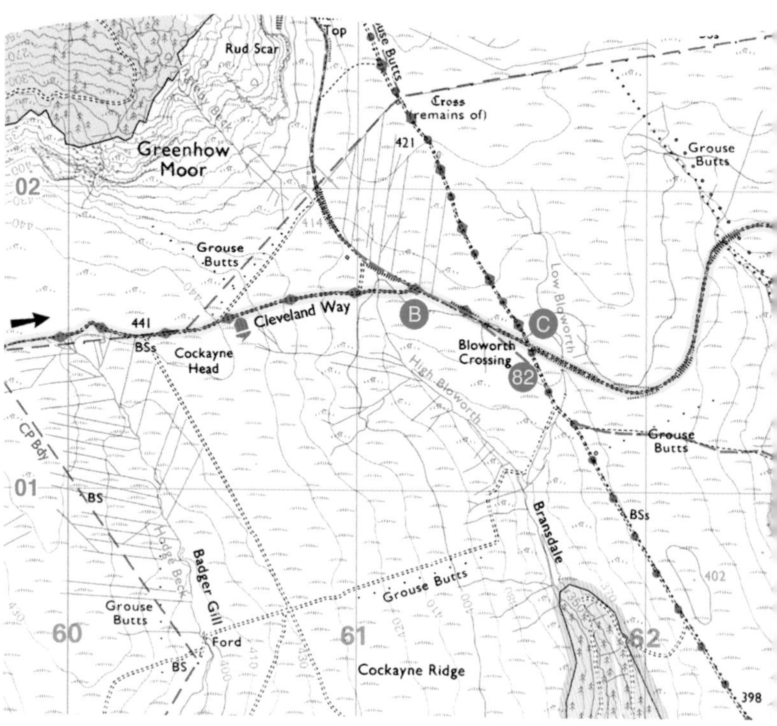

The walking is easy, with cindertrack replacing the sometimes uncomfortable stone chunks of the Urra Moor track. There is also plenty of small but interesting life. Watch for jewel-like green beetles and a dainty, day-flying moth which you may have seen earlier on the Cleveland escarpment. Plovers and lapwings feign injury in the breeding season to lure you away from their nests, or circle above giving those mournful cries which are so much part of the moorland scene. After a whole day of this, mind, you may wish they would give you a break. Ditto the midges in summer.

Rust from mineral seams in a beck on Farndale Moor.

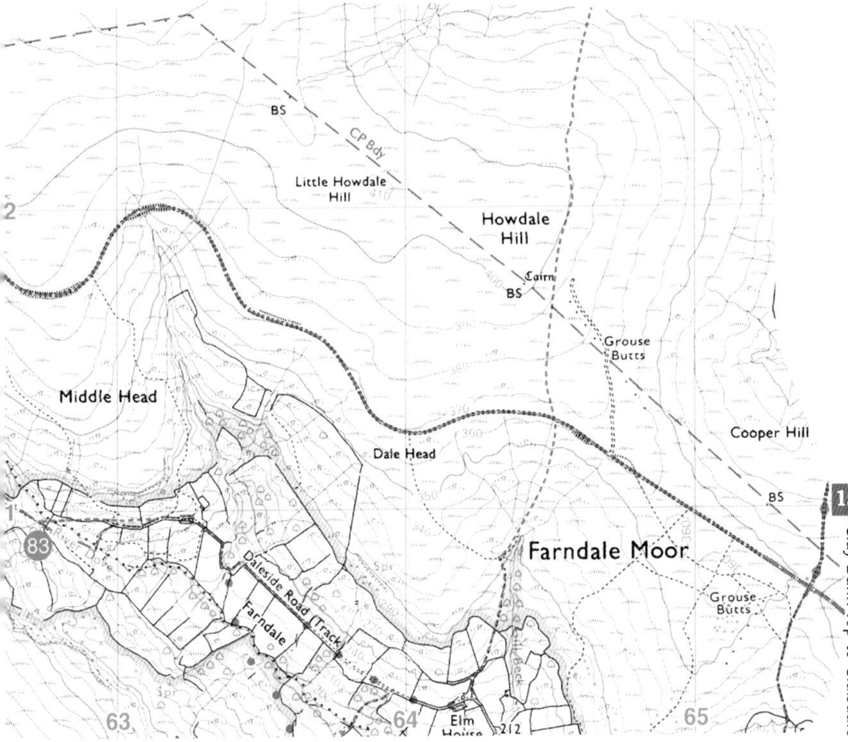

Noisy or not, the old railbed is so comfortable that the miles go by easily, crossing a succession of streams coloured orange with minerals which tumble away down the moorside. One section of the railway near the summit has its own vividly

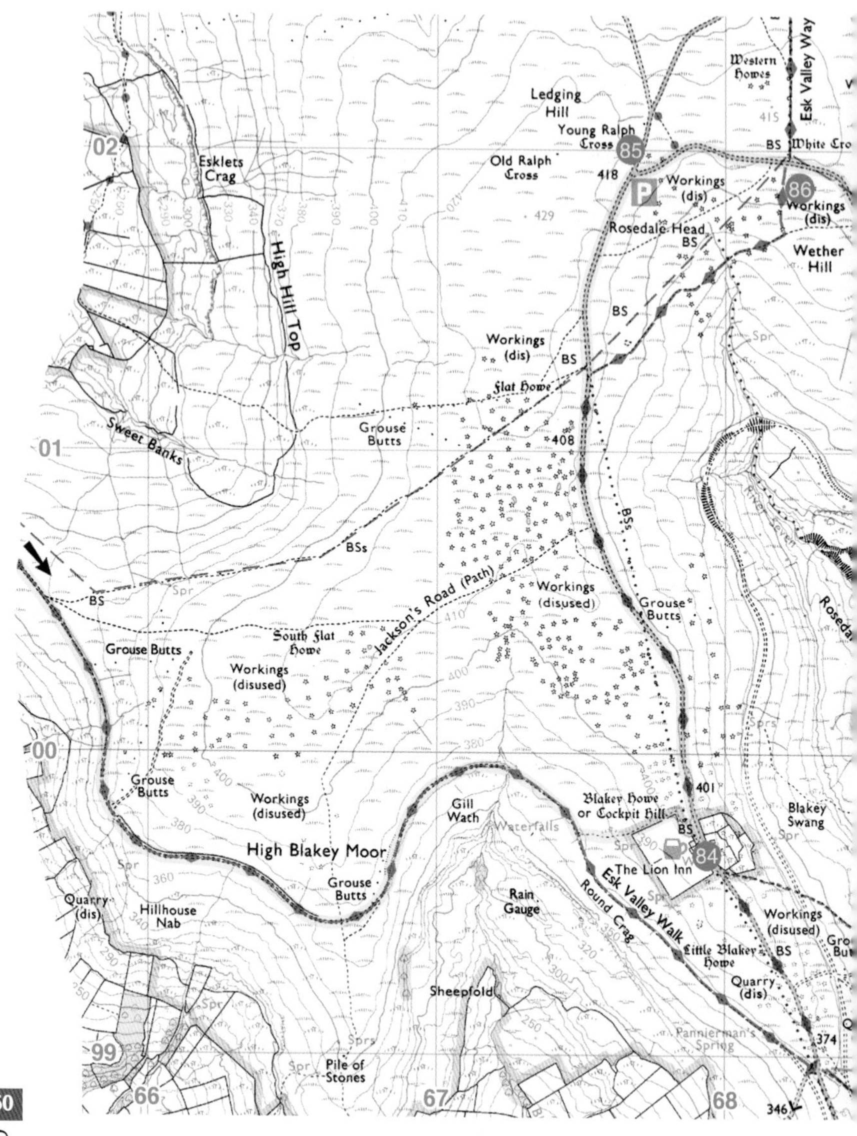

coloured ditch gleaming alongside. Here and there, old sleepers or other bits of rail detritus lie in the heather, which also shelters occasional heaps of grit left to help the grouse's digestion. Best of all, the sometimes oppressive landscape is relieved by gentle, constantly changing views of Farndale below to the right. This is a lovely characteristic of the North York Moors; however wild and monochrome the great plateaus, the deep green valleys which intersect them are never far away.

Around yet another gentle curve through a cutting, the view opens up again, and there – a mirage which gradually resolves itself into reality – are the low-slung buildings of The Lion inn **84**. Right on the horizon, they appear at exactly the right psychological moment for those who failed to bring picnics. The railway runs below the pub's intake, where a track runs up to the left at an LWW waymark and a sign about the old ironstone line and things to be seen around it. Bid farewell to Lyke Wakers here; they march off with their coffins and dirges to the far side of Rosedale. Your path angles right at a mound once used for cockfights and drops down to The Lion's entrance, past skips usually filled with empty bottles and cans. Civilisation. But it is welcome after the long hike from Clay Bank Top – and ahead of a considerable way still to go.

The first section after leaving the pub is one of the Coast to Coast's occasional stretches of just-too-much road-walking in one chunk. There are wide grassy verges but it is a slog up to Ralph Crosses **85** – the slender Young Ralph by the road to Danby, and his smaller Old mate a little further down the moorside to the left – then on via the Rosedale road to a stretch of the minor road down to Great Fryupdale. There are several diversions across the heather but they are boggy and often tortuous and miss out the Ralphs, which is a pity. There isn't an ideal combination.

Shortly before the crosses, you pass two other monuments on the left: one is the beautifully carved memorial to Frank Elgee (1880–1944), premier historian of the moors, which he learned to love during childhood sickness which confined him for a time to a wheelchair. The other is a plain but ancient menhir known as Margery Bradley and part of a rollicking series of legends involving the two Ralphs and Fat Betty **86**, a stout wheelcross-topped stone ½ mile (800 metres) further along the route on the Rosedale road. Tubby indeed, Betty is regularly given an almost luminous whitewash dress and is often decorated with sprays of flowers from anonymous well-wishers, possibly couples who know that when Margery, Betty and the Ralphs meet at night, as they are said to do, a wedding invariably follows.

Wayfarers traditionally left coins, food or drink on top of the crosses for others, in thanks for safe travel – a tradition which continues sporadically. A careful look at Young Ralph shows the joins where the cross was mended after falling and snapping into three parts when a thief clambered up in the 1960s to see what was there. On my visit, a party of woolly caterpillars was also heading towards the top.

The former cockpit at Blakey Howe, just above the Lion Inn, marked by its standing stone.

The tarmac is finally left on a clear, signed track **D** across the heather, cutting the corner between the Rosedale and Fryupdale roads. At the top of a gentle rise, drop to the right down a stony track to the disused but well-maintained shooting lodge of Trough House **87**. Here the stones give way to a pleasanter path through peat, grass and heather, faithfully skirting the head of Great Fryupdale with its mounds of grassed-over spoil from 19th-century coal mines **88**, another example of mineral working on the moors. The excellent, breakfasty name has developed much as Elephant and Castle did from Infanta de Castile; it originally meant the remote valley (*hop* in Old English) of the Norse goddess Freya. She was famously beautiful and so is the dale.

Can You See the Sea?

Who will see the North Sea first? Be on your toes as you approach the gliding strip on Carlton Moor. In good visibility, that's your likeliest first chance.

The path joins another minor road after about a mile. Go left for almost a further mile, ignoring a farm track down to the right, until you see a trig. point up ahead **E**. The road angles left, while a clear track goes ahead, keeping the trig. point to the left.

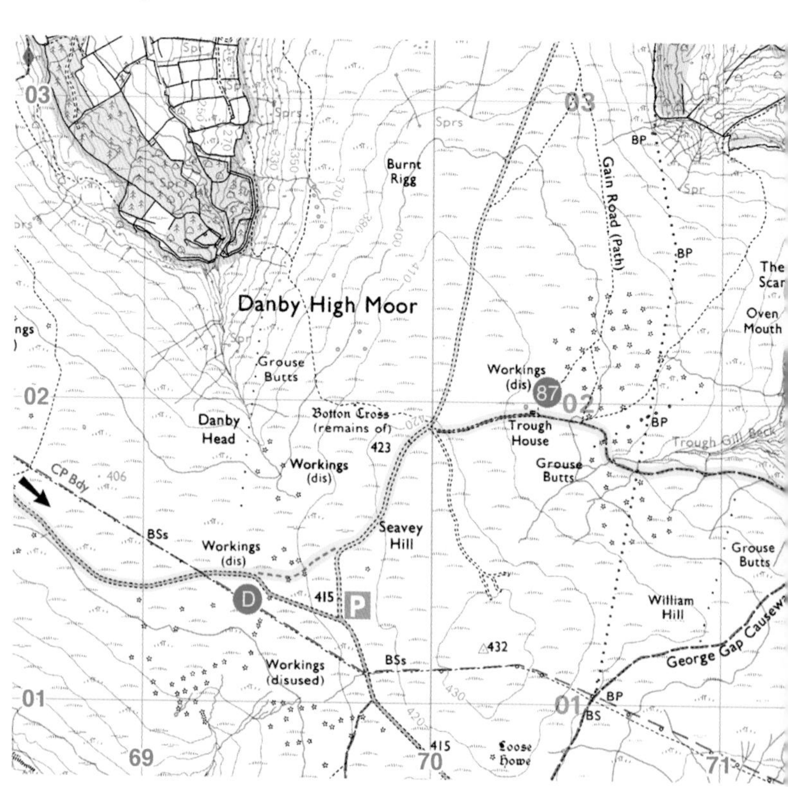

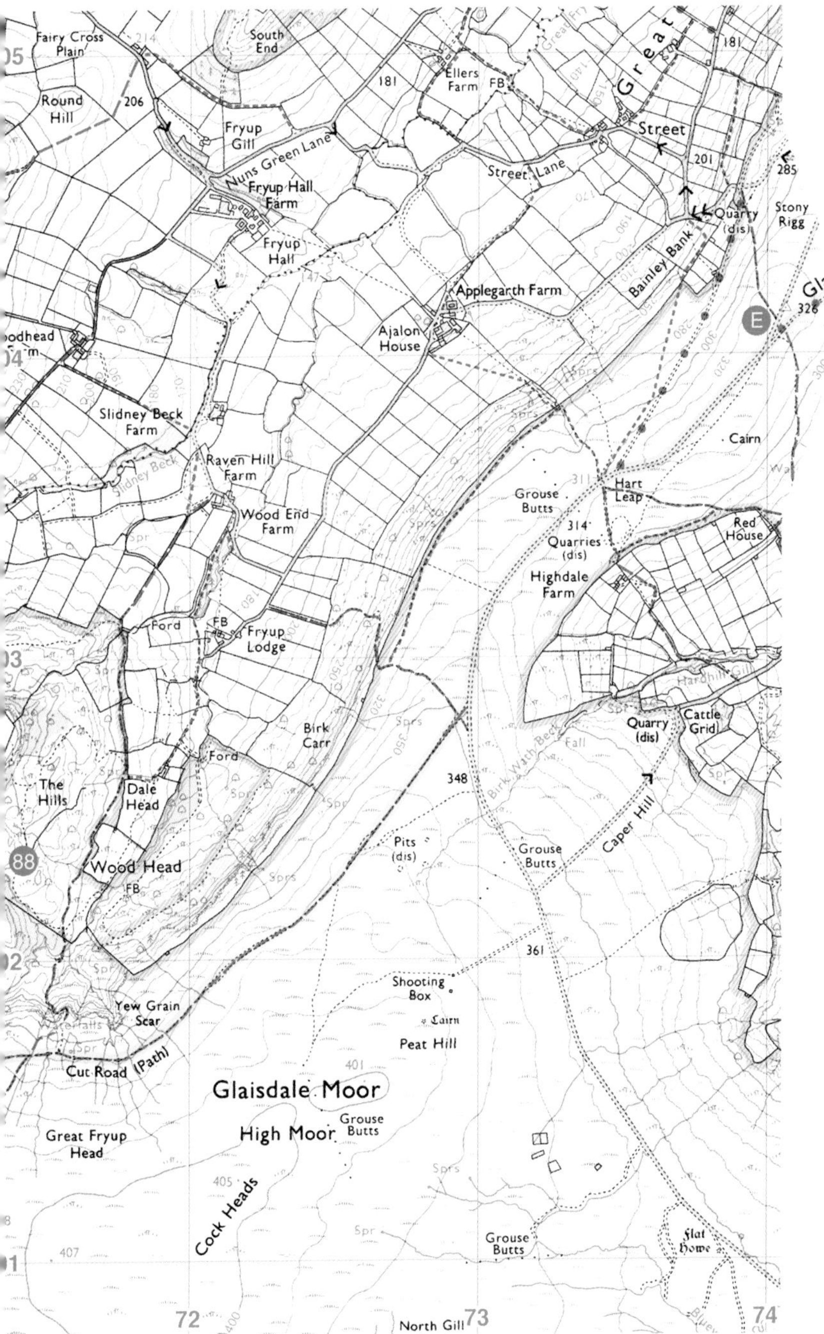
Fairy Cross Plain
214
South End
Round Hill
206
Fryup Gill
181
Ellers Farm
FB
Great Fryup
Street
Nuns Green Lane
Street Lane
201
285
Fryup Hall Farm
Fryup Hall
Quarry (dis)
Stony Rigg
147
Bainley Bank
Applegarth Farm
Glaisdale Rigg
326
E
Ajalon House
Woodhead Farm
Slidney Beck Farm
Slidney Beck
Cairn
Raven Hill Farm
311
Hart Leap
Grouse Butts
Wood End Farm
314
Quarries (dis)
Red House
Highdale Farm
Ford
FB
Fryup Lodge
Hardhill Gill
Quarry (dis)
Cattle Grid
Birk Carr
Birk Wath Beck
Fall
Ford
348
The Hills
Dale Head
Caper Hill
Pits (dis)
88
Wood Head
Grouse Butts
FB
361
Shooting Box
Yew Grain Scar
Waterfalls
Cairn
Peat Hill
Cut Road (Path)
401
Glaisdale Moor
Grouse Butts
Great Fryup Head
High Moor
405
Cock Heads
Grouse Butts
Flat Howe
407
72
North Gill
73
74
05
04
03
02
01

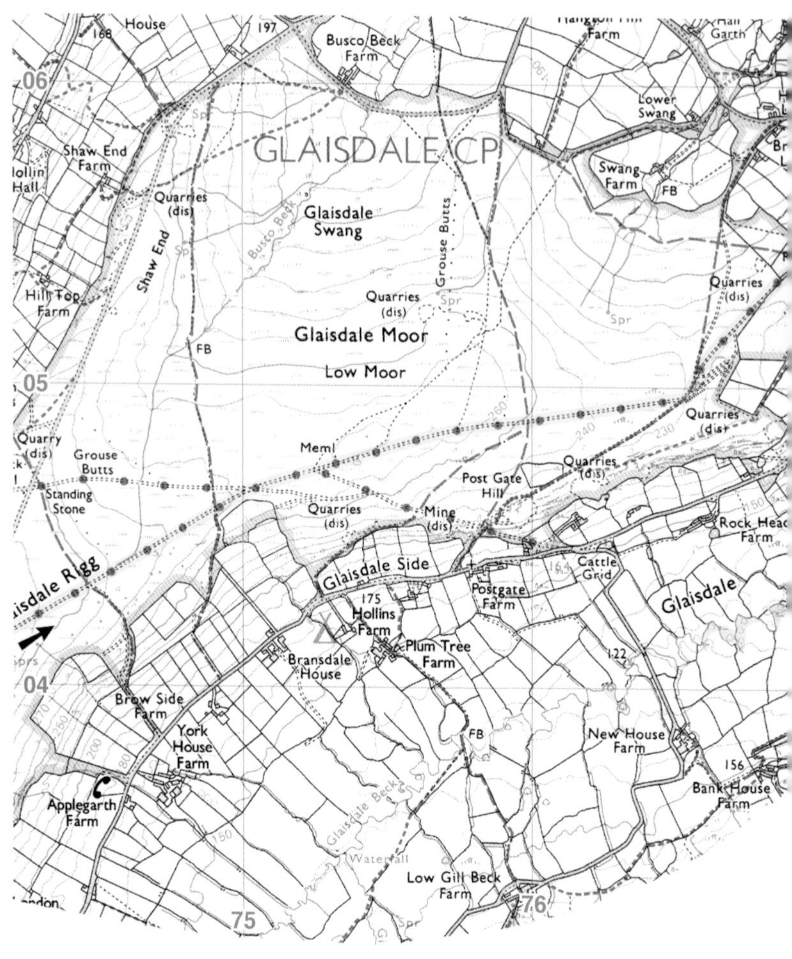

Follow the track gently down the spine of Glaisdale Rigg past a fine line of stone pillar waymarks and an area of grassy hummocks where locals saunter on summer evenings. A final cattle grid and you are in the outskirts of Glaisdale village. Turn right at the main road and then take the left turn marked Access Only and thread steeply down through the houses to a lane which leads to Glaisdale Station and its welcome pub and café. Past pubs in Glaisdale included The Moon and Sixpence, whose name accounts for an otherwise ordinary terrace house being called, intriguingly, Moon View.

Hard to Imagine . . .

Between 1869 and 1875 three blast furnaces made steel in the now peaceful village of Glaisdale.

In late summer, heather fills Blakey Ridge and the central high moors with vivid purple and the scent of honey.

Ironstone, alum and jet

The three old industries of the North York Moors are a fascinating combination. Between them, they created the lumps and bumps beside so many stretches of the path, as well as tunnels bored into the hills, quarry-workings slashed away from the escarpment and the railway which speeds walkers from Urra Moor to Blakey Ridge.

Ironstone, smelted for iron ore, was worked here, appropriately, in the Iron Age, 2,000 years ago, but first proliferated among medieval monks, who had some 120 bloomeries or small-scale smelting furnaces around the moors. The big breakthrough came in the 1830s when large Industrial Revolution companies began exploitation on a grand scale (Charles Dickens' novels often feature ironmasters, nouveau riche and strong-minded opponents of a decadent aristocracy). In 1852 lonely Rosedale saw an iron Klondyke; the population went from 550 to 3,000. Now it is below 300 and peace has long fallen on the mighty furnaces and the railway. The latter was built in 1861 and is a model of skilful contouring – although each end, at Rosedale and down the Cleveland escarpment at Ingleby Greenhow, culminates in a giddily steep incline where the ore trucks were uncoupled from their locomotives and lowered on iron cables, which occasionally and disastrously snapped. The railway was often blocked all winter by snow, but brought unexpected life to

The old ironstone railway's cindertrack offers easy walking for 5 miles, contouring round the head of Farndale to the welcome haven of The Lion inn.

Hacking out alum clay near Whitby in 1814 before treatment with seaweed and urine.

the moors. The lonely junction of the line and the Coast to Coast at Bloworth Crossing once had a linesman's cottage, with vegetable patch, pigs and hens, and the North Eastern Railway company's initials embossed even on the taps. The line ran for the last time in January 1929.

The story of alum is extraordinary. It comes from a frost-resistant clay once known only in Rome, which gave the Pope a monopoly of the process which makes alum a crucial chemical in tanning, dyeing and papermaking. A Yorkshire landowner, Sir Thomas Chaloner, discovered the same clay on the North York Moors in 1600, smuggled some of the Pope's craftsmen to Britain in wine barrels and started production. The price of alum fell from £52 a ton for the Pope's special to only £11 for Yorkshire's equally effective rival. The other curious feature of alum production, prior to 20th-century processes, was the boiling of the liquid product for hours in a mixture of seaweed and human urine – vast amounts of which were brought from London as ballast in returning North-East coal ships. As local historian Harry Mead says, 'The industry cannot have contributed much to local charm', but it lasted for 252 years, with side products of whitewash and rock salt, until cheaper sources of alum shale from deep coal mines undercut the last local works in 1867.

Jet is a fossilised wood about 180 million years old which lies in narrow seams along the coast and moorland escarpments inland from Whitby. It has been used to make jewellery since pre-Roman times, shining, hard enough to carve very precisely and – in a term to which it gave its name – jet black. It became fashionable in Victorian times when the mourning monarch led a fashion for black rings and necklaces. The Jet Miners' inn at Great Broughton, below the Cleveland escarpment, flourished mightily and an annual Jets' Holiday saw horse-racing on Whitby and Sandsend beaches. In the way of fashion, the black stuff fell out of favour in the early 20th century and attempts to revive it, most recently in 1966 when a Whitby man commissioned a range of jewellery in jet, gold and diamonds, have all failed. Old carving workshops may still be seen in Whitby and there is a good souvenir shop at the foot of the abbey steps which specialises in jet.

12 Glaisdale to Robin Hood's Bay

via the Littlebeck valley • 7–8 hours
19 miles (30.4 km)

Ascent 1,640 (500 metres)
Descent 2,296 feet (700 metres)
Lowest point Robin Hood's Bay: 33 feet (10 metres)
Highest point Sleights Moor: 919 feet (280 metres)

Two lovely valleys alternate with the last exhilarating strides over heather moor until a curious diversion through a caravan site brings you to the North Sea cliffs, quaint Robin Hood's Bay and . . . from Coast to Coast.

The route from Glaisdale starts with a brief but essential diversion to look at the slender arch of Beggar's Bridge **89** over the River Esk. Juggling your viewfinder to keep the standard modern bridge out of the picture, you may be lucky enough to capture one of the trains which still come up this valley – not many on the timetable, but a boon if you have time for a quiet day and fancy combining a short walk along the line with a train there or back. The Beggar's Bridge was supposedly built by Tom Ferris, a humble villager who fell in love with the squire's daughter, Agnes Richardson, but was sent packing by her father as too poor. Undeterred, the couple met secretly, with Tom fording the Esk at night for what must have been uncomfortable trysts. Determined to marry his love, Tom went to sea, captured a galleon from the Spanish Armada and returned in triumph to marry Agnes and, more prosaically, become Mayor of Hull. He built the bridge to make trans-Esk courting easier for other swains.

Retrace your route briefly under the railway bridge and go left on a signed path and footbridge over Glaisdale Beck by the ford and up a steep flight of stone steps. The Coast to Coast now enters a serene spell of woodland, climbing and descending gently on one of the paths known as trods, made up of stone flags laid in medieval times for pannier-ponies, which traded between villages and monastic settlements. Wildlife and flowers abound alongside the Esk, for a long time the only salmon river in Yorkshire, although clean-ups further south have changed that in recent years. After about a mile you reach a quiet lane which leads down to Egton Bridge, past a well-sited wooden seat **A** with a plaque kindly maintained by the parish council.

The Horseshoe will soon be maintaining you, unless you are in a rush or have an iron will. It is a lovely old pub with a pretty garden and interesting architecture – note the unusual windows and chevron cuts in the walls, typical of almost all locally quarried stone in these

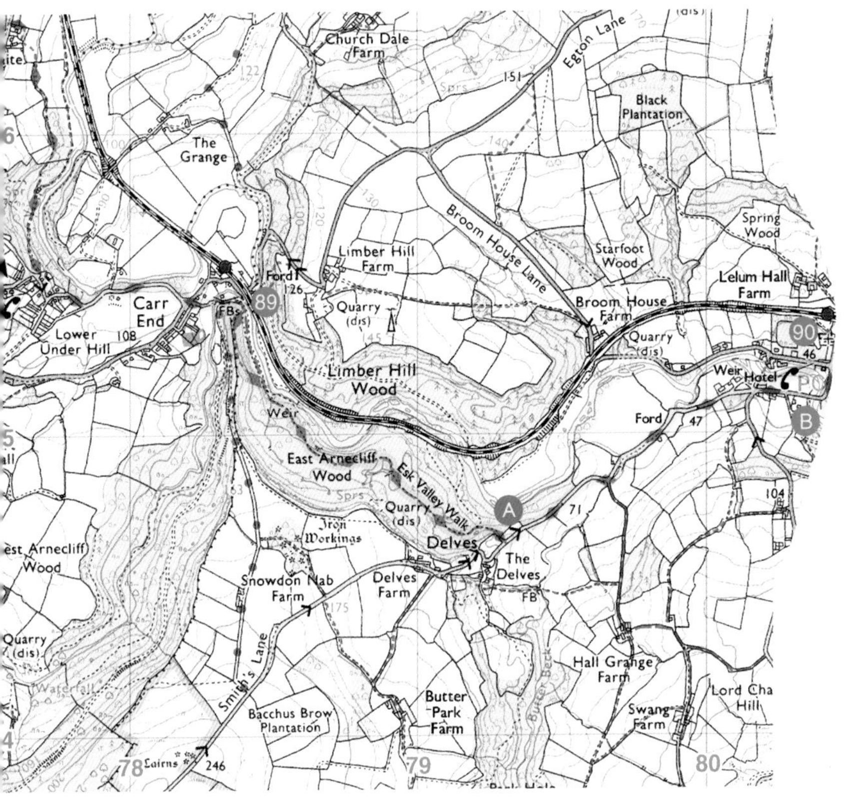

parts. At Glaisdale, you had to wait until the end of the village for the pub. Here it is one of the first buildings after a house and a barn, down a short lane to the left. Glory be.

Shortly beyond it, a signed path **B** drops down to stepping stones over the Esk and beyond an apparent dead-end caused by new riverside building – but actually a ginnel sidles between the houses and on to a lane where you turn right. Passing beautifully kept gardens and public lavatories, this takes you to the main road and a left turn to look at St Hedda's Roman Catholic Church **90**. Egton Bridge is a famous stronghold of the faith, nicknamed 'the village the Reformation forgot', and the home of a celebrated martyr, the Blessed Nicholas Postgate. A good and simple priest, he was hung, drawn and quartered at the age of 82 in 1679, when the fake 'Popish Plot' alleging a conspiracy to overthrow the Protestant monarchy led to panic and anti-Catholic hysteria. It was the last occasion in Britain on which Catholics were legally put to death for their faith.

The church has colourful decorations inside and out, a lovely garden and many mementos, including a model of a secret loft chapel in Egton, up the hill, which was only rediscovered in the

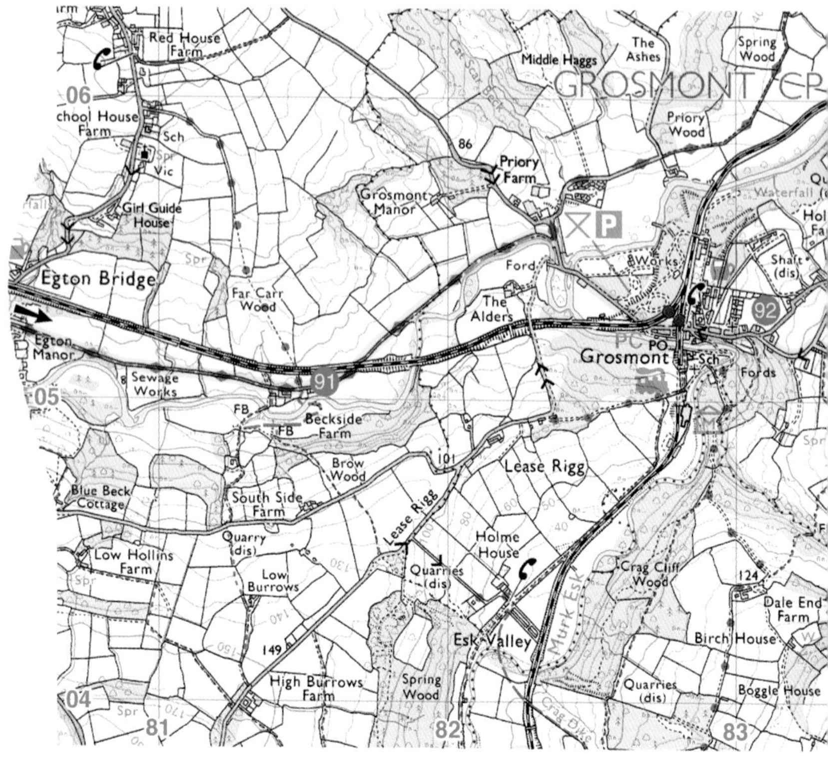

18th century when a servant pushed her hand through plaster hiding the entrance. The neighbouring primary school is the setting for Egton Bridge's other great claim to fame: the Old Gooseberry Show on the first Tuesday in August, which sees unimaginably vast fruits and desperate competition. For all the village's rather grand Victorian air, there are hidden gardens and allotments here and in Egton where amazing necromancy with manure and other potions goes on.

Retrace your steps and fewer than 50 yards south of St Hedda's church, go left through the Egton Estate's white-fenced and stone-columned entrance on the private unmade road, with a timber yard immediately on your left. This permissive right-of-way along the valley bottom has replaced an old toll road, whose rates, for everything from a cart to a coffin, are printed on a lovingly preserved sign on the side of the old toll house a little further on **91**. The road allows lovely glimpses of Egton Manor, banks of rhododendrons and other flowering shrubs, and a field sloping down to the river and populated by friendly donkeys. The route saunters between wild-flower verges until a loop in the Esk below Priory Farm brings you to the road leading over the river and under the railway into Grosmont.

In a miniature way, this ancient settlement is a famous railway junction with a claim to the world's oldest rail tunnel, a castellated structure for the old horse-drawn line to Pickering. The track of this runs beside the steam (and diesel) trains of the North York Moors railway which was memorably saved by local community spirit after the Beeching closures of 1965. Restoration took eight years but has proved an enormous success, especially since recent bridge-strengthening has allowed the puffing giants into Whitby. You will see from the map that there are two stations in Grosmont; the NYM connects with the conventional rail link between Whitby and Teesside (and thence the national network). Increasing co-operation means that steam trains now sometimes run up to Glaisdale, a stretch with a claim to be the most beautiful railway in Britain. Specialist shops abound, along with cafés and galleries which make Grosmont the Esk Valley's tourist capital.

You must pay for indulgence, however, by a steep haul out of the village up Fair Head Lane, past a tier of pastel-painted Victorian villas which look like something from a south-coast seaside town or even San Francisco **92**. More tarmac, alas, as

Old steam trains have brought new life to Grosmont and the Esk Valley.

you fork right twice, following signs to Pickering and Goathland until the open moor is reached. Here branch to the right to take in two prehistoric stone circles **93** on the way to the busy A169, the highway from the south to Whitby. The Low Bride Stones can be boggy but the High Bride Stones, a little further up, are more prominent and redolent of that awed, timeless feeling which can grip a traveller so strongly on the North York Moors. A little further along the road from Grosmont, a track **C** heads left across the heather to a stile on to the verge of the A169. Trudge right alongside the hurtling traffic for ¼ mile (400 metres) until a stile on the other side of the road leads to a path **D**, widening to a stony track, down the moorside, with Hillside Farm on the left as you reach a metalled lane. This leads quickly and steeply into the tucked-away hamlet of Littlebeck.

Holiday cottages with their own canoes line the stream, close to the Devil's Hole, where the informer who betrayed Nicholas Postgate drowned himself (and supposedly no fish have ever been caught since). There is a slight excess of Private notices about, but a friendlier sign to Falling Foss marks the way ahead **E**, up a long valley of mixed and in some places almost tropically dense woodland

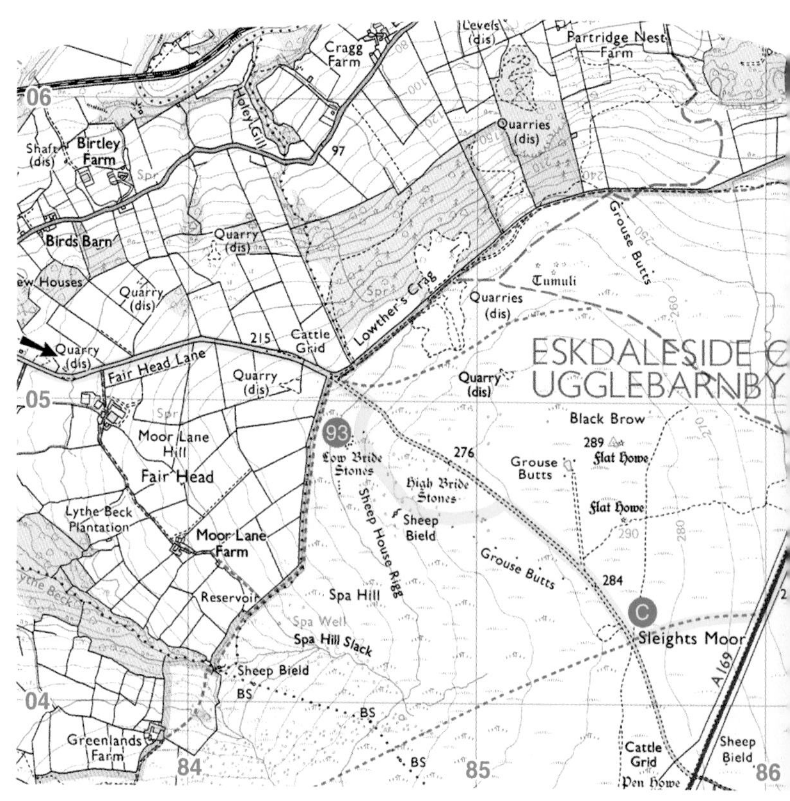

to the dramatic waterfall. Part of the wood honours the memory of a young naturalist killed in a road accident and a signboard usefully summarises the plants and wildlife which abound. History is everywhere too; the path climbs intriguingly past an excavated mineral-workers' cave and then over the top of the resulting spoil heap. In places there are precipitous drops to the stream, startlingly far below, and dank crevices are filled in almost jungle-profusion with moss and ferns.

Schoolmaster Chubb's two-storey Hermitage. Seats on top if it's full up inside.

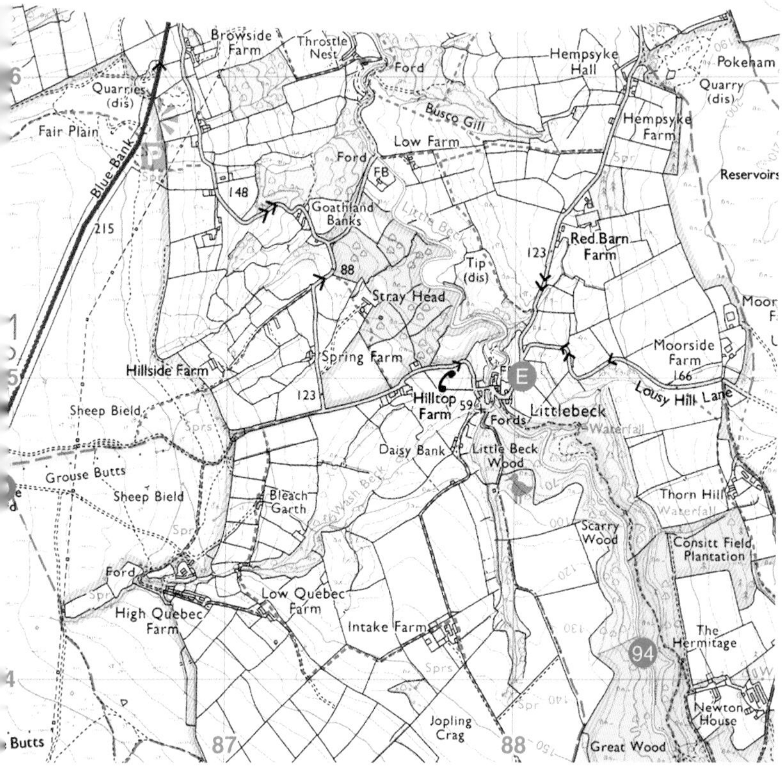

At the top of the main climb, a huge boulder on the left was hollowed out in 1754 for a Littlebeck schoolmaster, George Chubb, whose initials are carved alongside the date and the curious structure's title of The Hermitage **94**. The seats inside and also above the roof are comfy places for a rest. Then take the higher of two paths, followed by a right fork for Falling Foss **95**, which tumbles over a high rock face in front of Midge Hall, long boarded up but now restored with a very welcome tea garden, reminiscent of the building's Victorian heyday. Two daytrippers' car parks are near here and a confusing number of different coloured arrows mark short circular walks rather than the Coast to Coast.

The route goes left in front of Midge Hall, crossing a footbridge to the right bank of a lovely pool in front of the bridge carrying a farm track. Keeping this to the left, head onwards, fording the stream on stepping stones, and continue on the right bank through woodland and a growing number of glades, one with a pond full of bulrushes, until the path finally leaves the shade of the trees opposite picnickers at May Beck car park. On a clear day, the return to sunshine is welcome and the views back show the impressive length of the narrow, wooded defile from Littlebeck.

The path follows the metalled road left in a hairpin uphill to a half circle round New May Beck Farm, where a track leaves right on a signed path **F** marked by occasional posts, straight across Sneaton Low Moor to join the B1416 from Ruswarp at a stile opposite a copse and Soulsgrave Farm. Turn right and put up with rushing traffic (this is a well-known short-cut) for 500 yards to where a waymarked stile and gate leads to the long, final moor of Graystone Hills, a sting in the Coast to Coast's tail. The path curves across the moor, marked by three posts marked CtoC in various stages of dilapidation. It can seem unduly long and in murky weather the path may be indistinct, but the noise of the A171 Scarborough–Whitby road is very nearby to the right, should you feel lost. Shortly after the third post **G** it divides; both ways will get you there, but the one on the right is best, crossing a very boggy hollow on fine new duckboards. It then rises to a prominent gate and stile in a fence not far to the left of a gentle

Decoy Town

Seaton Moor above the Littlebeck Valley was unusually heavily bombed in the Second World War after a fake 'Middlesbrough' was built there, complete with subdued street lighting and rigged explosions.

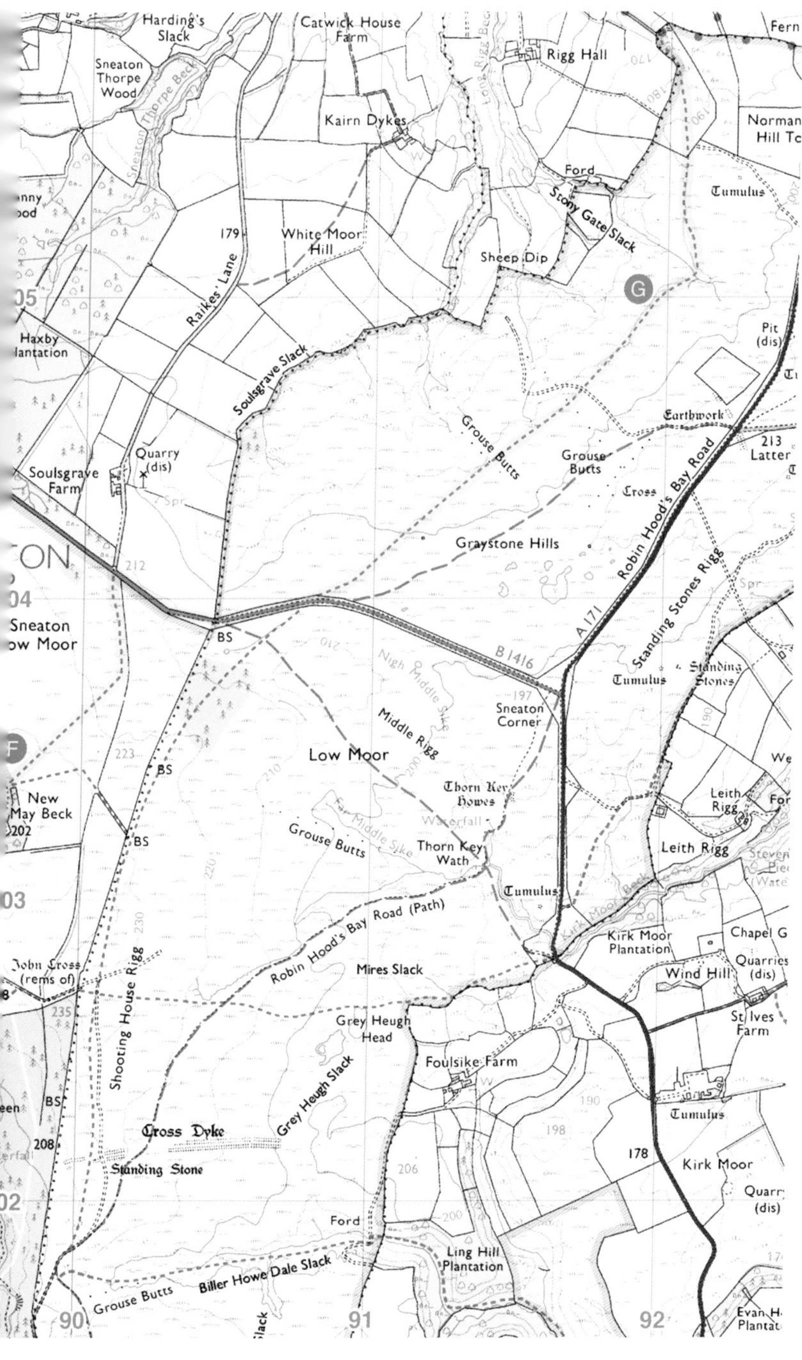
Harding's Slack
Catwick House Farm
Rigg Hall
Fern
Sneaton Thorpe Wood
Thorpe Beck
Sneaton
Kairn Dykes
Long Rigg Beck
Norman Hill
Ford
Tumulus
Stony Gate Slack
179
White Moor Hill
Sheep Dip
Raikes' Lane
G
05
Haxby Plantation
Pit (dis)
Soulsgrave Slack
Earthwork
Grouse Butts
213
Latter
Quarry (dis)
Soulsgrave Farm
Grouse Butts
Cross
Robin Hood's Bay Road
Graystone Hills
212
04
Sneaton Low Moor
A171
Standing Stones Rigg
BS
B1416
Nigh Middle Sike
197
Sneaton Corner
Tumulus
Standing Stones
Middle Rigg
F
Low Moor
223
BS
New May Beck
202
Thorn Key Howes
Leith Rigg
Waterfall
BS
Grouse Butts
Far Middle Sike
Thorn Key Wath
Leith Rigg
03
Tumulus
Kirk Moor Beck
Robin Hood's Bay Road (Path)
Kirk Moor Plantation
Chapel G
John Cross (rems of)
Mires Slack
Wind Hill
Quarries (dis)
235
Shooting House Rigg
Grey Heugh Head
St Ives Farm
Foulsike Farm
Grey Heugh Slack
BS
Tumulus
190
198
208
Cross Dyke
Standing Stone
178
Kirk Moor
02
206
Quarry (dis)
Ford
200
Ling Hill Plantation
Biller Howe Dale Slack
Grouse Butts
Slack
Evan Howe Plantation
90
91
92

mound topped with scrubby gorse – the ancient tumulus marked on the map. A brief stretch of grass follows, turning into deep ruts amid heather and gorse as you descend to the obvious gate at the end of the little 'thumb' of moorland on the map. Flanked by hedges, the track continues down to the road, where you turn right and continue ahead at a junction.

Take the first turning right on the road towards Low Hawsker, forking right after Mitten Hill Farm for the final uphill stretch, across the A171 and into High Hawsker – pub on the left.

The village has the air of commuterland and little to detain you, although a small well engraved with initials TC and 1790 hides in the

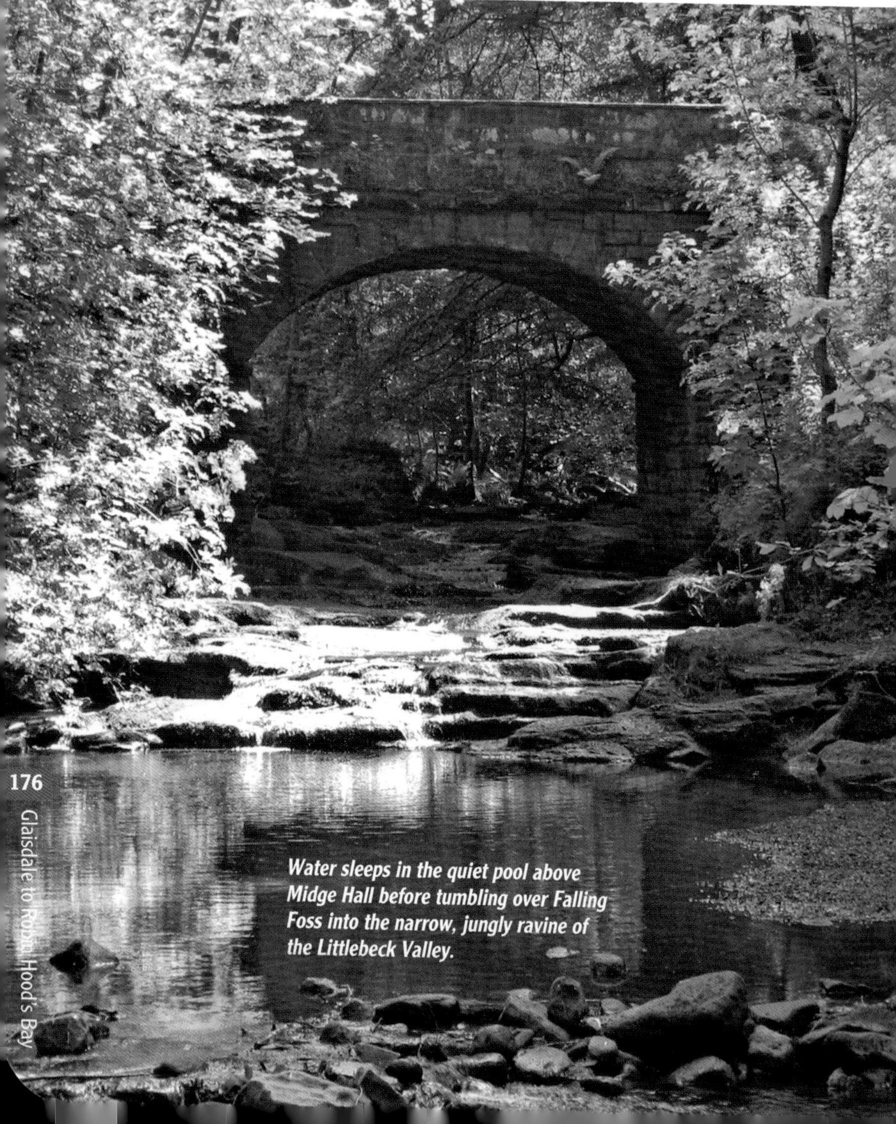

Water sleeps in the quiet pool above Midge Hall before tumbling over Falling Foss into the narrow, jungly ravine of the Littlebeck Valley.

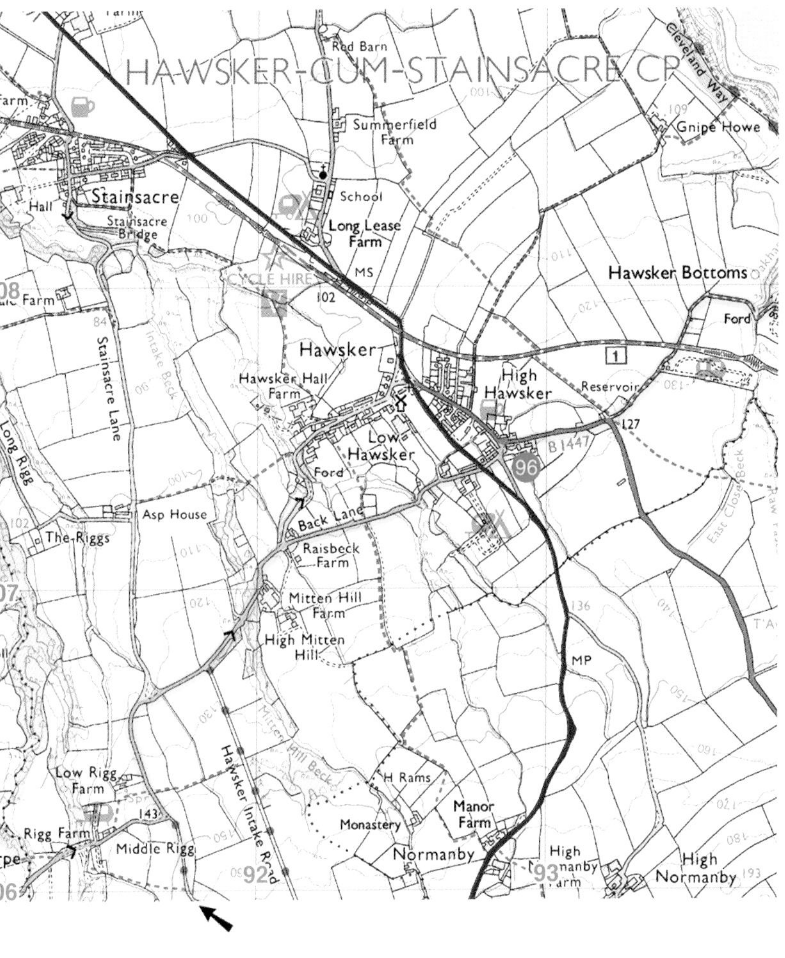

hedge on the right as you leave **96**. There are also two fields named after Robin Hood and Little John, after an alleged archery contest staged at the local priory. But something is likely to be urging you onwards now: ozone, or sea air. Head for its source along the road signed Robin Hood's Bay (Hooray! At last!) until a right-hand bend where a lavish sign and extremely neat, mown verges point you ahead to a couple of caravan sites. These provide a contrast to all your wild roamings which many Coast to Coasters find pleasantly incongruous, especially as the footpath goes right through the second site with its neat and completely immobile 'mobile homes' on both sides (the small tree with a hole in its trunk halfway down often hides a bird's nest, which accounts for people solemnly putting their ears to its bark). There are cafés at High Hawsker and the second caravan site, although the latter is often closed after 2pm.

After the second caravan site, with the North Sea grandly ahead, the path runs down and to the left of a sewage plant to rejoin our friend the Cleveland Way **H**. Together, the two great paths circle and switchback to the right along the very top of the cliffs, splendidly high above sea-wracked inlets such as Maw Wyke and Homerell Holes and Castle Chamber. Stunted trees remind walkers lucky enough to have a still, peaceful day that this is a sometimes tempestuous stretch. It also involves a final tribute to the genius of Alfred Wainwright. He did not design the coastline, but he lit on a destination which hides until the great walk's very last mile. Only after you round Ness Point, or the bay's North Cheek, do the superlatively pretty roofs and gardens of 'Bay Town' appear, perched right above the sea. The path drops to Rocket Post Field, where a replica of the pillar used by clifftop rescuers for target practice still stands **97**. Their rockets carried lines to wrecked ships, allowing a breeches buoy on a hawser to bring the crew to safety: accuracy was a matter of life and death.

The Rocket Post, used to train life-saving crews who fired rescue lines to foundering ships.

A kissing-gate stands in the field corner, followed by a brief corridor through hawthorns, and here, in the form of gently suburban Mount Pleasant North, is our destination. Residents have generously refrained from growing big hedges to hide their pretty gardens and magnificent sea views, as you walk down the street and, following a brief section with houses on both sides, reach the main road and turn left for the old village.

Steeply downhill, the townscape gets quainter and quainter, until you can go no further at The Dock, with Wainwright's Bar **98** on the left, where, remember, you have to buy your own pint rather than relying on the late author's largesse. A satisfying sign on the wall says The End, but delay this until you have dipped your boots in the sea. The slipway is not the place to do this. It is notoriously dangerous and has been the scene of drownings, so carry out your rituals by taking the steps up to the right, round the back of a row of cottages and down to the town's beach.

Here you can also leave the shell or pebble which you have brought from St Bees, playing your part in a steady geological transfer which may one day baffle scientists. Then celebrate and don't feel let down by the absence of cheering crowds. Robin Hood's Bay is a mecca for trippers who are unlikely to know about your amazing feat and wouldn't care if they did. But there may be a few, instantly recognisable, fellow-Ancient Mariners slumped about who will exchange yarns. And anyway, *you* know what you have achieved, and that is all that matters in the end.

Maw Wyke Hole
Pursglove Stye Batts
Pursglove Stye
Waterfalls
Limekiln Slack
White Horse
White Stone Hole
High Scar
Normanby Stye Batts
Hilda's Howe
Far Jetticks
Pits (dis)
Bottom House
Clock Case Nab
Bottom House Lane
Craze Naze
Homerell Hole
Rain Dale
Spring Farm
Cow & Calf
Raw Pasture
Castle Chamber
Raw Pasture Lane
Bulmer Steel
Raw Pasture Bank
Bulmer Steel Hole
Smails Moor Farm
Bay Ness
High Lane
Quarry (dis)
Ness Point or North Cheek
Reservoir
Ness Ruck
Green Hills
Hook's House
Copsella
Church Lane Farm
Dungeon Hole
Robin Hood's Bay
Church Lane
Hotel
Ground Wyke
West Scar
Ground Wyke Hole
Landing Scar
Thorpe Hall
East Scar
Fisher Head
Thorpe Green
Fylingthorpe
Dab Dumps
Cowfield Hill
Cowling Scar
Park Gate
Middlewood Farm
Yaddow Mills
Middlewood Lane
Robin Hood's Bay
Mark Lane
Farsyde House
94
95
96

Sailors and smugglers

Robin Hood's Bay is self-evidently very pretty, but there is more to it than meets the eye. At one time almost every cottage was connected underground through cellars, sewers and cubby-holes. This was where the smugglers unloaded their contraband and hid it, and themselves, from the Excise men. 'Bay', as they call it, was supposedly where Robin Hood retired from time to time, when bored of outmanoeuvring the Sheriff of Nottingham, and lived simply as a fisherman. He also is said to have defeated an invading force of Norsemen, proving as adept at inshore naval fighting as he was with his longbow in the greenwood.

Journey's end. Leave your Irish Sea pebble here if you haven't lost it on the way.

The little town has an heroic fishing and sailing tradition and a great name for rescuing ships which fell foul of the scaurs, jagged fingers of rock which reach out from this part of Britain's coast. The most famous occasion was in 1881 when the brig *Visitor* foundered in a blizzard off the town and adverse seas made it impossible to launch the nearest lifeboat at Whitby. In deep snow, 50 pairs of horses lent by local farmers dragged the lifeboat for 6 miles (10 km) to Robin Hood's Bay – including the final section of the Coast to Coast Walk. Women and children held flares and provided food and drink as the men slithered and pulled with the horses before the boat ran down the final, iced-over street to The Dock and rescued six despairing crew from the ship.

Such dramas were captured by the novelist Leo Walmsley in his 1930s trilogy *Three Fevers, Phantom Lobster* (memorable title) and *Sally Lunn*, based on a well-known local family, the Storms. A tradition of sea names also accounts for Storm Jameson, another successful novelist of the 1930s, who grew up on the final stretch of the Coast to Coast. Today, Robin Hood's Bay may sometimes seem insufferably twee and little more than holiday cottages, but 'real' people are living and working here. The internet has brought new arrivals who do not need to commute to work by driving for hours or waiting for irregular trains. They just plug in their computer and modem and enjoy the view.

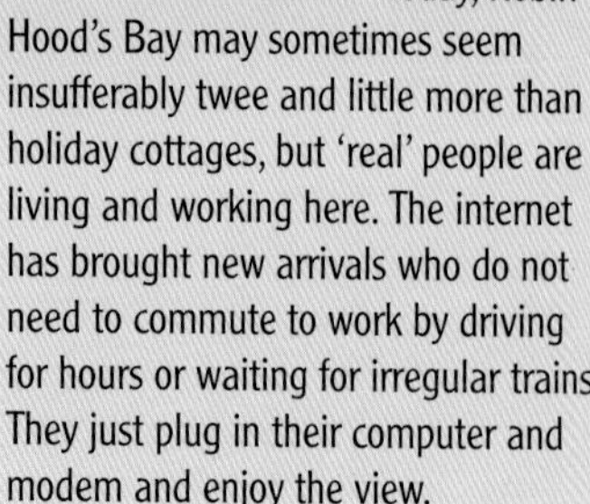

Coast to coast – the North Sea washes against the eroding, fossil-rich cliffs between Hawsker Bottoms and North Cheek, the gateway to Robin Hood's Bay.

Useful Information

Planning

The Coast to Coast rapidly adopted the starting and stopping points selected by Wainwright to begin and end each day's march and those are used as the structure here. But very large numbers of walkers who tackle the entire 192 miles (307 km) in one go adjust this basic programme to suit their time, energy and the unexpected. For most of its length, the route is amenable to all sorts of variations, just as Wainwright wished.

The fastest-ever crossing is under 48 hours, which comes at the far extreme of peak-bagging. I was passed at a fine pace by a group of paratroopers, who were taking a more sensible (for the extremely fit) eight days. The commonest allocation of time is a fortnight, which allows a day or two 'spare' for resting, spending extra time in the Lakes or Richmond, or holing up in foul weather. If you have the time, a further couple of days can easily be spent seeing more at a pleasantly leisurely pace.

Judging by previous walkers' accounts, a cheerful amount of 'cheating' goes on. Driven to despair by bad weather, walkers have phoned for a taxi to bridge dreary bits or cut out the Vale of Mowbray 'flat part' under the misapprehension that it is a yawn. Conversely, a lot of people add extra bits by, for example, overnighting in Osmotherly rather than Ingleby Cross, or walking down from Clay Bank Top to the village B&Bs a mile or two away (and back up again in the morning).

The most commonly used variations to Wainwright's (and this book's) basic layout include dividing the second day into two, spending a night at Grasmere. This gives time for average walkers to take the splendid variant to the route up the shoulder of Helvellyn and down Striding Edge, or to go over St Sunday Crag and Birks on the other side of Grisedale. It also helps boots, toes and rucksack straps to settle down. Another typical modification is to break up the very long fourth and fifth days by stopping at Bampton and Orton instead of Shap and Kirkby Stephen. Other possibilities are legion and part of the fun of the project is poring in an armchair over alternatives, balancing a stage's length with the whereabouts of places to stay, eat or wash your clothes.

The walk has developed a fascinating culture over four decades; invitations to restaurants, B&Bs and even an holistic healing centre discreetly adorn fences, trees and barns along the way. The range of waymarkers could form an exhibition entitled '1001 Ways to Stop Ramblers Going Astray'. Typing 'Coast to Coast' into an internet search engine will also keep walk-planners absorbed – and possibly horrified – by the experiences of others. An American family who stayed feisty in the face of every kind of disaster (most, it must be said, self-inflicted) will remain for ever in my mind.

Self-sufficient or support party

This is one of the first decisions you will need to make. Two weeks is a very long time to carry all your kit, although laundrettes or hotel/hostel washing machines occur often enough to prevent you causing a stink when you finally buy your pint at the Bay Hotel or St Bees. Many walkers organise kind friends or relations to act as support parties, ferrying heavy stuff to one or more points along the route. There are also several specialist companies which will take all your gear every day to your next stop. Equally usefully, they arrange drop-off and pick-up if required at both ends of the walk. This can be very helpful, as the rail service to St Bees is very limited and Robin Hood's Bay lost its train to Dr Beeching in 1965.

Leading companies are:
Sherpa: www.sherpavan.com;
☎ 0871 520 0124; London-based
Packhorse: www.c2cpackhorse.co.uk;
☎ 01768 371777; Kirkby Stephen
Coast to Coast Holiday & Baggage Services: ☎ 01642 489173
Brigantes Walking Holidays:
☎ 01729 830463

It is also entirely practicable to make your own arrangements with local taxi firms and/or some overnight stopping places in advance at a discount rate.

Accommodation

There is a terrific range, much of it generated by the walk, which helps in terms of drying sopping clothes or yarning about your amazing adventures to mine host. Most of the hoteliers, hostel wardens and B&B proprietors have become very knowledgeable about the route and the needs of its walkers. One of them, the celebrated Doreen Whitehead of Butt House in Keld, has written an excellent B&B guide to the trail, in between robust advice sessions with her local MP, the former Conservative leader William Hague.

Walkers may have been worried about the Youth Hostels Association's decision to close both Keld and Kirkby Stephen because of low demand. Although sad, this reflects modern walkers' increasing demand for privacy and comfort as opposed to budget stays. But Kirkby Stephen is still in the YHA Handbook as an independently-run hostel, and Keld is now Keld Lodge, a hotel.

The most flexible, cheapest but least comfortable way to stay is camping and there are sites at most of the obvious stopping points. 'Wild camping' on your own may be done at high altitude in the Lake District, e.g. at Grisedale or Angle Tarns, and many landowners will permit it elsewhere, but it is absolutely essential to ask them first. Hotels, hostels, bunkbarns and B&Bs are also well distributed along the route, although at Clay Bank Top you need to divert a mile or two down to the Cleveland plain. Many businesses will come to collect you and drop you back if you are whacked.

Youth hostels, including the star overnight site of the whole walk, Black Sail, are usually closed between October and March inclusive, except to pre-booked parties. A group of friends can take advantage of this. Contact the Youth Hostels Association, Trevelyan House, Dimple Road, Matlock, Derbyshire DE4 3YH, www.yha.org.uk or ☎ 01629 592600 because details may change. Lake District hostels have their own booking line: ☎ 01539 431117. Much general information and contact details are available on a number of websites devoted to the path and tourism in the wider area. You will also find that booked-up premises almost always pass you on to neighbours who cater to the Coast to Coast.

Information

The walk crosses two counties, both with vigorous tourist boards, and three national parks which are long-practised at catering for visitors. They are good early ports of call for detailed, up-to-date information on places to stay and local facilities. Many of the towns and villages on or near the path have their own websites, for example www.richmond.org.uk, which are best traced (if only because their webmasters sometimes change arrangements) via a search engine.

Cumbria Tourism, Windermere Road, Staveley, Kendal, Cumbria LA8 9PL;
www.cumbriatourism.org, www.golakes.co.uk;
☎ 01539 822222

Welcome to Yorkshire, Dry Sand Foundry, Foundry Square, Holbeck, Leeds LS51 5DL;
☎ 0113 322 3500; www.yorkshire.com

The Lake District National Park, Brockhole, Windermere, Cumbria LA23 1LJ

Lake District National Park Authority, Murley Moss, Oxenholme Road, Kendal, Cumbria LA9 7RL. ☎ 01539 724555.
www.lakedistrict.gov.uk

Yorkshire Dales National Park, Colvend, Hebden Road, Grassington, Skipton, North Yorkshire BD23 5LB

North York Moors National Park, Bondgate, Helmsley, York YO62 5BP; ☎ 01439 770657; www.northyorkmoors.org.uk

There are local official Tourist Information Centres at the following places. Opening times are seasonal and may vary from year to year.

Egremont: 12 Main Street, Egremont, Cumbria CA22 2DW; ☎ 01946 820693

Kirkby Stephen: Market Square, Kirkby Stephen, Cumbria CA17 4QN; ☎ 01768 371199

Richmond: Friary Gardens, Victoria Road, Richmond, North Yorkshire DL10 4AJ; ☎ 01748 825994

Northallerton: The Applegarth Car Park, Northallerton, North Yorkshire DL7 8LZ; ☎ 01609 776864

Whitby: The Moors Centre, Lodge Lane, Danby, Whitby, North Yorkshire YO21 2NB; ☎ 01439 772737

Whitby: Langbourne Road, Whitby, North Yorkshire YO21 1YN; ☎ 01723 383636

Websites dealing specifically with the path include: www.coast2coast.co.uk

www.coasttocoastguides.co.uk

The Ramblers' Association, Second Floor, Camelford House, 87–90 Albert Embankment, London SE1 7TW; www.ramblers.org.uk; ☎ 020 7339 8500 is an excellent national walkers' association with facilities such as map-lending for members and much useful general advice.

There is internet access on the route in hostels, cafés or pubs at Grasmere, Patterdale, Kirkby Stephen, Richmond, Ingleby Cross, Grosmont and Robin Hood's Bay, and many overnight places will let you go online if your onward journey needs sorting out. The maps mark phone boxes along the way.

Useful contacts

Backpackers' Club, 29 Lynton Drive, High Lane, Stockport, Cheshire SK6 8JE; www.backpackersclub.co.uk

British Trust for Ornithology, The Nunnery, Thetford, Norfolk IP24 2PU; www.bto.org.uk; ☎ 01842 750050

Cumbria County Council, The Courts, Carlisle CA3 8NA; www.cumbria.gov.uk; ☎ 01228 606060

Cumbria Wildlife Trust, Plumgarths, Crook Road, Kendal, Cumbria LA8 8LX; www.cumbriawildlifetrust.org.uk; ☎ 01539 816300

English Heritage: www.english-heritage.org.uk

North-West: Third Floor, Canada House, 3 Chepstow Street, Manchester M1 5FW; 0161 242 1400; North-East: Bessie Surtees House, 41–44 Sandhill, Newcastle upon Tyne NE13 3JF; ☎ 0191 269 1200

Forestry Commission, Silvan House, 231 Corstophine Road, Edinburgh EH12 7AT; www.forestry.gov.uk; ☎ 0131 334 0303

Long Distance Walkers' Association, www.ldwa.org.uk

National Trust:
North-West: The Hollens, Grasmere, Ambleside Cumbria LA22 9QZ; ☎ 01539 435 599

Yorkshire: North-East: Goddards, 27 Tadcaster Road, Dringhouses, York YO24 1GG; ☎ 01904 702021

Natural England, 1 East Parade, Sheffield, S1 2ET; www.naturalengland.org.uk; ☎ 0300 060 2745

North Yorkshire County Council, County Hall, Northallerton, North Yorkshire DL7 8AD; www.northyorks.gov.uk; ☎ 01609 780780

Ordnance Survey, Romsey Road, Maybush, Southampton SO16 4GU; www.ordsvy.gov.uk; ☎ 0845 605 0505

Royal Society for the Protection of Birds, The Lodge, Sandy, Bedfordshire SG19 2DL; www.rspb.org.uk; ☎ 01767 680551

Weathercall (Meteorological Office): www.weathercall.co.uk Cumbria and Lake District: ☎ 09068 500419 Yorkshire: ☎ 09068 500417

Transport

Train details are on www.nationalrail.co.uk; ☎ 08457 484950. Note that the last arrival in St Bees from either Barrow or Carlisle is late afternoon/early evening and remember that it is a request stop – you must tell the guard in advance that you want to get off there. National Express coaches go as far as Whitehaven, 4 miles (6.44 km) from St Bees, and to Whitby and other points along the route: www.nationalexpress.com; ☎ 08717 818181. If you drive, most B&Bs will let you leave your car, although they may charge. The nearest station to Robin Hood's Bay is Whitby, but Scarborough has more and better trains and the bus journey from there, at 40 minutes, takes only 20 minutes longer than the bus from Whitby. Other stations on the route are at Kirkby Stephen, Glaisdale and Grosmont.

Local bus services are operated by Arriva North East, ☎ 0844 850 4411and Stagecoach, ☎ 0871 200 2233. The National Park Moorsbus service on the North York Moors has timetables on www.northyorkmoors.org.uk. The national Traveline, ☎ 0871 200 2233 between 7am and 9pm, covers all public transport.

Rural buses are often very expensive and a shared taxi may be a better bet. You will often also learn a lot about the area from the driver. Taxis are available all along the path, with hubs at Kirkby Stephen, Richmond and Northallerton.

Local facilities

The tourist boards and local information centres can supply more detail but, in simple terms, towns and villages are equipped as follows:

St Bees all types of accommodation, shop, PO, ☎, cash machine
Sandwith bunkhouse, pub should reopen 2012
Moor Row shop, café, pub
Cleator shop, B&B, pub, ☎, doctor and dentist at Cleator Moor
Ennerdale Bridge all accommodation, shop, pubs, ☎
Seatoller all accommodation, shop, pub, ☎
Rosthwaite all accommodation, shop, pubs, ☎
Grasmere all accommodation but camping limited, shops, PO, pubs, ☎, cash machine
Patterdale all accommodation, shop, PO, pubs, ☎
Bampton accommodation, PO, pubs, ☎.
Shap all accommodation, shops, PO, pubs, ☎, doctor, bank, cash machine
Orton B&B, camping, shops inc. chocolate factory, PO, pub, ☎
Kirkby Stephen all accommodation, shops, PO, pubs, ☎, doctor, dentist, bank, cash machine
Keld B&B, hostel, campsite, café-shop, ☎
Muker B&B, pub, ☎
Gunnerside B&B, pub, ☎
Reeth all accommodation, shops, PO, pubs, ☎, cash machine
Marrick B&B, camping
Richmond all accommodation except camping, shops, PO, pubs, ☎, doctor, dentist, bank, cash machine
Colburn pub, ☎
Catterick Bridge hotel, camping, B&B, ☎
Danby Wiske B&B, camping, pub, ☎
Ingleby Cross B&B, shop, PO, pub, ☎
Osmotherly B&B, shop, PO, pub, ☎
Clay Bank Top B&Bs in local villages, min. walk 1½ miles (2.5 km), most will collect
Blakey Ridge B&B and camping at pub, ☎
Glaisdale B&B, camping, shop, PO, pub, ☎
Grosmont all accommodation, shops, PO, pubs, ☎
Littlebeck B&B, camping
Hawsker B&B, camping, pub, ☎
Robin Hood's Bay all accommodation, shops, PO, pubs, ☎

Many shops en route will give cashback, particularly if you buy a reasonable amount of goods. They and pubs may also cash cheques.

Some nearby places of interest

There are many attractions within easy reach of the path, as you would expect on a route which crosses three national parks. Here is a selection of some of the best. The leisurely walker will find an even greater choice further afield, with Carlisle, Ambleside, Windermere and Whitby among 'off-path' centres which are particularly worth visiting.

Sellafield Visitors Centre, Sellafield, Seascale, Cumbria CA20 1PG; ☎ 01946 727027. Nuclear power is back on the political agenda. Find out all about it in this slightly spooky setting.

Whitehaven Haig Colliery Mining Museum on former Haig Pit in Solway Road, Kells; 01946 599949; open all year, 9.30am–4.30pm. The Beacon on West Strand houses Whitehaven Museum; ☎ 01946 592302; local history plus a Met Office weather gallery; Apr–Oct, Tues–Sun, 10am–5.30pm. The Rum Story, Lowther Street; ☎ 01946 592933; the history of the rum trade and slavery, including a simulated rainforest and slave ship.

Egremont Lowes Court Gallery, 12 Main Street; ☎ 01946 820693; good gallery and gift shop in 18th-century town house which is also home to the local Tourist Information Centre.

Honister Slate Mine, Honister Pass, Borrowdale, Keswick, Cumbria; ☎ 01768 777230; a must for getting your breath back, warming up, drying out; there are regular mine tours as well, lots to buy and a licensed restaurant.

Lodore Boat landings, Derwentwater, Borrowdale; ☎ 01768 777282; tuition/hire in canoes, kayaks, sailing boats and even a Chinese dragon boat and Viking longship.

Keswick Cumberland Pencil Museum , Southey Works; www.pencilmuseum.co.uk; ☎ 01768 773626; if you didn't think that pencils could be fascinating, think again. The Theatre by the Lake, ☎ 017687 74411; consistently good programme; it developed from the Blue Bus touring theatre, an extraordinary convoy of trucks which were dismantled and fitted together to form an auditorium at stopping places. Bus and taxi serve Keswick from Borrowdale.

Grasmere and area: Dove Cottage, Grasmere; ☎ 015394 35544; William Wordsworth's smallest but most famous home, where his best poems were written, now supplemented by a fine modern gallery and restaurant extension. Rydal Mount and Gardens, Rydal; ☎ 01539 433002; Wordsworth moved here when he got successful and settled down for 37 years in the large, fine house, including his stint as Poet Laureate to Queen Victoria, appointed at the age of 74. The Heaton Cooper Studio, Grasmere; www.heatoncooper.co.uk; ☎ 01539 435280; gallery and shop exhibiting the work of four generations of a famous family; patriarch William Heaton Cooper's russet and straw landscapes of the fells are particularly beautiful – and expensive.

Ullswater Steamers, The Pier House, Glenridding, Penrith, Cumbria; ☎ 01768 482229; the graceful *Raven* and *Lady of the Lake* glide between three different ports: Glenridding, Howtown and Pooley Bridge.

Orton Kennedys Fine Chocolates, The Old School, Orton; www.kennedys-chocolates.co.uk; ☎ 01539 624781; watch the choccies being hand-made, for real and on a short video, before eating some in the café and buying more in the shop.

Kirkby Stephen Railway Station, Kirkby Stephen; www.settle-carlisle.co.uk; fully restored Victorian station a short step from the town which won the 2005 Railway Heritage Trust Conservation Award.

Hawes a bus or taxi ride away but it has the Wensleydale Creamery Visitor Centre, ☎ 01969 666210, in the creamery saved from closure by a fierce local campaign and the marketing effects of the cartoon Oscar-winners and cheese-eaters Wallace and Gromit; open all year. Dales Countryside Museum, ☎ 01969 666210; excellent and comprehensive; a stash of information and exhibits on 10,000 years of settlement in this characterful part of Britain; open all year.

Reeth Swaledale Museum, Reeth; ☎ 01748 884118; wholesome displays of Dales life and work in the 1836 Methodist schoolroom, plus family archives; open Easter–October or by appointment.

Richmond Castle, ☎ 01748 822493; all year apart from Christmas and New Year; stupendous bastion with unusual and moving exhibition on conscientious objectors jailed here during the First World War. Georgian Theatre Royal and Museum, Victoria Road; ☎ 01748 823710; box office ☎ 01748 825252; the oldest theatre in Britain to survive in its original form; built by actor/manager Samuel Butler in 1788, it houses enjoyable collections of playbills and painted scenery. Richmondshire Museum, Ryders Wynd; ☎ 01748 825611; thorough guide to local history with lots of original exhibits; open Easter–October. Green Howards Museum, Trinity Church Square; ☎ 01748 826561; the famous regiment's history right up to present-day service in Iraq and Afghanistan; open February–November.

Robin Hood's Bay Smugglers, Albion Road; one woman's take on the vivid history of Bay Town, with miniature scenes and recreated streets with the sounds and smells of the 18th-century smuggling past; open all year.

Bibliography

A Coast to Coast Walk, A. Wainwright (revised and updated by the painstaking Chris Jesty for Frances Lincoln, 2010; first published by the Westmorland Gazette, 1973). The original Bible.

Wainwright's Coast to Coast Walk (Michael Joseph, 1987). The coffee-table version with outstanding photos by Derry Brabbs.

Fellwanderer, A. Wainwright (*Westmorland Gazette*, 1966). The story behind the guidebooks and the great man's nearest, typically wry and quirky, go at an autobiography.

Coast to Coasting, John Gillham and Ron Turnbull (David & Charles, 2000). Eight different walks between the seas.

Coast to Coast – the original B&B accommodation guide, Doreen Whitehead (Butt House, Keld, Richmond DL11 6LJ).

Wainwright: the biography, Hunter Davies (Michael Joseph, 1995). A fascinating portrait.

The Modern Antiquarian, Julian Cope (Thorsons, Harper Collins, 1998). Opinionated, fascinating tour of stone circles and the prehistoric past.

Collins Bird Guide (Collins, 1999).

Wild Flowers of Britain and Europe, Andrew Branson (Bounty Books).

Cumbrian Discovery, Molly Lefebure (Batsford, 1964). Thorough and personal guide by a mate and rival of Wainwright.

The North Yorkshire Village Book and *The Cumbrian Village Book* (Federation of Women's Institutes, 1991). A modern Domesday Book full of fascinating facts collected by women in the know.

Building the North Riding, Lynn F. Pearson (Smith Settle, 1994). Readable introduction to the county of pantiles and honey-coloured stone.

A History of Lead Mining in the Pennines, Arthur Raistrick and Bernard Jennings (Longman, Green & Co., 1965). The authoritative study, although fresh discoveries have been made since.

A Walker's Guide to Swaledale, A. David Leather (Smith Settle, 1992).

The Lake Counties: Cumberland and Westmorland, Arthur Mee (Hodder & Stoughton, 1937). A fine old patriotic read.

Inside the North York Moors, Harry Mead (David & Charles, 1978). A very good collection of vignettes on the life and landscape of the moors.

Houses of the North York Moors (Royal Commission on the Historical Monuments of England, 1987). A sumptuous and comprehensive record, from cottage to stately home.

Where the Wainstones Stand, John G. Mawer and Basil Webster (Great Broughton and Kirkby Queen's Silver Jubilee Committee, 1977). One of many excellent local histories of communities along the path.

Ordnance Survey maps covering the Coast to Coast Walk

Having the complete map is very useful in terms of the wider context of the walk or making deviations off the path. There are rather a lot of them, but it is well worth poring over the route and its surroundings in advance.

Whitehaven & Workington Explorer 303

The English Lakes NW Area Explorer OL4

The English Lakes SE Area (very small section of route) OS Explorer OL7

The English Lakes NE Area Explorer OL5

Howgill Fells & Upper Eden Valley Explorer OL19

Yorkshire Dales N & Central Areas Explorer OL30

Darlington & Richmond Explorer 304

Northallerton & Thirsk Explorer 302

North York Moors W Area Explorer OL26

North York Moors E Area Explorer OL27

Alfred Wainwright's original guides to A Coast to Coast Walk and to the *Lakeland Fells*

9780711230637

9780711233683

9780711224650

9780711224667

9780711226142

9780711226586

9780711226678

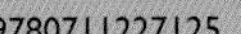

9780711227125

9780711221994

The Official Guides to all of

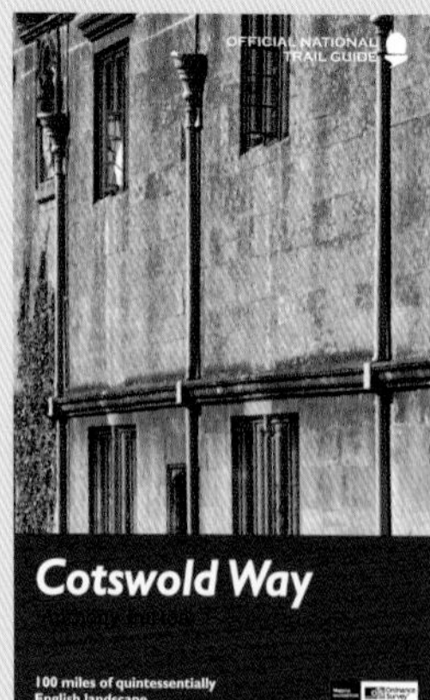

ISBN 978 1 84513 785 4

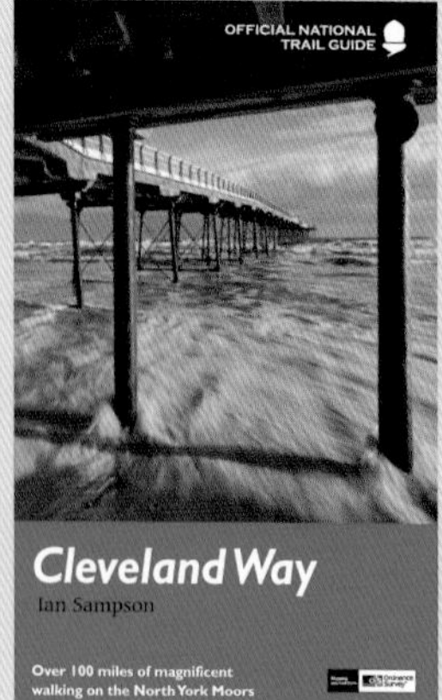

ISBN 978 1 84513 781 6

ISBN 978 1 84513 718 2

ISBN 978 1 84513 643 7

ISBN 978 1 84513 602 4

ISBN 978 1 84513 565 2

ISBN 978 1 84513 567 6

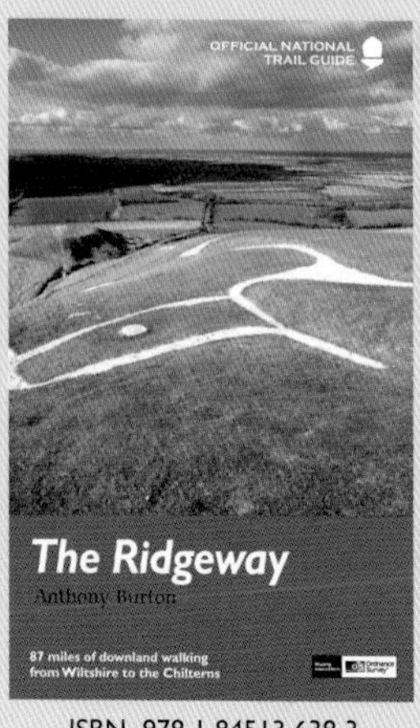

ISBN 978 1 84513 638 3

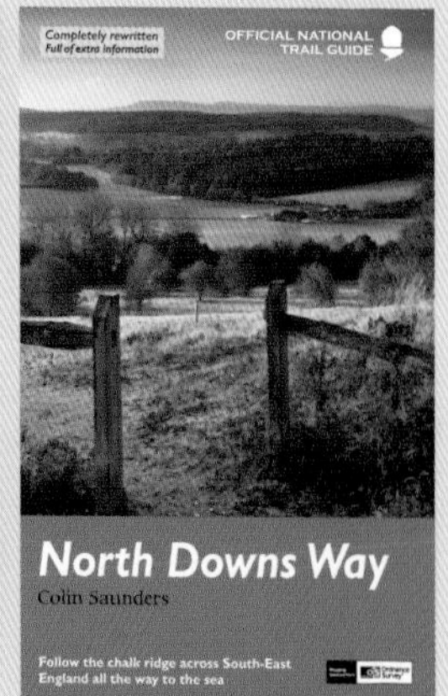

ISBN 978 1 84513 677 2

Britain's National Trails

OFFICIAL NATIONAL TRAIL GUIDE

Thames Path
in the Country
David Sharp and Tony Gowers
From the source to Hampton Court

ISBN 978 1 84513 717 5

OFFICIAL NATIONAL TRAIL GUIDE

Thames Path
in London
Phoebe Clapham
From Hampton Court to Crayford Ness: 50 miles of historic riverside walk

ISBN 978 1 84513 706 9

OFFICIAL NATIONAL TRAIL GUIDE

Peddars Way and
Norfolk Coast Path
Bruce Robinson with Mike Robinson
90 miles from Breckland to salt marsh and sea cliffs

ISBN 978 1 84513 784 7

OFFICIAL NATIONAL TRAIL GUIDE

South West Coast Path
Minehead to Padstow
Roland Tarr
160 miles of coastal walking from Exmoor to North Cornwall

ISBN 978 1 84513 640 6

OFFICIAL NATIONAL TRAIL GUIDE

South West Coast Path
Padstow to Falmouth
John Macadam
From golden beaches to rugged coves around Britain's southernmost tip

ISBN 978 1 84513 641 3

OFFICIAL NATIONAL TRAIL GUIDE

ISBN 978 1 84513 561 4

OFFICIAL NATIONAL TRAIL GUIDE

South West Coast Path
Falmouth to Exmouth
Brian Le Messurier
172 miles of dramatic coves, cliffs and beaches from Cornwall to Devon

ISBN 978 1 84513 564 5

OFFICIAL NATIONAL TRAIL GUIDE

South West Coast Path
Exmouth to Poole
Roland Tarr
From Jane Austen's Cobb to Lulworth Cove – over 100 miles of historic coastline

ISBN 978 1 84513 642 0

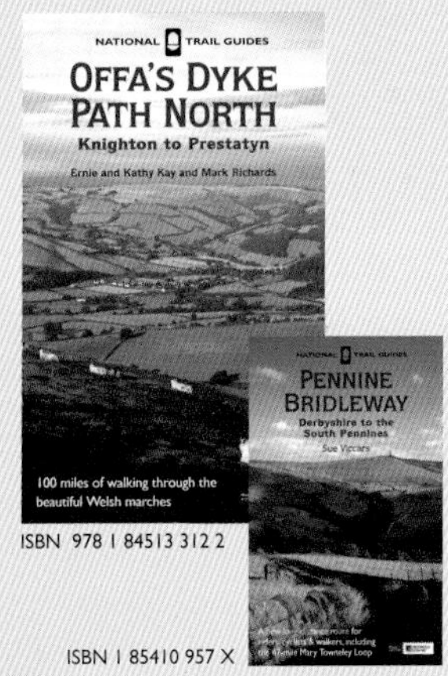

ISBN 978 1 84513 312 2

ISBN 1 85410 957 X

Definitive guides to other popular long-distance walks published by Aurum

ISBN 978 1 84513 708 3

ISBN 978 1 84513 786 1

ISBN 978 1 84513 787 8

The classic high-level walk from Irish Sea to North Sea

ISBN 978 1 84513 560 7

ISLINGTON LIBRARIES
3 0120 02532654 7
A & H
05-Oct-2012
796.51
£12.99
CL
796.51
3657891